Troubleshooting
Your Web Page

Evan Callahan

Microsoft®

PUBLISHED BY
Microsoft Press
A Division of Microsoft Corporation
One Microsoft Way
Redmond, Washington 98052-6399

Library of Congress Cataloging-in-Publication Data
Callahan, Evan, 1966-
    Troubleshooting Your Web Page / Evan Callahan.
        p. cm.
    Includes index.
    ISBN 0-7356-1164-5
    1. Web sites. I. Title.

  TK5105.888 .C346   2000
  005.7'2--dc21   00-048684

Printed and bound in the United States of America.

1 2 3 4 5 6 7 8 9   QWT   6 5 4 3 2 1

Distributed in Canada by Penguin Books Canada Limited.

A CIP catalogue record for this book is available from the British Library.

Microsoft Press books are available through booksellers and distributors worldwide. For further information about international editions, contact your local Microsoft Corporation office or contact Microsoft
Press International directly at fax (425) 936-7329. Visit our Web site at mspress.microsoft.com. Send
comments to *mspinput@microsoft.com*.

FrontPage, Microsoft, Microsoft Press, PowerPoint, Visual InterDev, and Windows are either registered
trademarks or trademarks of Microsoft Corporation in the United States and/or other countries. Other
product and company names mentioned herein may be the trademarks of their respective owners.

Unless otherwise noted, the example companies, organizations, products, people, and events depicted herein
are fictitious. No association with any real company, organization, product, person, or event is intended or
should be inferred.

Acquisitions Editors: Christey Bahn and Alex Blanton
Project Editor: Judith Bloch

Quick contents

Contents

Acknowledgments

- Margaret and Fiona, for their sweet love and support.

- Jim and Judy Callahan, for exemplary parenting—and grandparenting.

- Rob MacDougall and Jacques Ropert, for design inspiration.

- Melissa Callahan, Luke Woodward, Matt Luxon, and Fiona McNair, for all sorts of inspiration.

- My editors at Microsoft Press: Christey Bahn, Alex Blanton, Jenny Benson, Judith Bloch, and Wendy Zucker.

- The editing and production team at Siechert & Wood Professional Documentation (*www.swdocs.com*): Carl Siechert, Robert Tennant, Jeff Wagner, and Paula Berg.

- The people behind all the web resources I've turned to in my own web learning, especially Microsoft Developer Network (*msdn.microsoft.com*), Microsoft Product Support Services (*support.microsoft.com*), WebReview.com, Webmonkey (*hotwired.lycos.com/webmonkey*), and the World Wide Web Consortium (*www.w3.org*).

This book is dedicated to Gracie (right), whose arrival made our schedule a bit more exciting.

- Web designers around the globe, for their contributions to the ever-changing World Wide Web. For all its growth and commercialization, the web still belongs to everyone—from corporate workgroups to small business owners, community organizations to university students, political activists to home hobbyists. Let's keep it that way!

About this book

Troubleshooting Your Web Page presents a new way to diagnose and solve problems when creating web pages. Web design involves a variety of skills and different software programs, and chances are you don't have time to learn all the background information for each program or technology you use. Instead, you want to dive right in and create web pages. Then, when you come across a problem or obstacle, you need an answer.

That's where this book steps in. Through my own work, as well as discussion with self-taught web designers, I've found that there are a few dozen issues that people are likely to encounter on the path to web enlightenment. Unfortunately, the solution to these common problems can be tough to find in a traditional how-to or reference book. In *Troubleshooting Your Web Page*, I'll help you identify your problem, describe what might be causing it, and lead you to a solution as quickly as possible.

Who this book is for

This book is for anyone creating web pages for fun or business. It is ideal for self-starters who have software experience but haven't yet moved beyond the pitfalls and hurdles inherent to web design.

Because web pages are based on HTML and graphics standards, it doesn't matter what software tools or versions you use—most of the solutions work equally well across a wide range of software. The book covers popular web browsers (Microsoft Internet Explorer and Netscape), web authoring tools (such as Microsoft FrontPage and Allaire HomeSite), and graphics programs (such as Adobe Photoshop and Macromedia Fireworks).

If you use FrontPage 2000, you'll find special sections covering the common issues you're likely to come across—whether you use only the design tools, or also switch to HTML view for more control of your page.

How to use this book

Good news! You don't have to read this book from cover to cover or even in any particular order. It's designed so that you can jump in, quickly diagnose your problem, and then get the information you need to fix it, whether you've just begun to learn about operating systems and programs or whether you're knowledgeable enough to get right to the source of the problem. We've grouped the problems you're most likely to encounter into chapters with short, straightforward titles, listed alphabetically, that let you see at a glance what kinds of topics the chapter covers. Each chapter is broken down into two specific elements: the flowchart and the solution spread.

Flowcharts

The first thing you'll see when you turn to a chapter is a dynamic, easy-to-use flowchart. It starts by asking you a broad question about a common problem and then, as you answer a series of yes-or-no questions, guides you toward a diagnosis of your problem. If the solution to the problem is a simple one that requires only a few steps, you'll find a quick fix right there on the flowchart. Take a few minutes to work your way through the steps, and presto—your problem is solved and you're back to work (or play) with a minimum of down time. If the solution to your problem requires a little more explanation and a few more steps, you'll find a statement that describes the problem, along with the page number of the solution spread you need to go to. And if you can't find your specific

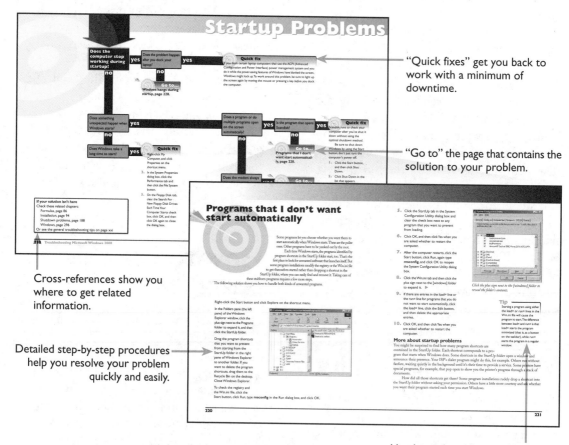

"Quick fixes" get you back to work with a minimum of downtime.

"Go to" the page that contains the solution to your problem.

Cross-references show you where to get related information.

Detailed step-by-step procedures help you resolve your problem quickly and easily.

Handy reader aids expand on the issue to help avoid future problems.

problem in the series of questions on the flowchart, look through the list of related chapters for another area where your problem might be addressed.

Solution spreads

The solution spreads are where the real troubleshooting takes place. I provide you with some brief information about the source of the problem you're experiencing, and then, with clear, step-by-step instructions, show you how to fix it. The solution spreads contain screen shots that show you what you'll be seeing as you move through the steps, and you'll be happy to see that most of the solutions take no more than two pages.

Although my goal is to give you just the facts so that you can quickly get back to what you were doing, in some cases we've provided more detailed background information that you might or might not want to read, depending on whether you're looking for a deeper understanding of what caused your problem. Also scattered throughout the solution spreads are tips that contain related material or advice that you might find helpful, and a few warnings that tell you what you should or shouldn't do in a given situation.

Troubleshooting Tips

Troubleshooting is the art of narrowing down possible causes of a problem, pinpointing what's wrong, and fixing it. Consider a lamp that won't turn on. You might try the switch, replace the light bulb, and check the circuit breaker. "Hmm," you say, "still no light. Better take this lamp apart—I'll just unpl—" Oops. It wasn't plugged in.

Troubleshooting steps

1. **Explore the problem.** Perhaps the spacing is wrong. Or a hyperlink doesn't work. What software feature or HTML tag is involved?

2. **Pinpoint the cause.** Is it mistyped HTML? Use validation tools to help find errors. A problem with a file? Browse folders on your web server. A missing attribute or setting? Consult HTML reference tables.

3. **Fix it.** Retype incorrect settings. Replace files. Add style settings. Preview to test your solution.

Different problem types

Some web page problems are like the lamp: there are many possible issues, but once you narrow down the field, most problems have easy solutions. For example, fixing a broken hyperlink is usually an easy matter once you figure out where the issue lies—a file is missing or in the wrong place, there's a typo in the tag, and so on. In these cases, the challenge is to learn what issues contribute to specific types of problems—and how to rule each of them out. For a few ideas, read the sections below.

In other cases, you'll already know what the problem is—the lamp's switch is broken, for example—but you won't know how to go about solving it. This is fairly common in web page design, where so many tools and technology details are involved. You might know, for example, that a certain HTML tag offers limited formatting, but not know how to set a style to overcome it. For these types of problems, go directly to the section in this book that covers the problem element (backgrounds, borders, or images, for example) and follow the flowchart you find there.

The final type of problem has no easy solution—you need a new lamp, or an electrician.

In these cases, I'll try to point you in the right direction: install a new browser, call your Internet service provider (ISP) or network administrator, search the web for additional information, or rethink your strategy altogether.

Web design software

If you use a web design program, such as FrontPage or Dreamweaver, you'll find some of your answers lie with features of the program itself. When things aren't working, take the time to go back through a process or command and see if options are available to address your issue. In FrontPage, for example, most page elements have a property dialog box, where you might be able to select a setting to solve your problem.

Don't hesitate to search the program's online help or web support pages. You'll be surprised how many common issues are addressed on Frequently Asked Questions pages or in a searchable knowledge base.

When you can't get the design program to do what you want, switch to HTML view and try to figure out what is really going on. In some cases, you'll find that settings in your design program didn't have the effect you intended in HTML—or that your program doesn't allow you to control the certain settings without editing HTML directly.

Mistakes in your code

If you edit HTML code directly, on the other hand, you'll have more control—but also the potential for additional problems. When troubleshooting, it's important to rule out typos or missing information in your HTML, style sheet, or script. Errors can result in a page that doesn't appear at all, or simply in a setting that doesn't take effect.

Software tools can help you troubleshoot problems. First, HTML formatting tools can arrange and indent your HTML code logically so that errors are easier to locate. If you use HomeSite, try the CodeSweeper feature. Or, the HTML Tidy tool is available at *www.w3.org/People/Raggett/tidy*. (Always back up your page before using a formatting tool, just in case the tool introduces new problems when rearranging your HTML.)

An even more important tool is validation software, which checks your code for typos, missing elements, and adherence to standards. If you use HomeSite, the Validate HTML feature will do the trick. Or, an HTML validation service is available at *validator.w3.org*. Validation tools usually report both *errors*, which you must address, and *warnings*, which often don't matter but might shed light on your problem.

Browser compatibility

Every web browser is different. When your page doesn't work, it's important to try it in another browser—preferably the most recent one you can find. If you don't have the most recent versions of both Internet Explorer and Netscape, download them from *www.microsoft.com/windows/ie* and *home.netscape.com/browsers* (note that you might want to keep an older version on your computer as well, for testing). Preview your page in each browser—if it works in the new version, the problem probably lies with limitations of the older browser.

That's not to say you can rest once your page works in the most recent browser. On the contrary, you'll probably want your page to work and look good in every browser that viewers are likely to have. Still, browser testing allows you to move forward with troubleshooting, determining whether or not to investigate browser limitations and workarounds.

In the process of testing different browsers, you might head off other issues with your pages. Try changing font sizes in each browser, as well as color and font settings on your system. If your pages have forms, test them in each browser. Take notes in the process, noting any browser issues you might need to look into. For browser information, see "Browsers" on page 42, or search the web (or HTML-related web sites) for *browser compatibility*.

The missing link

Most web pages depend on more than one file—there are links to images, multimedia files, other web pages, and additional supporting files such as style sheets. When images don't appear, hyperlinks don't work, or multimedia files don't play, you have to track down the problem in order to move forward.

On the bright side, file problems present a classic troubleshooting scenario (like the lamp that doesn't light), because the issues involved in linking files are well defined. Look at the HTML tags and settings you've used, making sure they are valid and

specify a file that exists. Try the file outside of your page—you might not have the proper permission to view the file, or for a media file, the proper player. Also, check for a problem with the web server—or your Internet or network connection.

Many web design programs, such as FrontPage and HomeSite, can verify all the links in your page, project, or web in one step. In addition to helping you prevent broken links, these tools can also rule out problems with missing files when your page isn't working. For more information, see "Hyperlinks" on page 174.

Layout challenges

Layout is perhaps the trickiest part of page design. When items on your page don't line up properly, text doesn't wrap the way you want, or the page is arranged incorrectly, it might take some detective work to figure out the problem.

First rule out glaring problems in your HTML (typos, invalid attributes, or missing end tags) using the tools discussed above. Next take a look at the HTML for the problem area of your page. Consult the reference for the tags you've used, and check if different settings might solve the problem. If the problem is with an image, for example, look at the attributes for the <IMG> tag. Experiment with different settings, and then preview the page in your browser. Don't forget to resize the browser window to see the effect this has on the layout.

If you use a table for overall page layout, check the width you've specified for each column (<TD> tag). Make sure each column has enough space for its contents, and that the overall table width is the right size. For more information, see "Tables" on page 310.

When all else fails

When you run into a dead end with trouble-shooting, take a step back. If you aren't sure which element of the page is causing the problem, take out sections of your page temporarily and preview again. Or, try to reproduce the problem you're having on a brand new page—starting fresh and copying each part of your page one step at a time—this process might help you narrow down the possibilities. Also, look at the HTML source for web pages that are similar to yours. How do their designers manage to do it?

Finally, if you can't make something work in your web page, drop back and punt. In other words, don't spend too much time troubleshooting a problem if there is an easier way to reach your goal. For example, if you can't make a multimedia file play on your page, simply provide a link to the file. An alternative solution might not be quite as cool, but it gets the job done.

The Troubleshooting web site

If you've found this book so fascinating that you could hardly put it down, you're in luck because…there's more! With the purchase of this book, you now have access to the Microsoft Press Troubleshooting web site at *mspress.microsoft.com/troubleshooting*, which complements the book series by offering additional troubleshooting information that's updated monthly. You'll find that some of the flowcharts have been expanded to cover additional problems, and that entirely new flowcharts with accompanying solutions have been created to address some important but perhaps slightly less common problems than those addressed in this book.

You'll find the Troubleshooting web site as easy to navigate as this book, and it continues our goal of helping you locate your problem and its solution quickly and easily. To access the site, you need this code: **TSW0830**. (Those are zeroes, not letter Os.)

Web pages with action, animation, and dynamic effects are often more interesting than static pages. But animating your pages requires special skills and software—such as a graphics program that creates animated GIF files or a web design program that offers dynamic effects.

For general information on GIF animation and software, see "Getting started with GIF animation" on page 7. For an introduction to options for activating your pages and creating dynamic effects, see "Bringing your pages to life" on page 10.

If you're having problems with your GIF animations or FrontPage dynamic effects, follow the flowchart to find a solution.

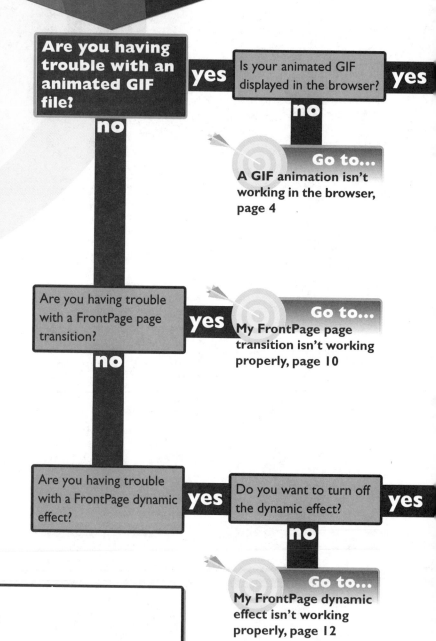

Are you having trouble with an animated GIF file?

yes → Is your animated GIF displayed in the browser? yes

no

no ↓

Go to... A GIF animation isn't working in the browser, page 4

Are you having trouble with a FrontPage page transition?

yes → **Go to...** My FrontPage page transition isn't working properly, page 10

no

Are you having trouble with a FrontPage dynamic effect?

yes → Do you want to turn off the dynamic effect? yes

no

Go to... My FrontPage dynamic effect isn't working properly, page 12

If your solution isn't here
Check these related chapters:
  Backgrounds, page 14
  FrontPage, page 154
  Hyperlinks, page 177
  Images, page 188
Or see the general troubleshooting tips on page xvii

Animation

Do you want the animation to stop repeating? — **yes**

Quick fix

Animations can be played once, can be repeated a certain number of times, or can loop forever.

In Fireworks:
At the bottom left of the Frames palette, click the GIF Animation Looping button and select No Looping, Forever, or a number of repetitions.

In ImageReady:
At the bottom left of the Animation palette, select Once, Forever, or Other.

no

Is the animation choppy? — **yes**

Go to...
A GIF animation is choppy, page 8

no

Does the animation take too long to load in a browser? — **yes**

Go to...
My animated GIF file takes too long to load, page 6

no

Is the animation too slow or too fast? — **yes**

Quick fix

Each frame of an animation has a duration or delay you can set. Specify 0.1–0.5 seconds (10–50 one-hundredths) for smooth animation, or 1–10 seconds when you want to incorporate a delay.

In Fireworks:
In the Frames palette, double-click each frame and then type the number of one-hundredths of a second you want that frame to display.

In ImageReady:
Just below each frame in the Animation palette, select a number of seconds of delay.

Quick fix

The trick is to display the Dynamic HTML Effects toolbar.

1. Click the paragraph or picture that has the effect you don't want.
2. On the Format menu, click DHTML Effects.
3. On the Dynamic HTML Effects toolbar, click the Remove Effect button.

A GIF animation isn't working in the browser

Source of the problem

Using GIF graphics software, such as Adobe ImageReady or Macromedia Fireworks, you can create GIF animations, which are like simple movies that can be played in a web browser. A GIF animation looks and works just like an ordinary GIF graphic, but if created properly, it comes to life on the page. (For an introduction to GIF animation, see "Getting started with GIF animation" on page 7.)

If your animated GIF isn't working, the problem might lie with the web browser, the procedure you used to create the animation, or with options you selected when saving. To diagnose and solve the problem, follow these steps.

How to fix it

1. In your web browser, check whether other GIF animations are working—banner ads on the typical home page, for example, are animated. If you don't see any animation, the problem is probably your browser. Some older browsers don't support GIF animation, instead displaying only a static picture. In addition, newer browsers give you the option to turn off animation altogether if you find it too distracting. To turn on animation in Internet Explorer 5, click Internet Options on the Tools menu, click the Advanced tab, select Play Animations, and then click OK. ▶

2. If your animation still doesn't work, open it in your graphics or GIF animation program. If possible, use the original artwork, such as a Fireworks or ImageReady file. Otherwise, open the GIF file—but be aware that a file exported in GIF format might not contain all the information your graphics program needs to edit it.

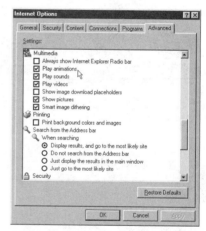

Make sure animations are turned on in your browser.

3. Look at the frames palette or list of frames in your animation. If there is only one frame, your GIF isn't an animation. To turn it into an animation, you can either add frames or duplicate the existing frame and make minor changes to each copy. ▶

4. If the animation has display errors, such as pixels or areas that are blurred or repeated during animation, it might be due to *optimization* options your GIF uses. In an effort to make your animated GIF files as small as possible, most graphics programs play a few tricks that might not be compatible with your browser. (Some AOL browser users, for example, have reported trouble with optimized animations.) If your animation has display problems in a browser, turn off optimization options. In ImageReady, for example, turn off the Bounding Box and Redundant Pixel Removal options; in Fireworks, turn off the AutoCrop and AutoDifference options.

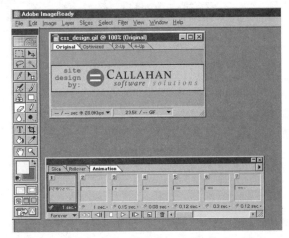

For animation, you need at least two distinct frames.

5. Preview your animation to make sure all is in order; then save or export it. Specify an adaptive palette, and select a setting with enough colors to display all your frames adequately. When reducing the number of colors, preview the animation again to make sure the available colors provide a smooth display. ▶

Tip

When you save or export an animation, be sure to select Animated GIF format. In some graphics programs, such as Fireworks, it's possible to save an ordinary (static) GIF file even after you've added multiple frames of animation.

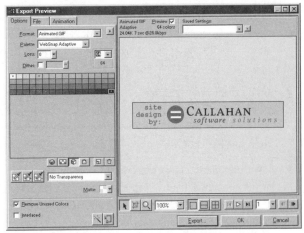

In Fireworks, export using Animated GIF format and the WebSnap Adaptive palette. For this animation, 64 colors are enough.

My animated GIF file takes too long to load

Source of the problem

GIF files compress image information fairly efficiently, especially when the file contains areas of solid color. What's more, animated GIF files use sophisticated methods for reducing size, storing a minimum of image information to reproduce your animation. Still, large or colorful animations contain a great deal of information. If you don't design and optimize them carefully, you could end up with a large file that is slow to load over the Internet.

To reduce the size of an animated GIF file, try the following steps. In steps 1 through 4, you'll consider changes to the animation. Then you'll make sure you've used optimal settings when saving or exporting the GIF file.

How to fix it

1. Open your animation in your graphics or GIF animation program. If possible, use the original artwork, such as a Fireworks or ImageReady file. Otherwise, open the GIF file—but be aware that if the file was previously optimized, it might not contain all the information your graphics program needs to edit it.

2. Using the frames palette or list, look to see how much change there is between frames. Are there more frames than necessary to represent the action? If so, delete intermediate frames, and then increase the delay between frames. ▶

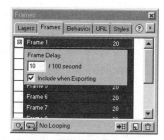

3. If your animation is an extremely large file, consider reducing action in the sequence. Try to keep the action to one area—leaving most of the background unchanged—and your GIF software will be able to optimize the animation more effectively.

Recipe for small GIF animations: less action and color, fewer frames, longer frame delay.

4. If possible, use fewer colors in your animation—GIF files with less color are much smaller. Specify an adaptive palette for your animation (or the individual GIF graphics it uses). Try reducing the color depth or number of colors, but preview the animation to make sure the available colors provide a smooth display.

5. Preview your animation to make sure all is in order; then save or export it to Animated GIF format. Make sure your program's GIF optimization settings are all selected—most programs select them by default.

Getting started with GIF animation

A GIF animation is like a small movie that can be played in a portion of your web browser. Most of the active pictures you see on web pages are transmitted to your web browser as GIF animations. The format is so popular because, unlike other forms of animation, nearly every browser can display GIF files without extra software. You can include a GIF animation in your pages just as if it were an ordinary GIF file—but in addition to the image, the file stores a series of *frames* to represent movement or changes to the image.

You can create GIF animations in two primary ways: the one-stop shop or the two-step process. Graphics programs such as Adobe ImageReady, Macromedia Fireworks, and Microsoft PhotoDraw (version 2) let you create graphics, specify frames of animation, and export compressed GIF files.

Some graphics programs don't have these animation capabilities. If this is the case, you'll need to create a series of separate GIF files for the frames of your animation. Then combine the frames into an animation using a GIF animation assembly tool. The following programs are inexpensive and available for download on the web: Ulead GIF Animator, Alchemy Mindworks GIF Construction Set, BoxTop Software GIFmation, and Jasc Animation Shop. For more ideas, search the web for *GIF animation software.* ▶

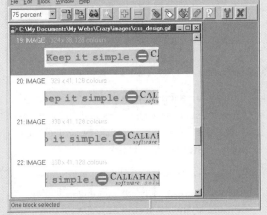

There's more than one way to assemble a GIF.

Here are some tips for getting started:

- Keep animations as small and simple as possible. Limit the amount of animation on your pages, because too much animation can distract from the rest of the content.

- In Photoshop or ImageReady, keep the background in a separate layer, as well as each of the objects you want to animate; in Fireworks, create symbols for the objects you'll animate.

- To fade objects in and out, create duplicate frames and then reduce the opacity of the objects in some of them.

- An animation can be run once or repeated. To break up the repetition—without adding to the size of the file—create a long delay on one frame.

- For animation examples and ideas—or perhaps to find the GIF you need without creating it yourself—search the web for *free animated GIF.* Or, study just about any advertisement you see on the web—it's most likely a GIF file!

A GIF animation is choppy

Source of the problem

Like motion pictures, GIF animation relies on the fact that individual frames presented quickly enough appear to the human eye as live motion. If you've created an animation that appears choppy or uneven, probably the film has too few frames to display convincing motion, or the projector isn't running at the right speed.

Follow these steps to make your animation smoother.

> **Tip**
>
> If your animation is slow and choppy when viewed over the Internet, but works fine on your computer, the GIF file is probably too big. For ideas on reducing file size, see "My animated GIF file takes too long to load" on page 6.

How to fix it

1. Open your animation in your graphics or GIF animation program. If possible, use the original artwork, such as a Fireworks or ImageReady file. Otherwise, open the GIF file—but be aware that if the file was previously optimized, it might not contain all the information your graphics program needs to edit it.

2. Examine the frames one by one. If your software supports *onion skinning*—display of more than one frame at a time—use it to compare frames. Wherever frames differ radically, the transition will be abrupt; for convincing action, every change or movement needs to occur over at least three frames, often many more. ▶

3. If there aren't enough frames in part of the animation sequence, insert new frames that display intermediate steps from one frame to the other. This process is called *tweening*.

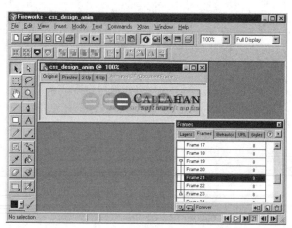

Onion skinning shows you more than one frame at a time.

4. In the frames palette or list for your animation, note the delay settings in seconds (or hundredths of a second). To speed up the action in your animation and reduce choppiness, reduce the amount of delay between frames. Most graphics programs allow you to select multiple frames and change the delay settings all at once. In most cases, you'll want the same delay between all frames to produce the smoothest animation. (A notable exception is when you want a pause in your animation sequence.) ▶

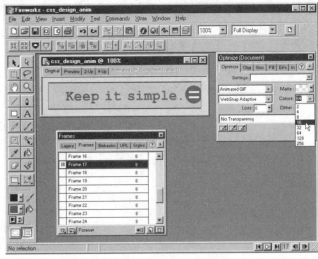

Reducing the delay between frames results in faster, smoother animation.

5. Animation typically involves quite a bit of trial and error. As you make changes, preview your animation frequently and judge the smoothness of action. However, be aware that the timing in a web browser often differs from what you'll see in your graphics program. For accurate timing, preview the GIF in each web browser.

Tip

Many graphics programs offer a *tween* feature that creates intermediate frames in an animation. In ImageReady, for example, if two frames share the same layer in a different position (or with a different opacity or effect setting), choose Tween on the Frames palette pop-up menu to add intermediate frames between them. In Fireworks, insert two instances of the same symbol (on a single frame) and change the position or other settings for the second instance. Then select the two and click Modify, Symbols, Tween Instances to create intermediate instances across frames.

My FrontPage page transition isn't working properly

Source of the problem

Using the Page Transition command, you can add fancy animations that run in Internet Explorer when viewers move from one page to another. FrontPage takes care of the programming for you, adding code that makes the effect work.

The trouble is, page transitions use special code in the <HEAD> section of your HTML that must be in just the right place to function properly, so they are prone to errors. In some cases, you can fix these errors; in others, you'll just have to live with the limitations.

If your page has a page transition that isn't working, follow these steps.

> **Tip**
> Page transitions don't work in Netscape—or in any browsers other than Internet Explorer 4 and later. If you want your site to work the same in all browsers, skip the transitions.

How to fix it

1. If you applied a page transition to a page that already has a dynamic HTML effect, it might not work because of the way FrontPage ordered the code in HTML. If this is the case, you can change the HTML manually to fix the problem. Switch to HTML view and find the line with a **<META http-equiv="Page-Enter" ...>** tag. Cut this line and paste it within the **<HEAD>** section but above any **<SCRIPT>** blocks.

2. Are you trying to apply a page transition to a page with frames? FrontPage adds the transition to the individual pages inside each frame, not to the frames page as a whole. To apply the transition to the frames page, you'll need to add a line to the HTML. First create a new web page and add the transition you want. Then switch to HTML view and find the line that begins with a **<META http-equiv="Page-Enter"...>** tag. Copy this entire line, switch to the frames page HTML, and paste the line into the **<HEAD>** section of that page (above any **<SCRIPT>** blocks).

3. If the page transition you want isn't working properly, remove it. Click Page Transition on the Format menu, select the event (such as Page Enter) in the Event box, select No Effect in the Transition Effect box, and then click OK.

Bringing your pages to life

As the web evolves, more and more action and interactivity appears on web sites. If you have the right tools, you can spice up your pages with movies, responsive menus, and special effects. Each tool requires a different set of web technologies for making it all work in a web browser—and one of your jobs as a web designer is to decide how much of this complexity to add to your pages.

The following list introduces popular methods for bringing your pages to life—with either animation or interactivity—along with some pros and cons of using each method:

- **Animated GIF files.** A GIF file is the simplest form of animation, and it works with nearly every browser. Animated GIFs aren't interactive and can't include sound. See "Getting started with GIF animation" on page 7 for more information.

- **Movies.** Using compressed video formats such as QuickTime, Microsoft Media, or RealVideo, you can create movies and embed them on your web page. Software tools include QuickTime, Adobe Premiere, and RealProducer Plus. See "Multimedia" on page 224 for more information.

- **Flash animation.** Growing in popularity, this flexible animation format requires that viewers have a Flash plug-in or control for their browser. Flash animations are compact, can include sound, and provide *interactivity*—your animation can respond to the viewer's actions. To create Flash animations, use Macromedia Flash or Adobe LiveMotion.

- **FrontPage effects.** Using page transitions, dynamic HTML effects, hover buttons, and other FrontPage features, you can add many popular effects quickly and easily. Disadvantages? Many of these features work only with Internet Explorer, and they aren't particularly flexible.

- **Effects in other programs.** Many programs help you add interactivity to your web pages. For example, Macromedia Fireworks and Adobe ImageReady create active buttons and *rollovers*—graphics that automatically change or perform *behaviors* when users click them or move the mouse over them. To make these behaviors work, the programs write JavaScript code that you copy into your web pages. ▶

    Web design programs such as Macromedia Dreamweaver and Adobe GoLive take this concept further, offering custom behaviors that can animate your pages in response to a variety of user interactions.

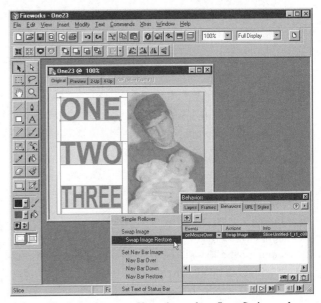

Many lively web page effects depend on JavaScript code to make them work. Fortunately, web design programs like Fireworks will write the code for you.

- **JavaScript and DHTML programming.** If you're up to the task, you can learn to program web browsers yourself. You will find plenty of free samples out there—to start, search the web for *JavaScript samples* or *DHTML samples*. For one example of rollovers in JavaScript, see "My page doesn't do anything when you move the mouse over links and images" on page 184.

My FrontPage dynamic effect isn't working properly

Source of the problem

Using the Dynamic HTML Effects toolbar, you can add custom animation and interactivity to your pages. FrontPage does the programming for you, adding to your pages scripts and other code that make the effects work in a browser.

The trouble is, these features use the same complex web technologies that they are designed to help you avoid. This means that they are prone to errors, and their behavior sometimes varies from browser to browser. In some cases, you can fix these errors; in others, you'll just have to live with the limitations.

If your page has dynamic effects that aren't working, follow these steps to diagnose and fix problems.

How to fix it

1. Have you deleted or moved files in your web? When you first add dynamic effects, FrontPage adds a file called Animate.js to your web. If your effects are broken, this file might have been moved or deleted. If you don't see it, open any page with a dynamic effect and click Save. FrontPage adds the file again.

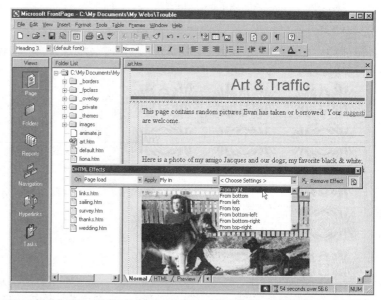

Dynamic effects can spice up your pages, but you might run into some inconsistent behavior.

2. Is a font not changing as you specified? Dynamic font effects work only on text that hasn't otherwise had its font set using the **<FONT>** tag or FrontPage font settings. If your dynamic font effect isn't working, switch to HTML view and delete the **<FONT>** and **</FONT>** tags around the text that has the dynamic effect. If you want both the font formatting and the dynamic effect, apply the font formatting using a style. (For an introduction to styles, see Appendix B on page 347.)

3. Are you trying to apply a dynamic effect inside a shared border area? To do this, open the shared border file separately. (See "I can't find the HTML file for a shared border" on page 40.) Add the effect there, and then save and close the border file. Also, to ensure that FrontPage includes the necessary JavaScript code, add a text effect somewhere on the main page. If you don't need any effect on the main page, insert a blank line on the page, press the Spacebar, and then apply any effect to the blank line.

4. Did you use the Include Page command to include a page that has a dynamic effect? To ensure that FrontPage includes JavaScript code to make the effect work, you'll need to add a text effect somewhere on the main page as well. (If you don't need one, add an effect to a blank line that contains a space.)

5. If the effect you want still isn't working, remove it. Click the paragraph or picture with the effect, click Dynamic HTML Effects on the Format menu, and then click the Remove Effect button.

Tip

When you use dynamic effects, be sure to test them in every browser you want to support—and be prepared to see different results. These features don't work in older browsers, and many of them won't work in any Netscape browser. If you want your site to work the same in all browsers, don't go dynamic.

Note

You can apply dynamic effects and transitions to paragraphs, pictures, and pages—but not to individual words. When you apply an effect to text, FrontPage applies it to the entire paragraph.

A background image is perhaps the easiest way to make your web pages more appealing. You can either use a single large image, or create a small image that tiles (repeats) across and down your whole page.

As you might have guessed, problems can arise once you start using a background. For example, your background image might not look right or work well with items on your page.

An important concept to explore is transparency—the ability for images to let the background show through. For an introduction, see "Many ways to let the background show through" on page 25.

Whether your backgrounds aren't working right or your text and images don't look right with the background, you'll find answers in this chapter.

Are you having trouble with the page background?

yes →

no ↓

Have you set the background color?

yes →

no ↓

Quick fix

Specify a background color using HTML color codes or the FrontPage color picker. If you use a background image, set the color to match the image background.

In HTML:

In the **<BODY>** tag, set the **bgcolor** attribute. For example:

```
<body
bgcolor="#cccc99">
```

In FrontPage:

1. On the Format menu, click Background.

2. Select colors in the Background and Text boxes, and then click OK.

Does an image appear on a white or colored box rather than show the background around it?

yes →

Go to...

The background doesn't appear around the edges of an image, page 24

If your solution isn't here

Check these related chapters:

Or see the general troubleshooting tips on page xvii

Backgrounds

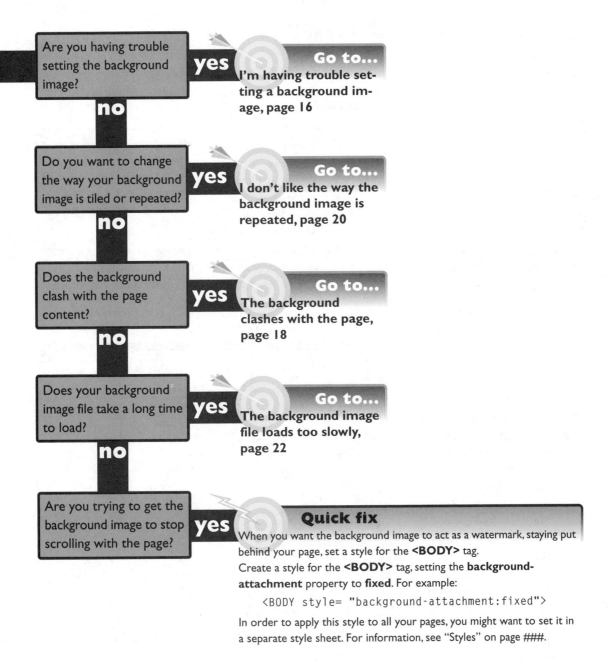

Are you having trouble setting the background image?

yes → **Go to...** I'm having trouble setting a background image, page 16

no

Do you want to change the way your background image is tiled or repeated?

yes → **Go to...** I don't like the way the background image is repeated, page 20

no

Does the background clash with the page content?

yes → **Go to...** The background clashes with the page, page 18

no

Does your background image file take a long time to load?

yes → **Go to...** The background image file loads too slowly, page 22

no

Are you trying to get the background image to stop scrolling with the page?

yes → **Quick fix**

When you want the background image to act as a watermark, staying put behind your page, set a style for the **<BODY>** tag.

Create a style for the **<BODY>** tag, setting the **background-attachment** property to **fixed**. For example:

```
<BODY style= "background-attachment:fixed">
```

In order to apply this style to all your pages, you might want to set it in a separate style sheet. For information, see "Styles" on page ###.

I'm having trouble setting a background image

Source of the problem

With graphics software and a simple addition to the <BODY> tag, you can enhance your web page—or a table on your page—with a background image. If you are having a problem displaying a background image, there are really only a few possible causes: the image isn't valid, the file isn't in the location you specified, or the HTML you used is incorrect. If you use a page-design program such as FrontPage, it's also possible you've used an incorrect procedure to change the background.

> **Note**
> Most web browsers give you the option to turn off the display of images. If you've turned images off, turn them back on to display the background.

If you have a background image but can't get it onto your page, follow these steps to fix the problem.

How to fix it

1. Using Windows, locate the background image file on your computer. You should store it in a folder along with your web pages or a subfolder. It's best if the file is in either GIF or JPEG format. (You can also use PNG format, but since most older browsers can't display this format, it's best to stick with GIF or JPEG.) To make sure your web browser can display the image, double-click the file or drag it to your browser window. ▶

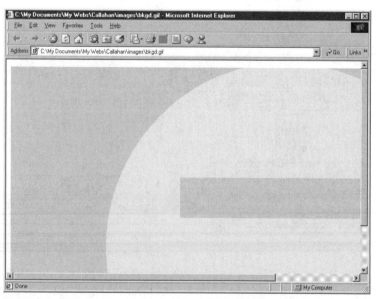

Make sure your background image is a GIF or JPEG file and is located in a folder with your web files.

2. If the image file isn't valid, edit or re-create the image in your graphics software, and then export the GIF or JPEG file into a folder with your other web files.

3. Set the **background** attribute of the **<BODY>** tag to the name of the image file with its extension. (On UNIX and Linux web servers, you must use the exact capitalization.) If the file is in a subfolder of your web's root folder, precede the file name with the folder name and a forward slash.

```
<body background="images/swirly.jpg">
```

4. Set the **bgcolor** attribute to the background color of the image. This way, the color will be displayed immediately when your page loads, even if the background image takes time to load. (Don't know about specifying color? See "Web color numbers" on page 67.)

```
<body background="images/swirly.jpg"
    bgcolor="#cccc99">
```

5. Preview your page to test the background.

Setting the background in FrontPage

1. Follow steps 1 and 2 above to ensure your background image file is valid, and then open your web page in FrontPage.

2. On the Format menu, click Background.

3. Under Formatting, select Background Picture. Click Browse, locate and select your picture file, and then click OK. ▶

4. Before closing the Page Properties dialog box, make sure the page background color matches your image background. In the Background box under Colors, select the closest color.

5. If you want all your web pages to share the same background and colors, you don't need to set these options in every file. Instead, set background options only in your home page. For each other web page, select the Get Background Information From Another Page option and specify your home page as the template.

Note

If your page uses a FrontPage theme, your page derives its background from the theme—you can't specify a background in HTML or using the ordinary FrontPage method described here. However, you can change the background image in the theme itself.

Tip

When you replace an image with a file of the same name—such as a background image—FrontPage sometimes continues to display the old image on your page. If this occurs, you can either rename the updated image, or close and restart FrontPage to refresh the file.

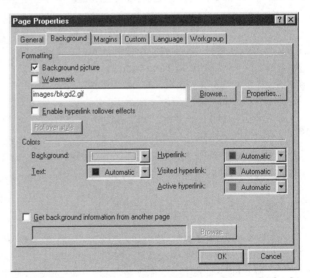

In FrontPage, you set page properties to change the background image and color.

If you subsequently change the background settings in your home page, FrontPage automatically makes the change to all pages that use the home page as a template.

The background clashes with the page

Source of the problem

Web pages with a background color or image are more interesting than those presented on plain vanilla white. Unfortunately, if your page has too much going on in the background, it can lose clarity or readability in the foreground. The same principle applies in a book or magazine—for easy reading, text is usually printed on a light, solid background, and seldom on top of a color picture.

On the web, there are even more reasons to keep the background simple. Text on a computer screen is difficult to read without good contrast. Because every computer monitor displays color somewhat differently, you are best off selecting a color scheme that's likely to provide good contrast on any system. ▶

Even if you choose a simple background, older web browsers and computer video systems might change your colors or *dither* the background color, creating a grainy effect that reduces contrast and readability with the foreground.

If your background clashes with the content of your page, don't despair. Follow these steps to strike a good balance between the content and background—providing a nice "parchment" on which to present your web pages.

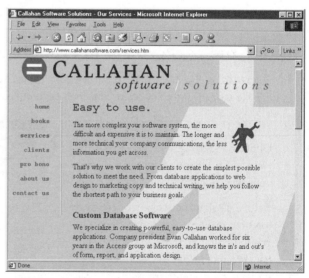

A simple background graphic with two web-safe colors provides good contrast with the text.

How to fix it

1. Choose a background color that contrasts well with the text—a light background for black text, for example. Be sure to select a *web-safe* color—one that can be displayed as a solid color in any web browser. (Don't know about web-safe colors? See "Web color numbers" on page 67.) The following **<BODY>** tag, for example, specifies a light olive-colored background that is web-safe and provides contrast with black text.

```
<body bgcolor="#cccc99">
```

2. If you use a background image, try to keep it simple. If necessary, edit the image in your graphics program. In graphic artwork, for example, reduce the number of colors to a minimum, selecting colors without much contrast. If possible, use only web-safe colors—while this is limiting, it is the best way to create a background that will be displayed clearly. Export this type of background image in GIF format, which displays solid areas of color clearly. (For more troubleshooting ideas, see "Colors in my GIF images are dithered or grainy" on page 74.)

3. If you've selected a colorful or photographic-style background, make it fairly muted. (Otherwise, it may be more suitable as an image on just one area of the page.) To tone down the background image and improve contrast with the foreground, edit the image in your graphics program. Increase brightness, reduce contrast, and reduce color saturation to give the background image a "washed out" appearance. (If your background is dark and your text is light, the same principles apply, but you'll need to decrease brightness instead.) Save this type of image in JPEG format for the smoothest color transitions.

4. If you decide to fill the page background with a colorful image or photograph— which isn't good for readability but might provide the look you want—try displaying text on a solid area of the page for good contrast. To do this, include the text in a table and set the background of the table or cell containing the text to a solid color. In this example, the page background displays a photo, while a table provides a solid-colored area to display text. ▶

With a colorful image in the background, a solid-colored table displays easily readable text.

```
<body background="boat.jpg">
<table bgcolor="#cc9933"
   align=right width=320
   cellpadding=8>

   .
   .
   .

</table>
```

5. By default, the browser *tiles* (repeats across the page) background images. If your background image is tiled in a way that clashes with the page, edit it to create a smoother pattern. (For ideas, see "I don't like the way the background image is repeated" on page 20.)

6. Preview your page each time you make a change to the background—it is difficult to tell how text will look on a background until you see it. Continue making adjustments until your page looks right and has the background/foreground contrast it needs.

I don't like the way the background image is repeated

Source of the problem

You can design a background image either to fill the whole browser window, or to be *tiled*, which means it will repeat across or down the page. By default, in fact, when you include a background image, the web browser repeats the image as many times as it takes to fill the window. But designing a graphic to be tiled can be tricky; if you don't line up pixels properly, you might end up with an undesirable effect on your page. It's easy to end up with jagged edges or a pattern that isn't consistent.

If a repeating background image is giving you trouble, follow the steps below.

Tip

Some graphics programs offer special features to help you create tiled backgrounds. In Adobe ImageReady, for example, you can apply the Tile Maker filter to transform a picture into a smooth tiled image.

How to fix it

1. If you've created your own background artwork and are having trouble making it tile properly, open it in your graphics program. Try to make the top and bottom edges of the repeating image line up, as well as the left and right edges. ▶

   To match the edges, copy elements from one side of the image and paste them on the other side so the graphic matches. Alternatively, you can create a kaleidoscopic-style image by duplicating your image into four copies, flipping the copies horizontally and vertically, and carefully matching the edges.

2. If your artwork primarily consists of areas of solid color, save or export it in GIF format. If it is a photographic-style image or has gradual color changes, use JPEG.

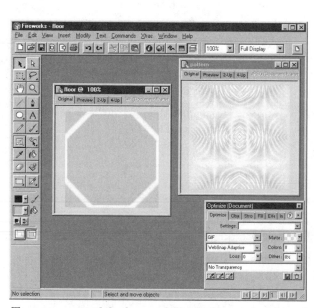

To create a smooth background tile, make sure the edges of your graphic line up from left to right and from top to bottom, as they do in these floor tile and swirl patterns.

Preventing the background image from repeating

1. The easiest way to keep a background image from tiling is to make it large enough to fill the browser window. Open the image in your graphics software. Change the canvas size to at least 1024 pixels wide and 768 pixels high—the largest pixel dimensions used by most computer video systems. (In Photoshop, click Canvas Size on the Image menu.) The drawback to using a large image is that you'll increase the size of the file, and it might load slowly. (For ideas on reducing this delay, see "The background image file loads too slowly" on page 22.)

2. Unless the image already has a background or canvas color, use the paint bucket tool in Photoshop to fill in the new area with the background color you want.

3. Some images can repeat down the page but not across. For example, this very short but wide image ends up displaying a colorful bar down the left side of the page. ▶

   Before saving this type of image, set the canvas size to one pixel high by 1024 or more pixels wide. (Or, if the image displays a pattern down the page, set the canvas height to just the number of pixels the pattern requires.) Making the image very wide prevents the bar from repeating horizontally.

4. Recent browsers—those that support cascading style sheets (CSS)—allow you to specify whether or not to repeat the background image. By using a style, you can prevent the browser from repeating the image even if the browser window is larger than the image. To display the image just once, set the **background-repeat** property of the **<BODY>** tag to **no-repeat**. Or, if you want the background to repeat in one direction only, set the property to **repeat-x** (to repeat across only) or **repeat-y** (to repeat down only). For example:

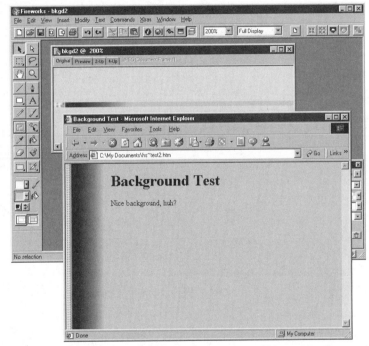

This image is only a few pixels high, but it repeats down to fill the screen. It doesn't repeat to the right because the image is wider than the window.

```
<body background="bkgd.gif" style="background-repeat: no-repeat">
```

The background image file loads too slowly

Source of the problem

If your background is a small image that is repeated to fill the screen, it is unlikely to be a very large file. But if you use a full screen image for the background, you might find that it takes too long to load in a browser—and once the image finishes loading, the background changes abruptly.

Through careful design and optimization of your background image, you can usually manage to reduce it to a workable size. Follow these steps to fix the problem. ▶

How to fix it

1. Open the background image file in your graphics program. If possible, use the original artwork, such as a Fireworks, Photoshop, or Illustrator file; otherwise, open the GIF or JPEG format file.

2. Evaluate whether your image includes a pattern that repeats across or down. If it does, you can reduce its size to one section and let the browser do the repeating. Crop the image to one section, making sure that the left and right edges match, as well as the top and bottom edges.

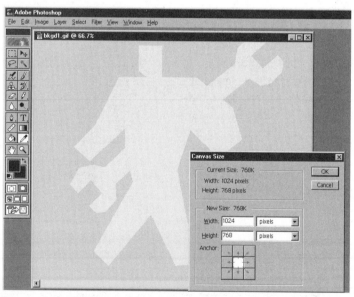

Even a large background image can load quickly if you minimize color and export using an optimal format.

---

3. Check the canvas size. If the image is over 1024 pixels wide or 768 pixels high, you might be able to reduce its size without having an effect in most browsers. If you don't mind it repeating in those cases where the browser window is very large, make the image even smaller. (To instruct browsers not to repeat the image, see "Preventing the background image from repeating" on page 21.)

4. Try to reduce the number of colors or contrast in the image. Remember that, in general, a background image should be simple to avoid clashing with the foreground.

5. If the image is a photograph or includes gradual color changes, use JPEG format. To make the image smaller, reduce the quality setting to 60 or less. ▶

6. If the image is primarily areas of solid color, be sure to export it in GIF format. Try to export using as few colors as possible without making the image look bad; a GIF image with 2, 4, or 8 colors is much smaller than one with the maximum 256 colors. Use *web-safe* colors where possible to ensure that all browsers can display the background appropriately. (Don't know about web-safe colors? See "Web color numbers" on page 67.)

7. Use any image optimization or preview features in your graphics program to try different settings. While there is no strict guideline, aim for a file size under 5 KB, and try never to use a background that's over 25 KB. ▶

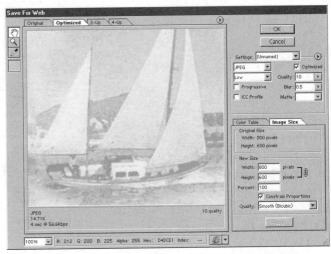

With the JPEG quality set to just 10, this muted sailboat image fills the whole page but is a small enough file to be practical.

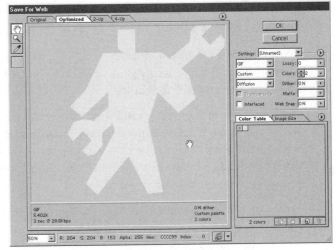

In Photoshop 5.5, the Save For Web feature allows you to experiment with different settings and compare the results of each.

The background doesn't appear around the edges of an image

Source of the problem

Even when your images illustrate items that are not square, all image files occupy a square area on the screen. But when an image has an irregular shape, you most likely want to display the page background around its edges. Otherwise, your image appears to be floating on a square matte (usually white) rather than blending in with the page. ▶

Fortunately, GIF images can include pixels or areas that are transparent. The transparent area is most often around the edges of an image, but it can also be inside the image, resulting in a see-through effect.

If your image isn't letting the background show through, follow these steps to specify transparency.

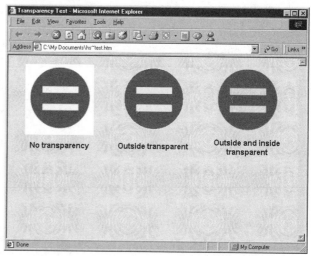

Without transparency, the image shows its true size.

How to fix it

1. Open the image file in your graphics program. If possible, use the original artwork, such as a Fireworks, Photoshop, or Illustrator file; otherwise, open the GIF format file.

2. Only one color in your image can be transparent; by the same token, all areas with that color will be see-through. Before exporting your image, decide on the color around the outside that will be transparent. If that same color—often white—also is used within your graphic, change the background or canvas to a different color. (Ideally, this should be the background color of your page, although it doesn't have to be.)

3. Export the file: for example, click Save For Web (Photoshop) or Export Preview (Fireworks). Select GIF format.

4. Select Indexed Transparency. The areas you intend to be transparent should be indicated with a gray checkerboard pattern. If they aren't, click the Add Color To Transparency button and then click the areas of the image that you want to be transparent. ▶

5. Export the file, and then preview the image on a page that has the background setting you want.

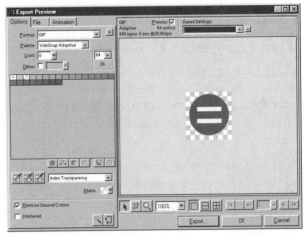

Most graphics programs indicate transparent areas with a gray checkerboard pattern.

Many ways to let the background show through

Most graphics programs use the simplest method of transparency, called *alpha* transparency. In this format, the edges of the image change abruptly from the image color to the background. If your graphics program offers it, you might be able to achieve a smoother look using *indexed* transparency instead. This method transitions the color smoothly at the edges, from the image color to the canvas or matte color you specify.

There is one drawback to indexed transparency, however, that arises when you place an image on a color other than the one you indexed to: the image might display a halo of color around the edges. The effect is especially apparent when an image intended for a light background gets placed on a dark page. This problem happens to a lesser extent with alpha transparency. The moral of the story? When saving a transparent GIF, always try to specify a canvas or matte color close to the page background; if you don't know the exact background color you'll use, choose alpha transparency. (For more information on this problem, see "The image has a slight halo" on page 204.)

There is a third type of transparency, called *8-bit* or *PNG* transparency, available only in PNG format files. Using PNG transparency, you can specify areas of your image that are partially see-through, creating a translucent effect and allowing the background to show through as much or as little as you like. What's more, PNG transparency solves the halo issue mentioned above: these graphics display equally well on any background. However, because not all browsers support PNG files—version 4 browsers offer partial support and earlier browsers don't display them at all—it might not be a good idea to use them just yet. In the future, PNG files could become the standard, adding improved options for transparency.

To continue with this solution, go to the next page.

The background doesn't appear around the edges of an image

(continued from page 25)

FrontPage makes transparency even easier

With FrontPage, you don't need to use a separate graphics program to specify transparency in an image.

1. Select the image on your page that you want to be transparent. ▶

2. On the Picture toolbar, click the Set Transparent Color button.

3. Click the outside area of the image to reveal the background.

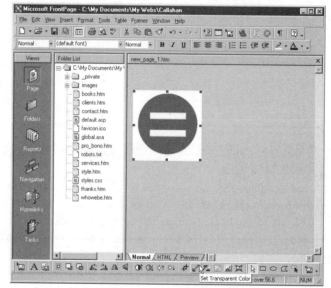

In FrontPage, getting the background back is a quick three-step process.

One way to make elements of the page stand out or to separate them is to put a border around them. Web browsers can display borders of varying widths around your tables, pictures, and other objects.

Unfortunately, the methods you use to specify borders are not consistent. For some objects, you can change a simple property or HTML attribute; for others, you'll have to use styles. What's more, there are some borders that browsers don't let you control.

If you use FrontPage, you'll probably discover shared borders, which don't border objects but instead provide standard content at the top, bottom, left, and right sides of your web pages.

If your solution isn't here

Check these related chapters:

Frames, page 140
Images, page 188
Tables, page 310

Or see the general troubleshooting tips on page xvii

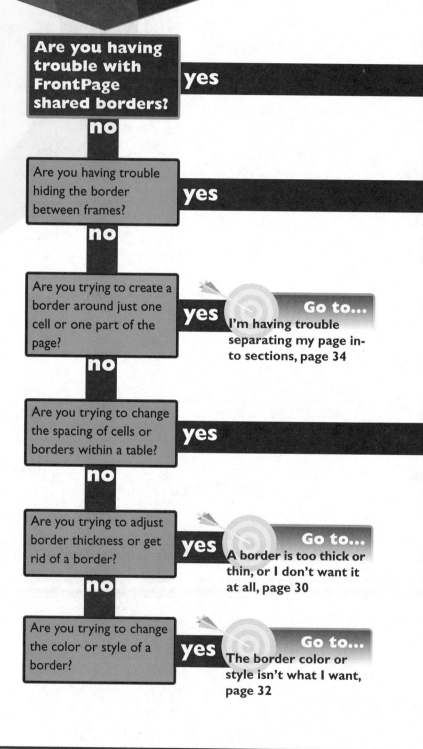

Are you having trouble with FrontPage shared borders?

yes

no

Are you having trouble hiding the border between frames?

yes

no

Are you trying to create a border around just one cell or one part of the page?

yes

Go to...
I'm having trouble separating my page into sections, page 34

no

Are you trying to change the spacing of cells or borders within a table?

yes

no

Are you trying to adjust border thickness or get rid of a border?

yes

Go to...
A border is too thick or thin, or I don't want it at all, page 30

no

Are you trying to change the color or style of a border?

yes

Go to...
The border color or style isn't what I want, page 32

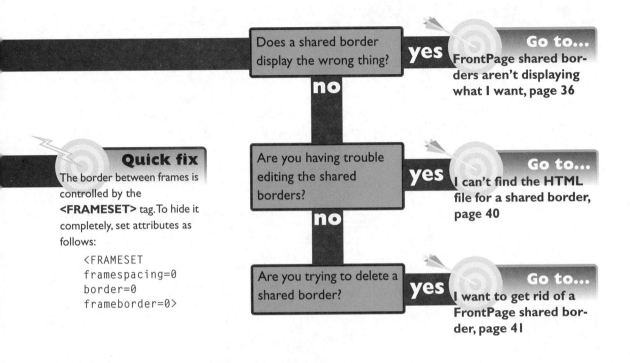

Does a shared border display the wrong thing?

yes → Go to... **FrontPage shared borders aren't displaying what I want, page 36**

no

Quick fix

The border between frames is controlled by the **<FRAMESET>** tag. To hide it completely, set attributes as follows:

```
<FRAMESET
framespacing=0
border=0
frameborder=0>
```

Are you having trouble editing the shared borders?

yes → Go to... **I can't find the HTML file for a shared border, page 40**

no

Are you trying to delete a shared border?

yes → Go to... **I want to get rid of a FrontPage shared border, page 41**

Do you want to close the gap between cell borders?

yes → **Quick fix**

You control the gap between the border lines inside a table with cell spacing. For example:

```
<table border=3 cellspacing=0>
```

In FrontPage:

1. Right-click the table and click Table Properties.
2. In the Cell Spacing box, type **0**, and then click OK.

no

Are the borders in a table too close to the text?

yes → **Quick fix**

If the contents of cells in a table are too close to the borders, increase the cell padding. For example:

```
<table border=3 cellpadding=6>
```

In FrontPage:

1. Right-click the table and click Table Properties.
2. Increase the value in the Cell Padding box, and then click OK.

A border is too thick or thin, or I don't want it at all

Source of the problem

Web browsers make it easy to display borders around images, tables, and embedded objects. But the border won't always look right on your page. A thick border might be too distracting, while a thin border might not show up well or frame your content as you'd like it to.

In many cases, you won't want a border at all. For example, if your image already includes a frame or border as part of the picture, you won't want an additional box around the image. Tables frequently have borders, especially when they display data organized in columns. But if you use a table for page layout, you probably won't want borders around the table or its cells. ▶

Fortunately, border thickness problems are easy to fix using either HTML or a web design program. Border thickness is controlled by the **border** attribute. To fix problems with the thickness of borders around images, tables, or objects on your page, follow these steps.

Sometimes table and image borders just don't look right.

How to fix it

Fix a border using HTML
If you prefer to edit the HTML directly, follow these steps.

1. In the HTML, find the tag that controls the border you'd like to change. You can specify a border for the contents of the following HTML tags: **<IMG>**, **<TABLE>**, **<OBJECT>**, and **<EMBED>**.

> **Tip**
> Using a table for page layout? Even if you don't intend to have a border for the table, it's a good idea to include a one-pixel border during the design and testing process. A border makes it easier to see what's happening with your page layout, and it's easy to turn off when you're ready.

2. Set the value of the **border** attribute to the width of the border in pixels; a value of 5 or more is a thick border, while 1 or 2 indicates a thin border. For no border, set the border attribute to 0.

```
<img src="images/frame.jpg" width=179 height=114 border=0>
```

Fix an image border using FrontPage

If your web design program is FrontPage, you don't have to change the HTML to fix an image border. Follow these steps instead.

1. Right-click the image and click Picture Properties.

2. Click the Appearance tab.

3. In the Border Thickness box, type the number of pixels you want the border to have. For no border, type **0**. ▶

4. Click OK.

Fix a table border using FrontPage

If your web design program is FrontPage, you don't have to change the HTML to fix a table border. Follow these steps instead.

1. Right-click the table and click Table Properties.

2. In the Size box under Borders, type the number of pixels you want the border to have. For no border around the table or its cells, type **0**. ▶

3. Click OK.

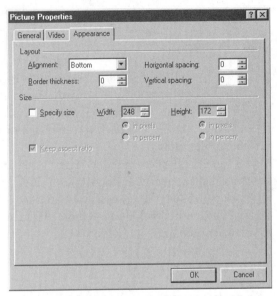

In FrontPage, you can change image and table borders by setting properties.

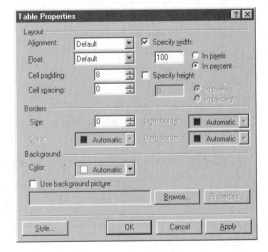

The border color or style isn't what I want

Source of the problem

When a table or image has a border, the border defaults to solid and black. If this isn't what you have in mind, you can adjust the border to the color and style you prefer. But the problem is complicated by the fact that different browsers support border color and style in different ways. (See the note at the right.)

To get the border color and style right—at least in browsers that support cascading style sheet (CSS) standards for borders—follow these steps. As support for styles increases, this method will become more effective in solving your border problems.

Note

Many browsers, including Netscape versions 4 and earlier, don't support border styles. If you want your pages to be displayed consistently in all browsers, don't use border styles. If you want to change only the color of a table border, there is a method that works in Netscape 4 as well as Internet Explorer: Set the **border color** attribute in the **<TABLE>** tag to the color you want.

How to fix it

1. Set the CSS **border** property for the table or other object, specifying three values: the border width (in pixels), the border style (solid, double, ridge, groove, dashed, dotted, outset, or inset), and a hexadecimal color number. (Don't know about color numbering? See "Web color numbers" on page 67.) ▶

   An easy way to set a border style is to add the **style** attribute to the HTML tag as shown here, substituting the style and color settings you want:

Newer browsers can display fancy border styles.

```
<table style="border:8px ridge #993300">
```

This method of setting styles is referred to as *inline*, and is best suited for occasional style settings. If you plan to use the same type of border throughout your web page or site, you're better off defining the border style either in a **<STYLE>** section of your page or a stand-alone style sheet. (For more information, see Appendix B on page 347.)

Fix border styles using FrontPage

If you use FrontPage, you can achieve the same styled borders without directly editing your HTML. Here's the procedure for creating or styling the border around almost any page element.

Tip
Tables and images aren't the only objects that can have borders. In fact, you can use the CSS border property to create borders around just about anything on a web page. For example, by enclosing a section of your page in a **<DIV></DIV>** block and setting styles, you can define a border around that section.

1. Right-click the image or table, and then click Picture Properties or Table Properties. Click Style, click Format, and then click Border.

Or, if you're setting a border style for a paragraph or cell in a table, click the paragraph or cell and then click Borders And Shading on the Format menu.

2. Click Box under Setting, set other options such as Style, Color, and Width, and then click OK. ▶

Tip
When you set border styles, FrontPage displays your settings in Page view. Remember that the styles may not look this way in your web browser. To preview the result of your style changes in Internet Explorer, click the Preview tab at the bottom of your page.

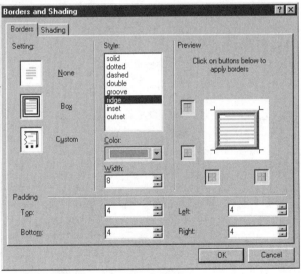

FrontPage helps you set border styles easily.

I'm having trouble separating my page into sections

Source of the problem

A common practice in page layout is to divide up your content into different areas on the page. To do this, you probably used a table that fills the whole page and organizes your content.

The problem arises when you try to create a colored border around an area of the page. If you specify a border for the table, a border appears around the entire table—you can't put borders around individual cells using ordinary HTML. You could use styles to create borders (see "The border color or style isn't what I want" on page 32), but not all browsers support them.

Fortunately, there is a clever solution to this problem that works in nearly all browsers. It allows you to create square borders around specific areas of the page. This is possible because HTML allows you to put tables *within* tables and specify the background color of each table and cell. ▶

If your page has sections that aren't set apart in the way you'd like, follow these steps to create borders to separate them.

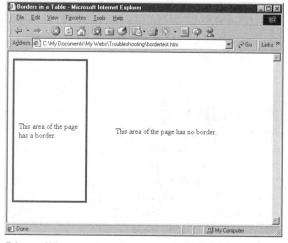

It's possible to create a border around just one area of the page.

How to fix it

1. If the body of your page isn't already enclosed in a table, create one. For this outer table, be sure to specify **border=0** and **cellpadding=0**.

2. In the cell for which you want a border, set the background color to the color you'd like for the border around the cell. (Set the **bgcolor** attribute of the **<TD>** tag.) Set the **width** and **height** attributes for this cell to the exact size you want. Otherwise, the size of the cell—and your border—could change with the width of the browser window.

3. Inside the cell—between the existing **<TD>** and **</TD>** tags—define a new one-cell table surrounding the existing cell contents. ▶

4. Set the **width** and **height** attributes of the inner table to a few pixels less than the cell that contains it. If you want a 4-pixel box around the cell, for example, set the width and height to **8** pixels less than the width and height of the cell that contains it.

5. Set the background color of the inner table to the same color as the page background. (Set the **bgcolor** attribute of the **<TABLE>** tag. If the page background is white, for example, type **bgcolor=#ffffff**.)

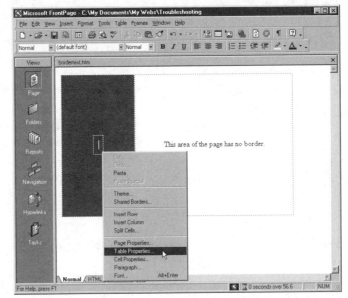

Within the cell for which you want a border, you'll insert a table—and then adjust its size and color.

Here's what your HTML might look like:

```
<!-- Outer table, provides overall page layout -->
<table width=500 border=0 cellpadding=0 cellspacing=0>
  <tr>
    <!-- Background color provides border around this cell -->
    <td align=center width=160 height=300 bgcolor="#003399">
      <!-- Inner table has white background -->
      <table width=152 height=29
        bgcolor="#ffffff"
        cellpadding=10 cellspacing=0>
        <tr>
          <td>
            <p>This area of the page has a
              border.
            </p>
          </td>
        </tr>
      </table>
    </td>
    <td align=center width=350>
      <p>This area of the page has no border.</p>
    </td>
  </tr>
</table>
```

Tip

When using HTML to specify the exact height and width for cells in a page-layout table, it's a good idea to specify the width of the entire table as well—and make sure the individual cell widths add up to the table width. Otherwise, browsers may distribute extra space inconsistently. If you use a page design program such as FrontPage, it most likely sets the cell widths appropriately.

FrontPage shared borders aren't displaying what I want

Source of the problem

When you add shared borders to your FrontPage web—or create a web site from a template that uses shared borders—all your web pages share the same content at one or more of the edges. For example, the top border of every page can display a page banner with the title of that page, while the bottom of the page might display your e-mail address or a copyright notice.

The trouble is, shared borders don't always display what you want, especially when you first add them to your web. You'll commonly see messages such as "[Add this page to the Navigation view to display a page banner here]." Or, if you do see titles and links in the border, they might not be the ones you want. Finally, as you edit shared borders or make changes in Navigation view, you might find that FrontPage fails to display those changes in the borders. ▶

If your shared borders aren't displaying the right thing, follow these steps to whip them into shape.

How to fix it

1. If you are working with a new page that you haven't yet saved, click Save on the File menu, type a name for your page, and click OK.

A common problem with new pages is that the shared border areas don't display titles or links.

2. Make sure you have the shared borders you want for your site. FrontPage can manage borders for all four sides of the page, or just one or two. If you don't see the borders you want, click Shared Borders on the Format menu. Select or clear the Top, Bottom, Left, and Right check boxes as desired. Select Include Navigation Buttons under the Top or Left box (or both) so that FrontPage will create navigation bars for you. Then click OK. ▶

3. Most shared borders include banners and navigation bars, which should automatically display page titles and links on each page in your web. However, these elements get their content from your web structure as defined in Navigation view. To switch views, click Navigation in the Views bar (at the far left). Make sure every page that you want to connect is shown in the navigation structure of your web.

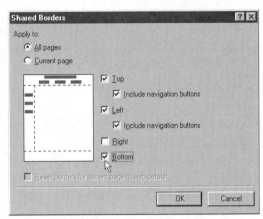

The most common shared borders are top and bottom. A left side border is often used for hyperlinks.

4. If you find any pages missing from the navigation structure, drag each page—including any new pages you've added to the web—from the Folder List onto the navigation structure and arrange your pages in a logical fashion. In a simple web site, for example, the Home page is at the top level, while other pages are included underneath. ▶

5. To return to your web page, click Page in the Views bar. In most cases, shared borders now display page titles and navigation links.

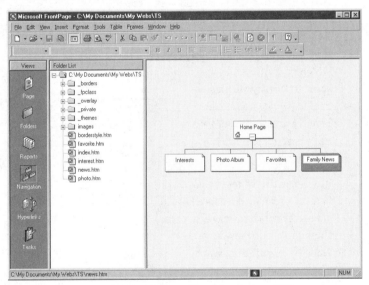

The solution to navigation bar problems is often to add your page to the Navigation view.

If this solution didn't solve your problem, go to the next page.

FrontPage shared borders aren't displaying what I want

(continued from page 37)

Source of the problem

You've made sure the correct borders are displayed and have added your pages to Navigation view. But your shared borders still aren't right. To fix the problem, you might need to make additional changes to the text, images, page banners, or navigation bars in the border areas.

How to fix it

1. For each page banner or navigation bar that isn't displaying what you want, you need to review and modify properties. Double-click the page banner or navigation bar. ▶ For a navigation bar, specify which part of the navigation hierarchy you want to display, such as Same Level or Top Level. FrontPage creates links on each page based on your selection.

2. Now that the banners and links are ready, edit your shared borders to make them look just the way you want—after all, they will be displayed on every page of your web site. For example, you may want to insert a logo or type some text, such as your name and address or a copyright notice. ▶

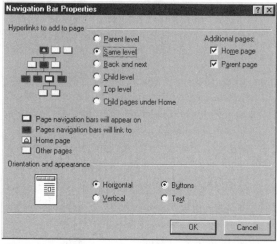

In the properties for a navigation bar, you can specify which pages it will link to.

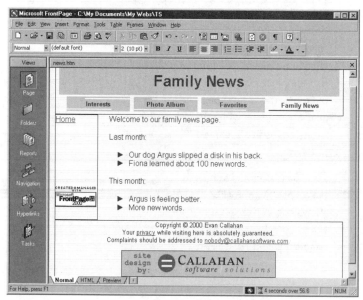

To add a consistent look to your site, insert logos and text in your shared borders.

3. The best way to test shared borders is in your web browser. On the File menu, click Preview In Browser. Click hyperlinks on your navigation bar to view each page. If your shared borders still aren't right, switch back to FrontPage and make additional changes.

Sharing page borders across an entire web site

Most web sites, whether or not they are created with FrontPage, have border areas at the top, sides, and bottom that are the same from page to page. FrontPage shared borders provide a great way to design this type of web site, because they ensure that the border areas always contain the same content. They also allow you to make changes in a single place rather than on every page.

You might be curious about how shared borders work, since the HTML they contain isn't stored with any individual page. FrontPage stores the HTML content of your borders separately (see "I can't find the HTML for a shared border" on the next page). Then, when you edit your web pages, FrontPage displays the shared borders around them so you can edit them. When you save a page, FrontPage automatically creates a table and lays out your shared border content as well as the main content of your page.

Even if you don't use the FrontPage navigation or banner features, you can still benefit from shared borders. Anything you repeat from page to page is a good candidate for placement in a shared border. Here are a few ideas for content you might put in a shared border:

- Your company logo

- A navigation bar, list of hyperlinks, or an image map that links to other pages

- Advertisements

- Logos of your partners, associations you belong to, or certifications you have

- Contact information, such as your name, address, phone, and an e-mail link

- E-mail address of the webmaster or person to contact about web site problems

- Special links to a search page, signup page, or privacy policy

- Copyright or legal notices—the fine print

I can't find the HTML file for a shared border

Source of the problem

When you add shared borders to a web, FrontPage creates and manages the HTML for the border areas of your web site. It creates four shared HTML files—Top.htm, Bottom.htm, Left.htm, and Right.htm—and automatically displays them when you view pages in a browser.

It's easy to change these borders in Page view. You just click in the border area of the page and insert text or graphics or make other changes. But when you switch to HTML view, you won't see the contents of these border areas of your page. FrontPage keeps the border files hidden away.

If you want to edit the HTML for the border areas, you'll need to open the shared HTML files directly rather than edit them as part of the pages that use them. To locate and open the border files, follow these steps.

How to fix it

1. On the Tools menu, click Web Settings. Click the Advanced tab, select Show Documents In Hidden Directories, and then click OK. If FrontPage asks whether you want to refresh the web, click Yes.

2. Click Folders in the Views bar (at the far left). Double-click the _borders folder to open it. If your web has shared borders, you'll see one or more of the following files: Bottom.htm, Left.htm, Right.htm, and Top.htm. ▶

3. Double-click the shared border file you want to edit. To view HTML, click the HTML tab at the bottom of the page. When you save the shared border file, remember that changes you've made will apply to every page in your web.

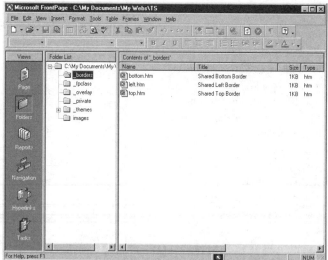

FrontPage hides the HTML files for shared borders.

I want to get rid of a FrontPage shared border

Source of the problem

When you add shared borders to a FrontPage web, every page shares the same thing around the edges. This can be very handy, since it helps you keep your web site consistent and easy to navigate. But for some pages on your web, you might not want the shared borders. ▶

Fortunately, FrontPage allows you to remove one or all of the shared borders from any one page or your whole site. To get rid of one or more shared borders, follow these steps.

How to fix it

1. On the Format menu, click Shared Borders.

2. Under Apply To, click Current Page. Or, if you want to remove shared borders from your entire web, click All Pages.

3. Clear the check box for each border you don't want, and then click OK. ▶

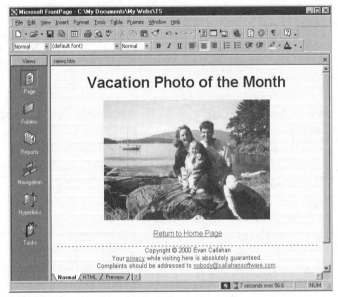

You can remove one or more of the shared borders from your whole web—or from just one page.

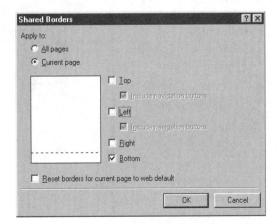

Over the past few years, web browsers have evolved a great deal, making web surfing and design more rewarding. But for all the advances, browser issues remain one of the major sources of trouble in web design.

On the bright side, new browser versions are coming closer to following the same set of web standards. But the compatibility challenge is growing as we ask browsers to present increasingly complex content and run interactive programs.

For an introduction to Internet networking, see "Internet connectivity basics" on page 47. For general tips on designing pages that are compatible with a variety of browsers, see "Designing pages for all browsers" on page 55.

When you run into trouble in your browser, follow this flowchart to a solution.

If your solution isn't here
Check these related chapters:

Are you having trouble displaying your web page in a browser?
yes →
no ↓

Are you having trouble accessing the Internet?
yes →

Go to...
I'm having trouble accessing the Internet, page 44

no ↓

Are you trying to view the HTML source of a web page?
yes →

Quick fix
Viewing the HTML source of web pages is an important way to learn. Right-click the page or frame you're interested in and click View Source.

no ↓

Are you having problems with Internet Explorer settings you've changed?
yes →

Quick fix
If Internet Explorer no longer works as you expect, you can reset your settings to defaults. On the Tools menu, click Internet Options. Click the Advanced tab and then click Restore Defaults.

no ↓

Do you need to download a version of Internet Explorer or Netscape?
yes →

Quick fix
It's a good idea to test your web pages in all popular browser versions. Download them from these web sites:

Netscape:
home.netscape.com/download/

Internet Explorer:
www.microsoft.com/windows/ie/

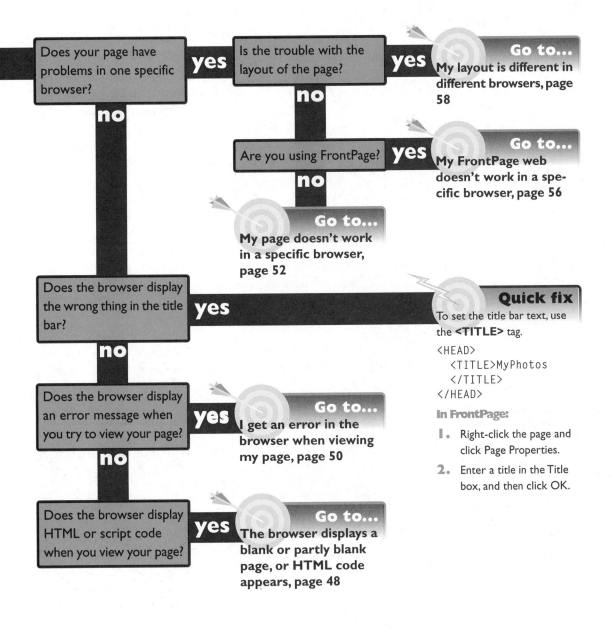

Does your page have problems in one specific browser?

yes → Is the trouble with the layout of the page?

yes → **Go to...** My layout is different in different browsers, page 58

no → Are you using FrontPage?

yes → **Go to...** My FrontPage web doesn't work in a specific browser, page 56

no → **Go to...** My page doesn't work in a specific browser, page 52

no → Does the browser display the wrong thing in the title bar?

yes → **Quick fix**

To set the title bar text, use the **<TITLE>** tag.

```
<HEAD>
   <TITLE>MyPhotos
   </TITLE>
</HEAD>
```

In FrontPage:

1. Right-click the page and click Page Properties.

2. Enter a title in the Title box, and then click OK.

no → Does the browser display an error message when you try to view your page?

yes → **Go to...** I get an error in the browser when viewing my page, page 50

no → Does the browser display HTML or script code when you view your page?

yes → **Go to...** The browser displays a blank or partly blank page, or HTML code appears, page 48

I'm having trouble accessing the Internet

Source of the problem

Your Internet connection is your gateway to the outside world. You can't afford to be without it. But the grand network that brings the bounty of the Internet to your computer is bound to give you trouble now and then. You might see error messages indicating trouble finding the server, experience trouble connecting to your Internet service provider (ISP), or run into problems when upgrading your computer or software.

What is it this time? Perhaps the server you're trying to access—or your ISP or Internet gateway—is temporarily down. The problem could lie with your computer's hardware, software, or settings. There are many factors involved with accessing the Internet, and in some cases, you might have to seek outside help. But the following steps will help you isolate and work through the most common problems associated with accessing web pages.

How to fix it

1. Try to open web pages on your own computer. In your browser, click Open on the File menu, click Browse, and select a valid web page (.htm) file. If you can't open web pages, reinstall your web browser to see if that fixes the problem.

2. Be certain you are working online. In Internet Explorer, click the File menu and make sure that Work Offline is *not* checked. In Netscape, click the File menu, point to Offline and click Work Online. Click the Refresh button.

3. Check to see whether your problem is with a single page, the server, or the whole Internet. In the browser's address bar, type **www.microsoft.com** or **www.yahoo.com**. If these reliable sites are successfully displayed by your browser, the problem lies with the server or page that you were attempting to access, and not with the whole Internet. Try the problem page again several minutes later, in case the server was temporarily offline. ▶

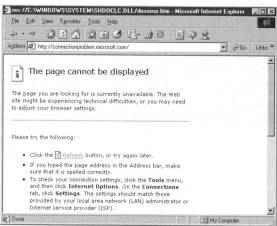

Uh-oh, Internet problem. In this case, it's just one server.

4. If your Internet connection is through your network, DSL, or ISDN—meaning you never dial using a modem—skip to the steps under "Connecting over a network, " below.

   Otherwise, check your dial-up connection. (In Windows, for example, an icon at the lower right corner of the screen indicates whether you are connected.) If you are connected to your ISP but no web pages are available, disconnect—it's possible something has gone wrong with the communication between the ISP and your computer.

Tip The quality of Internet service—from the small local companies to the international giants—varies quite a bit. If you have recurring connection problems related to your service, don't hesitate to switch to another ISP.

5. Connect using dial-up networking. (In Windows, double-click My Computer, double-click Dial-Up Networking, and then double-click a connection.) If you get an error message, check if there is a dial tone. If you don't hear anything from your modem, check your phone line and cables. If you still can't determine the cause of the problem, see your modem or browser documentation for ideas. (In Internet Explorer 5, click Contents And Index on the Help menu, click Connecting To The Internet on the Contents tab, and then click Fixing Connection Problems.)

6. If you hear the modem dialing but not connecting—you get a busy signal or there is no answer—check the area code and phone number settings. If everything is in order, it could just be that your ISP doesn't have enough lines or computer capacity. Try again later.

7. If it appears that the computer is connecting, but you get an error message about a password, check the user name and password settings you're using. If you believe they are correct and you still can't connect, contact your ISP.

Connecting over a network

1. Check with your coworkers, network administrator, or ISP to confirm that the network is functioning properly. It's possible that your network's connection to the Internet isn't working properly or the service is overloaded.

2. Most connections over a network go through a *proxy server*, also known as a gateway or firewall. Verify your proxy settings. In Internet Explorer, click Internet Options on the Tools menu, click the Connections tab, click LAN Settings, and then set options under Proxy Server. In Netscape, click Preferences on the Edit menu, double-click Advanced under Category, click Proxies, and then set options.

Tip If you're connected to the Internet and are using Internet Explorer— but can't view a web site—you might have corrupt cookies. To check, move the contents of the cookies folder (such as C:\Windows\Cookies or C:*windowsroot*\Profiles\ *username*\Cookies) to another folder temporarily. Try to browse the Internet again. If that solves the problem, move cookies back a few at a time to find the bad apple.

To continue with this solution, go to the next page.

I'm having trouble accessing the Internet

(continued from page 45)

Source of the problem

You've tried some of the easy solutions, but you're still not able to connect to the Internet. Use these steps to diagnose problems with your network configuration.

How to fix it

1. Check whether your computer's TCP/IP configuration—the protocol that allows you to access the Internet—is functioning properly. Open an MS-DOS window. (Click the Start menu, point to Programs, and click MS-DOS Prompt or Command Prompt.) Type **ping 127.0.0.1** and press Enter. This command asks your system to request a response from *itself*—using the TCP/IP protocol. You should see four lines of text beginning with "Reply from…" ▶

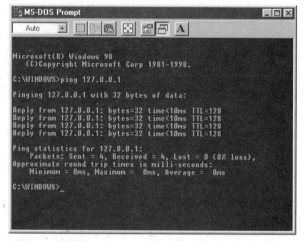

When you ping *a computer, it should reply as shown here.*

2. If these lines don't appear, you might need to reinstall TCP/IP. Not for the faint of heart, here are the steps (for Windows 98): Right-click Network Neighborhood and click Properties. Double-click the TCP/IP entry for your network card (you don't need to do this for dial-up adapters) and write down the settings on all tabs, especially the DNS, Gateway, and IP Address tabs. Next select each TCP/IP entry and click Remove. Click OK and reboot your computer. Again, right-click Network Neighborhood and click Properties. Click Add, double-click Protocol, click Microsoft under Manufacturers, click TCP/IP under Network Protocols, and click OK. Double-click the TCP/IP protocol entry to replace the settings you recorded. Click OK, and then restart your computer. ▶

3. Check if you are communicating with the Internet. Type **ping 208.20.99.165** at the MS-DOS prompt and press Enter. If you are communicating with the Internet, you'll see four lines of text beginning with "Reply from…"

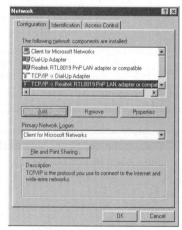

For successful communication, your TCP/IP protocol settings must be correct.

4. Check if you are communicating with a domain name service (DNS)—a computer, usually at your ISP, that translates the dot-com style names into Internet addresses. Type **ping callahansoftware.com** and press Enter. Again, you should see "Reply from…" If you get the response "Unknown host callahansoftware.com," either your server or your DNS settings aren't working. If DNS isn't working, it's probably time to contact your network administrator or ISP.

Internet connectivity basics

As the Internet grows and its use becomes increasingly widespread, it's easy to forget what an amazing accomplishment it represents. As most of us have experienced, even a small network between similar computer systems is prone to problems. By comparison, the global Internet is a huge project involving millions of computers of different types. As with any network, the computers that provide and relay information are called *servers*—they are on call to serve other computers that make requests over the network. The computer that you connect with at your ISP is a server, and every web site on the Internet is hosted on a server.

This vast network works through a *protocol*—a strict set of rules—called TCP/IP. This protocol allows computers to communicate, requesting and routing information from one to another across great distances. Each computer on the network has an *IP address* consisting of four numbers between 0 and 255, such as 207.46.131.137 (the address for *microsoft.com*). Every named network location, or *domain*, has a static IP address. By contrast, when you connect to your ISP or company network, your computer is assigned a temporary IP address so that servers can send information back in response to your requests.

Computers use the numeric IP address to access each domain on the network, but humans use a *domain name*, such as *microsoft.com*. In order to translate these names into numbers, the Internet uses the domain name system, a huge network of servers with the entire database of current names, numbers, and network routing information. And if you register your own domain name on the Internet, it will end up in this database so that web users everywhere can make requests of your web site.

Once your browser has the IP address of a web server, it uses another protocol—Hypertext Transfer Protocol (HTTP)—to request a web page. This protocol allows you to send or request information and get responses without staying directly connected to the server on the other end—which would be a difficult proposition given the number of computers on the Internet.

In summary, every time you type in a web address, your computer first resolves the domain name into an IP address, sends an HTTP request through your proxy server or ISP to the web server, and waits for the information to come back. Once the server sends back the data—an HTML or image file, for example—it closes the connection. And once your browser receives the HTML, it interprets and displays the web page.

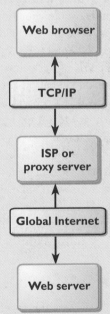

When you request a web page, there's a lot going on behind the scenes.

The browser displays a blank or partly blank page, or HTML code appears

Source of the problem

Generally speaking, browsers display what they're instructed to display—by reading and interpreting the HTML code you give them. If you see HTML code when viewing your page in the browser—or if you see nothing at all—there's probably something wrong with the HTML you've provided to the browser. ▶

The most likely cause of the problem is a typographical error or a syntactical error in your HTML. For example, if you leave out the closing bracket (>) after a tag, the browser will interpret the text up to the next tag as part of the previous HTML tag. If you leave out the opening bracket (<) before a tag, the browser won't know it is a tag and might display it as ordinary text. Leaving out certain closing tags—for comments or scripts, for example—might cause the browser not to display the remainder of the page. And in strict browsers such as Opera, even a minor HTML error can prevent the browser from displaying all or part of your page.

To fix your page, follow these steps.

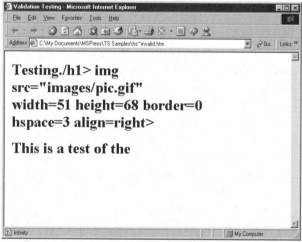

When HTML code shows up or the page contents stop suddenly before the page is fully rendered, something in your HTML has misled the browser.

How to fix it

1. In case the page failed to load completely, reload it in your browser. In Internet Explorer, click Refresh on the View menu. In Netscape, click Reload on the View menu. If you still get a blank or otherwise messed-up page, something is wrong with your HTML. (If the browser displays an error message, see "I get an error in the browser when viewing my page" on page 50.)

2. Check your HTML carefully for correctness. For example, make sure that all tags have opening and closing brackets (< and >). Be certain that all tags that open a block of code have corresponding closing tags. If the browser displays HTML or cuts the page short, the place in your page where the problem begins is a good spot to inspect. Fix any formatting problems you can find, add missing closing tags, and then preview your page again.

3. Diagnose problems in your HTML code by using an HTML validation tool. If you use HomeSite to edit your page, validation is built into the program. On the Tools menu, click Validate Document; results appear at the bottom of the screen. Otherwise, you can use an online validation tool such as the one at *validator.w3.org*. ▶

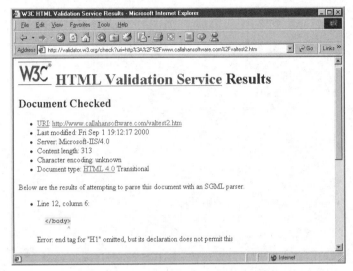

    If the validation software reports any missing or invalid tags, correct them and preview the page again. (For ideas on correcting other errors you find, see "An HTML validation tool reports errors in my code" on page 86.)

HTML validation software looks for missing tags and rule violations in your code.

4. Code that is disorganized or poorly formatted can make it hard for you to diagnose errors. If you'd like to clean up your code—indenting code for easy reading, for example—use an HTML formatting tool. If you're using HomeSite, try the CodeSweeper feature—the "HTML Tidy" option often produces the best results. On the Tools menu, point to CodeSweeper, and then click Allaire Default HTML Tidy Settings.

5. If your page has script code, it might be causing errors in the page without letting you know. In Internet Explorer 5, look for a warning icon at the lower left corner of the window. In Netscape, type **javascript:** in the address bar to open the JavaScript console, where errors are displayed. If your script is causing errors, remove it from your page or see "Scripting" on page 280 for ideas on solving problems.

Tip
Before you run an HTML formatting tool, save a copy of your web page so you can revert to the original if necessary. In some cases, you may not like the formatting the tool uses. Also, reformatting can create new problems on your page—make sure to preview your page carefully after reformatting your code.

I get an error in the browser when viewing my page

Source of the problem

Web pages seldom cause a browser to display an error. That's because most browsers simply ignore any HTML code they don't recognize. If you do see an error when viewing your page, the problem is probably with the browser itself or with your Internet connection.

Recent browser versions are designed to recover from programming errors, stopping bad scripts without reporting errors to the viewer. If your browser is configured to display script errors, however, you'll see an error message when a script performs an illegal operation or is invalid. ▶

Errors are not always easy to track down and solve, but identifying the cause is often the first step. If you're getting an error message, follow these steps.

How to fix it

If the browser crashes

1. If the browser displays the Windows "Illegal operation" message, you probably won't be able to fix the problem by changing your page. It might be an isolated incident. Reboot your computer and then try viewing the page again.

Invalid JavaScript can cause a disturbing interruption for viewers of your page.

2. If you still can't view the page, you might need an updated browser. (Look for the latest from Microsoft at *www.microsoft.com/windows/ie* or Netscape at *home.netscape.com/download*.) Another likely source of trouble is your video card or software—you might try updating your video driver or checking with the browser manufacturer to see if your video hardware is supported.

If the browser says it can't find or display the page

1. Browsers use a variety of different messages to tell you that they can't display a page. In any case, the first thing to check is whether you have mistyped the domain name or page name. Be sure you have the right file name extension—web pages aren't always .htm—and the right domain syntax, such as www.w3.org. ▶

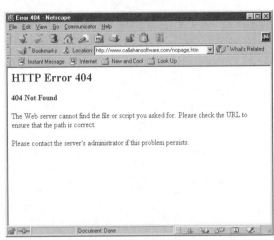

If you type the wrong name or the file isn't in the right place, your browser won't find it.

2. If you typed the correct address, it's possible the file isn't in the correct location. Using your FTP software—or Windows Explorer for local files—check to make sure you saved or published your page to the right place on your web server.

3. If you're trying to open the default page on your server—by typing **www.yahoo.com**, for example—it's possible that the web server isn't configured to find the file name of your page. Check which file name(s) your web server is looking for—often index.htm or default.htm.

4. If the browser can't find the domain of the server you specified, your Internet connection or web server could be down. Check to make sure you are connected to the Internet. If you are, try your server again later or contact your ISP or web server administrator.

If the browser displays a security warning

1. There are two sources of security errors—permission settings on the server and security precautions taken by the browser. If your browser displays a message such as "401 Unauthorized," "403 Forbidden," or "You are not authorized to view this page," the web server has permission settings that don't allow you to view the page. To solve the problem, update security settings to allow anonymous access (or access to appropriate users).

2. If the browser displays its own security warning for your page, it means that browser settings don't allow some feature of your page. ▶ If your page tries to run an ActiveX control, for example, security settings might not allow it.

 To view the page, you can loosen browser security restrictions. To address

Browser security settings can result in warnings.

the problem for viewers, however, make sure you use only "signed" controls from reputable sources—and provide an alternative page for viewers who have strict security settings.

My page doesn't work in a specific browser

Source of the problem

There's a strong tendency for people to design pages for the browser they use most—perhaps Internet Explorer, perhaps Netscape—and for the most recent version. While designing your site, you'll frequently preview pages with that browser. Later, when you test them in another browser or version, you might find that your tags, styles, scripts, or embedded objects aren't working. Welcome to browser incompatibility!

Problems arise either because the other browser doesn't support some features you've used, or because it requires a different syntax or tag to perform the same function. If a browser doesn't support an HTML tag or attribute, it generally won't tell you. Instead, it will ignore the part it doesn't understand and just display the page as best it can. In some cases, the effect won't be too noticeable—for example, if you provide a background sound that plays in only some browsers; in others, the problem could cause errors or prevent viewers from seeing your page.

To address your browser compatibility problem, follow these steps. For design strategy ideas, see "Designing pages for all browsers" on page 55. If your page uses scripts and they aren't working, see "My script works in one browser but not in another" on page 290.

How to fix it

1. Evaluate the seriousness of the problem. If your page isn't working in a recent version of Netscape or Internet Explorer (4 or later), you clearly need to find a solution. If it's in a less popular browser, on the other hand, consider whether you can live with the problem. For example, if your graphics don't line up in the WebTV browser—which isn't very popular, especially for business use—you might choose to ignore the problem.

2. If your HTML editor offers easy external previewing, be sure to set up the browser for viewing the page that's giving you trouble. As you change your code to fix the problem, perform frequent checks of your page in that browser. In FrontPage, for example, click Preview In Browser on the File menu, and then click Add if the browser you need isn't listed among those available. ▶ In HomeSite, click Configure External Browsers on the Options menu and add the browser you need. Then, every time you preview a page, you'll have the option to see how it looks in that browser.

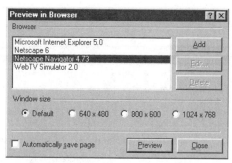

Preview frequently, and in more than one browser.

3. If your HTML has errors, they could trip up the browser. Check your HTML carefully for correctness—for example, do all tags that open a block have corresponding closing tags? Diagnose problems in your HTML code by using an HTML validation tool. ▶

    If you use HomeSite to edit your page, validation is built into the program. Click Validate Document on the Tools menu; results appear at the bottom of the screen. Otherwise, you can use an online validation tool such as the one at *validator.w3.org.* (See Appendix C for other suggestions.) For ideas on correcting errors you find, see "An HTML validation tool reports errors in my code" on page 86.

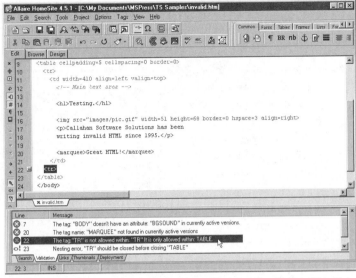

HomeSite validation results help you follow standards. Double-click each message to jump to that line of HTML.

4. Some of your HTML might be too advanced for the browser or might apply only to a specific browser. The **<MARQUEE>** tag works only in Internet Explorer, for example, while **<BLINK>** works only in Netscape. Many validation programs report tags or attributes that work with only one browser, and many HTML reference sources list browser compatibility. Find the tag on your page that has the problem in the browser you're testing. Can you achieve the same effect using another method that is better supported? In place of the **<BLINK>** tag, for example, you might use JavaScript or create an animated GIF image.

> **Tip**
> If you want to display different pages—or different elements on the page—for viewers with specific browsers, you can do this using a script. See "My script works in one browser but not in another" on page 290.

To continue with this solution, go to the next page.

My page doesn't work in a specific browser

(continued from page 53)

5. If your page uses cascading style sheets (CSS), they might be the problem. Where possible, use ordinary HTML tags and attributes to create the effect you want. For example, use **<BODY>** tag attributes, such as **bgcolor** and **link**, to set background properties and link colors, even though these attributes are often better controlled using CSS. For more information, see "The styles don't work in a certain browser" on page 304.

> ## Which browsers should you design for?
>
> How popular is each browser? It just so happens that many web sites track browser-use statistics. (To find them, search the web for *browser statistics*.) Estimates as of this writing—the numbers can change rapidly—suggest that around 75 percent of viewers use Internet Explorer 4 or later, around 20 percent use Netscape 4 or later, and the remaining 5 percent or so use older versions or other browsers such as WebTV, Opera, or Lynx.

6. If your page uses embedded objects, plug-ins, or Java applets, be aware that they might not work in older browsers or on systems that don't have the required software components installed. ActiveX controls, for example, run only in Internet Explorer for Windows. Even if components do work elsewhere, viewers might have to download plug-ins to support them.

   If you want to be sure that none of your viewers have been excluded, substitute alternatives that are more compatible or widely supported. Also, see "Understanding sound and video formats" on page 229 for information on how best to make multimedia available.

7. If you can't do without advanced features, you might need to create special links or separate pages for users who can't view them. For example, you might provide a link for downloading a new browser or plug-in, or a link to a simpler version of your page or multimedia file.

Designing pages for all browsers

There are four basic strategies for dealing with the differences among browsers:

- **Keep it simple.** This strategy, referred to as "designing
  for the lowest common denominator," involves using
  only HTML that's been supported for many years—no
  styles, scripting, or plug-ins, of course. Also, test your
  pages in an older browser to make sure that viewers using such browsers can access your site.

- **Go cutting edge.** The opposite strategy is to assume
  that everyone is using the latest browser, such as
  Netscape 6 or Internet Explorer 5.5 or later. You can then
  use all the latest features: styles to format and position
  objects, dynamic HTML effects, and enhanced content
  such as Flash animations. If you go this route, you really
  should indicate on your home page which browser version your viewers will need in order to access your page.

- **Create separate web pages for each browser.**
  Many large web sites use this labor-intensive strategy to
  deliver the best content to each viewer. You'll need to
  create three or more versions of your pages, one for
  each browser or group of browsers. For example, build
  a low-tech set of pages for older browsers, a feature-
  rich set of pages for recent browsers, and a third set
  just for Netscape 4. Then use scripts—either JavaScript
  in your pages or scripts on the server—to display the
  proper pages.

- **Adopt a balanced approach.** Create a single set of
  pages that work for most of the browsers you want to
  support, using cutting-edge features where they help
  you get the message across. Meanwhile, make sure your
  pages aren't badly flawed in any other browsers. For
  specific compatibility problems, make compromises or
  find workarounds.

My FrontPage web doesn't work in a specific browser

Source of the problem

Many features of FrontPage are designed to work only in Internet Explorer 4 and later. When you try them in Netscape or another browser, they might look wrong or they might even cause errors. Because many users have other browsers, these features are not practical for general web use.

In an attempt to mitigate this problem, FrontPage includes options that can help you avoid creating a web that isn't compatible with the browsers you want to support. For example, you can disable all FrontPage features that don't work in Netscape.

Follow these steps to get your page working in other browsers and to prevent the problem from happening again.

Tip

Disabling features (using step 3 on the facing page) does *not* remove them from your pages. In some cases, disabling them may even prevent you from removing them—for example, you must remove all positioning and dynamic HTML effects before turning the features off, or else you won't be able to use the toolbars that control these effects.

How to fix it

1. If you've used page transitions, dynamic HTML effects, border styles, background sounds, marquees, certain font effects, or absolute positioning of objects, they're unlikely to work in Netscape 4 or earlier. If these features simply fail to work—but otherwise don't create havoc with your page—keep them for the benefit of Internet Explorer users. If, on the other hand, they do cause problems, remove them from your page.

2. If your page uses a FrontPage theme, reapply the theme without using styles. On the Format menu, click Theme. Click All Pages or Selected Page. Clear the Apply Using CSS check box, and then click OK.

3. To avoid using features that are incompatible with some browsers, disable them.

On the Tools menu, click Page Options. Click the Compatibility tab. In the Browsers box, select Both Internet Explorer And Navigator. Under Technologies, clear check boxes for those features you want to avoid, such as CSS 2.0 (Positioning) and Dynamic HTML. Click OK. ▶

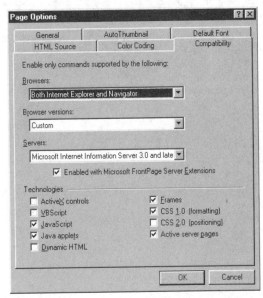

You can tell FrontPage to disable features that don't work in Netscape.

This web designer's compatibility solution

In designing my own web pages for *www.callahansoftware.com*, I used style sheets to format my content in a consistent and flexible way. I had a tough time getting everything to look right in Netscape 4, but I desperately wanted to avoid having separate pages to support different browsers. Too difficult to maintain!

Because of browser differences with CSS support, I decided to compromise. I have one set of pages, but two separate style sheets—one for Netscape 4, another for all other browsers. A simple JavaScript routine at the top of each page causes links to be made to one style sheet or the other. Meanwhile, if a browser doesn't support JavaScript or CSS—an increasingly unlikely scenario—the viewer sees the pages with a plain but acceptable appearance.

My layout is different in different browsers

Source of the problem

With each new version, web browsers evolve and develop a unique sense of style. Each browser has idiosyncrasies in layout and presentation, and when you're trying to make pages look right for every viewer, these can drive you crazy. Perhaps you've got the layout just right in your browser. Then when you try another browser, everything gets thrown into disarray: fonts are different sizes; the spacing is off; the content doesn't fit in the cells of a table as you intended, and so forth. ▶

To solve a few common layout problems, follow these steps. For design strategy ideas, see "Designing pages for all browsers" on page 55.

How to fix it

1. If your HTML editor offers easy external previewing, be sure to set up the browser for viewing the page that's giving you trouble. As you change your code

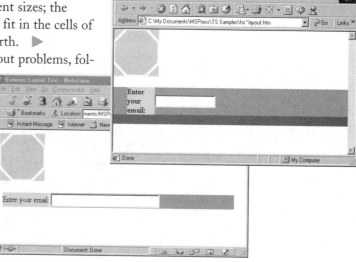

The same HTML can produce a very different display.

to fix the problem, frequently check your page in that browser. In FrontPage, for example, click Preview In Browser on the File menu, and then click Add if the browser you need isn't listed among those available. In HomeSite, click Configure External Browsers on the Options menu and add the browser you need. Now while you experiment with your page, you'll have the option to see how it looks in each browser.

2. Perhaps there is a problem with the page margin. By default, browsers insert spaces in the top left corner of each page. Netscape and Internet Explorer use different attributes of the **<BODY>** tag to change this margin, so to change it back, you will have to insert some redundant code. Use the following **<BODY>** tag to start the page immediately at the top and left.

```
<body topmargin=0 leftmargin=0 marginheight=0 marginwidth=0>
```

3. Perhaps you're getting an extra line or excessive space at the end of a cell, hyperlink, or other element. Many browsers add extra spaces if you put the end tag (such as **</TD>** or **</A>**) on its own line (although this shouldn't happen under HTML specifications). This problem is especially apparent if you have two images that need to be adjacent to each other. To close up the space, move the end tag to the end of the previous line.

```
<a href=other.htm>
   <img src="ralph.gif" width=50 height=50></a>
```

Also, to avoid extra space between cells in Netscape, set both the **cellspacing** and **border** attributes to 0 in the **<TABLE>** tag:

```
<table cellspacing=0 border=0>
```

4. Make sure that Netscape correctly displays a table with empty cells. Some versions of Netscape collapse empty cells even if you've specified a width or height. (For more on this problem, see "Empty cells aren't being displayed properly in Netscape" on page 316.) To keep a cell from collapsing, put an element inside it, such as a nonbreaking space:

```
<td width=50> </td>
```

> **Tip**
>
> If you create a stretching table—one that changes column sizes with the width of the window—browsers may size the columns differently. For help, see "I specified column widths, but they still seem to vary from the size I gave" on page 320.

5. You might have a problem with the spacing of columns across the page. It's common to limit page width or create columns across the page by enclosing your whole page in a large table. Unfortunately, browsers apply cell widths somewhat differently. To make your table appear the same among browsers, set the **width** attribute for every **<td>** tag, giving each column enough space for its contents. If you specify a table width, make sure that cell widths add up to that same value; otherwise, Netscape distributes extra space to every cell. Here is an example:

```
<!-- Table for overall page layout -->
<table width=600 cellpadding=0 cellspacing=0 border=0>
   <tr>
      <td width=200>
         Insert narrow column HTML here.
      </td>
      <td width=400>
         Insert wide column HTML here.
      </td>
   </tr>
</table>
```

To continue with this solution, go to the next page.

My layout is different in different browsers

(continued from page 59)

6. Differences in text size might be goofing up the display of your page. For browsers that support CSS, you can set font size precisely in points or pixels. For example, this style sheet entry sets the font size to exactly 16 pixels:

```
body, td { font-size: 16px; }
```

7. If you create a form, you'll find that Netscape and Internet Explorer set text fields (**<INPUT>** tags) to different widths; in Netscape, these fields might not fit your page or cell width. Change the value of the **size** attribute so the fields fit properly in Netscape. Then, if you like, use a style to specify an exact field size and font:

```
<input type="text" name="email" size="20"
    style="width:300px; font:10pt arial">
```

8. If you can't get the page to be displayed properly in all browsers, try to compromise so that you provide the best possible layout in the most common browsers and a reasonable facsimile in others.

> **Tip**
>
> If you want to display different pages for viewers with specific browsers, you can do so using a script. See "My script works in one browser but not in another" on page 290.

Color is a critical factor in designing effective web pages. You can select colors for nearly every element of your pages, including text, hyperlinks, backgrounds, and borders.

Because there are many different methods for setting color, it's easy to run into problems. In addition, color presents tough issues because people view your web pages on different systems, and colors don't always look the same from one system to another.

If you are having trouble getting the color you want, follow the troubleshooting flowchart here. And if possible, try out your web color scheme on a variety of computers.

For an introduction to a few important color concepts, see "Web color numbers" on page 67.

If your solution isn't here
Check these related chapters:
Borders, page 28
Frames, page 140
Hyperlinks, page 174
Images, page 188
Text formatting, page 322
Or see the general troubleshooting tips on page xvii

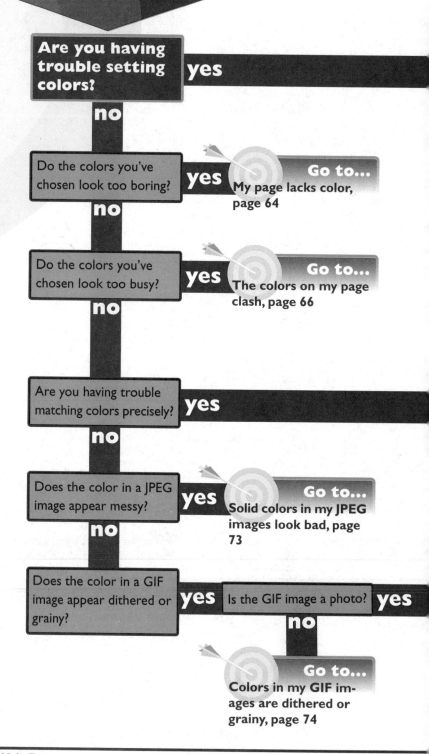

Are you having trouble setting colors?

yes

no

Do the colors you've chosen look too boring?

yes Go to... My page lacks color, page 64

no

Do the colors you've chosen look too busy?

yes Go to... The colors on my page clash, page 66

no

Are you having trouble matching colors precisely?

yes

no

Does the color in a JPEG image appear messy?

yes Go to... Solid colors in my JPEG images look bad, page 73

no

Does the color in a GIF image appear dithered or grainy?

yes Is the GIF image a photo? **yes**

no

Go to... Colors in my GIF images are dithered or grainy, page 74

Are you using a FrontPage theme?

yes

Quick fix

When you use a theme, FrontPage controls the background, text, and hyperlink colors. To control them yourself, change or remove the theme.

1. On the Format menu, click Theme.
2. Select a theme with colors you like, or select (No Theme).

no

Are you having trouble setting basic text and background colors?

Quick fix

Specify basic page colors using HTML color codes or the FrontPage color picker. Select a background color that contrasts well with the content of your page.

In HTML:

In the **<BODY>** tag, set the **text** and **bgcolor** attributes. For example:

```
<body text="#003300"
bgcolor="#cccc99">
```

In FrontPage:

1. Open the page you want to change.
2. On the Format menu, click Background.
3. Select colors in the Background and Text boxes, and then click OK.

no

Are you having trouble setting the color of specific text, backgrounds, or borders?

yes

Go to...
The color of a specific element isn't what I want, page 68

Do your colors look different on some computers?

yes

Go to...
My colors look wrong on 256-color computer systems, page 70

no

Go to...
Colors in my images don't match other colors on the page, page 72

Quick fix

For photos, the JPEG image format is usually your best bet. To create small image files with smooth color, save as JPEG.

1. Open the original high-quality image file (or rescan) using your graphics software.
2. Save as a JPEG file with Medium or High quality.
3. In your web pages, replace the old GIF file with the new JPEG file.

My page lacks color

Source of the problem

By default, web pages don't have any color; like an ordinary printed page, they are black text on a white background. Unless you've specified colors for elements of your page, it probably looks rather plain and boring.

On the other hand, you can have too much color. Your goal is to find a happy medium between a boring page

design and one that is so colorful that it distracts from the content. ▶

If your web page is lacking in color, the following steps will help you put a good finishing coat on your pages.

How to fix it

1. The easiest way to add color to a boring page is to specify a background color. Decide whether you want a light-colored background with dark (or black) text, or a

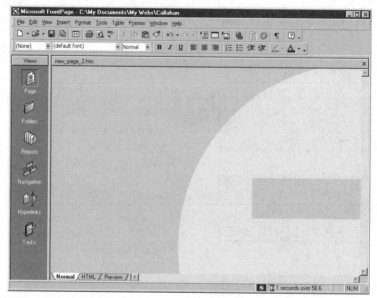

A two-color background image is one way to add color that looks good but isn't too distracting.

dark-colored background with light text. Dark text on a light background is usually easier to read. To set the background color, specify a value for the **bgcolor** attribute in the **<BODY>** tag. (Not familiar with hexadecimal color numbers? See "Web color numbers" on page 67.)

2. Create a background image for your page and save it in the folder with your web page (or another folder where you store images for your web site). Set it as the background using the **background** attribute in the **<BODY>** tag. A background image should be fairly simple—using just two colors, for example—and its primary color should be the background color you selected in step 1. Design the image either to fill the entire screen or to repeat (tile) across or down the page. (For more information on background images, see "Backgrounds" on page 14.)

```
<BODY text="#003300" bgcolor="#CCCC99"
   background="images/bkgd.gif">
```

3. If your page still doesn't have just the color you want, surf the web to look at color in some of your favorite sites. Do they use a background image? What basic colors do they use for background, text, and images? Apply the color ideas you like to your site. (See "Borrowing a color scheme" below.)

Tip

If you use a background image, set the background color to match the image. This way, viewers will see the matching background color while the image loads.

Borrowing a color scheme

It can be tough to find the right colors through experimentation. Often, the best solution is simply to copy someone else's color scheme. It's perfectly legal—and besides, they'll never know!

If you see a web color scheme you like, try to discover what colors the page uses. For most pages, you can find out what colors they use by viewing their HTML source code. In your web browser, on the View menu, click Source (or Page Source). Make a note of the color numbers in the **<BODY>** tag, and then try them in your own pages.

If colors you like are in a GIF or JPEG image, copy the image from within your web browser: right-click the image and then click Copy. Then paste the image into your graphics software and "borrow" its colors. In Adobe Photoshop, for example, click New on the File menu, click Paste on the Edit menu, click the eyedropper tool, and then click the color you like to select it as the foreground color. To discover its hexadecimal color number for use in your web page (in Photoshop 5.5), click the foreground color box; the Color Picker indicates the value with a # sign. ▶

Borrow colors from images you like by copying them into your graphics software.

The colors on my page clash

Source of the problem

By and large, web viewers value clearly presented information over a fancy appearance. If you've used too many colors or colors that don't work together well, viewers might be distracted or find your text difficult to read. Intense colors can look hideous on a computer screen, so it is important to use them sparingly.

If your web page has too much color, follow these steps to tone it down.

Tip

If you use FrontPage, a theme is the easiest way to select a complete color scheme. To apply a theme, on the Format menu, click Theme. Preview themes to find one you like, trying different options such as Vivid Colors and Background Picture.

Note that once you apply a theme, you can no longer change the background or default text colors. Instead, you customize the theme itself.

How to fix it

1. If the colors you chose make the text hard to read, change the color scheme to dark or black text on a light-colored background. Don't use an intense background color—muted is better!

   For web-safe dark colors, try the following color values: #993333, #000099, or #996666. And don't be afraid to use black (#000000) if you have too much color. For light colors, use muted tones, such as #CCCC99, #99CCCC, or #FFFFCC. Or use gray (#CCCCCC) or white (#FFFFFF).

2. Try to use colors that are appropriate for your topic and audience: dark blue, gray, and white are very corporate, while one or two bright colors like pumpkin orange, sea green, or maroon work well on a personal page or a consumer-oriented site.

3. If you use a background image on your page, make sure it is simple and uses colors that contrast well with the text.

4. If you have any GIF or JPEG images, place them on the page so you can see how they look with the colors you choose. If the colors don't look right together, try a plainer background or text color.

Tip

Newer versions of graphics programs, such as Photoshop 5.5 and Fire-works 3, can display RGB notation in either decimal or hexadecimal—and help you select web-safe colors without giving it any thought.

Tip

You might want to use a calculator (such as the Calcula-tor program included with Windows) that converts val-ues to and from hexadecimal.

Web color numbers

By now, you've probably run across a few of those six-character color codes, such as #CCCCFF (pale lavender) or #000066 (deep navy). How do you make sense of these codes, anyway?

Here's how it works. Computer color uses a notation called RGB, short for red-green-blue. Each color consists of three values between 0 and 255: the first is the amount of red the color contains, the second the amount of green, and the third the amount of blue. The combination 0-0-0 represents black, and 255-255-255 represents white. To keep the color codes to a smaller number of characters, HTML uses hexadecimal (base 16) notation. In *hex*, 00 is 0, and FF is 255; so just six characters can describe any RGB color value. The code for black is #000000, and white is #FFFFFF.

Using RGB notation, you can specify more than 16 million different colors. However, when you want to limit yourself to the 216 web-safe colors, there's an easy way to recognize them. Web-safe RGB colors consist of combinations of only the following two-character hexadecimal values: 00, 33, 66, 99, CC, and FF. (This is why there are only 216—not 256—web-safe colors: For each component color—red, green, and blue—there are six values in the web-safe palette. Six times six times six produces 216 unique combinations.) In other words, #99CC33 is safe, but #4ED3FC is not.

Your graphics software might require you to specify RGB color values in decimal (base 10) notation. If so, use the following decimal values for web-safe RGB color: 0, 51, 102, 153, 204, and 255.

The color of a specific element isn't what I want

Source of the problem

You can change the color of many web page elements: text, backgrounds, borders, and lines. If you aren't seeing the colors you expect on your page, chances are you've either specified colors in the wrong place or used incorrect HTML to set them.

The general strategy for setting color is simple: First, set the primary colors for the page. Then add color accents sparingly and consistently. The best way to add consistent accents is to create a *style* for each color or color combination you want to use, and then apply the style to individual objects on your page. Styles allow you to control the color of many more page elements than does ordinary HTML.

When an element of your web is the wrong color, follow the steps below to create and apply a style that provides the color accent you want.

How to fix it

1. For clearer code, remove any HTML tags and attributes that try to set color but aren't having the effect you want.

2. For each color combination you want to use, decide on a style name and note the colors you'll specify. (See "Web color numbers" on page 67.)

3. Create the styles by adding a **<STYLE>** section to the **<HEAD>** block of your HTML file. For each style, provide a style name preceded by a period and set the **color** and **background-color** attributes using hexadecimal color numbers. For example, you could add the following lines to the **<HEAD>** section:

```
<style><!--
.hilite {
    background-color: #FFFF00;
}
.blues {
    color: #0000CC;
    background-color: #99CCFF;
}
--></style>
```

4. Apply the style to individual elements on your page by setting the **class** attribute of each tag: ▶

```
<p class=blues>This paragraph has the
blues.</p>
```

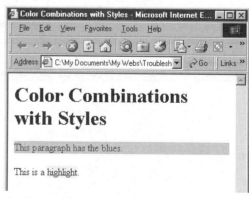

Styles provide an easy way to apply colors.

5. If you want to apply a style to a section of text that isn't already defined by a tag such as **<P>** or **<TD>**, surround the text with its own **<SPAN>** tag and set its **class** attribute accordingly:

```
<p>This is a <span class=hilite>highlight
  </span>.</p>
```

Tip

Remember that much of the color on web pages comes from graphics or images, which you can't change using HTML. To change color in images, edit them in a graphics program such as Photoshop.

Elements you can color

The following table lists the elements you can color and provides style samples for each. Also, in case you want to support older browsers that don't support cascading style sheets (CSS), the table also lists the ordinary HTML code you could use to set the same color (where available).

To color this web item	Set and apply a CSS style	Or use HTML without a style

Page text and background	`BODY, TABLE, TD {`
	`    color: #006600;`
	`    background-color: #CCCC99; }`
		`<BODY text="#006600"`
		`bgcolor="#CCCC99">`

Specific text	`.blue { color: #0000CC }`
	Apply in HTML:
	`<H1 class=blue>Blue Header</H1>`
		`<H1><FONT color="#0000CC">`
		`  Blue Header`
		`</FONT></H1>`

Text highlight	`.hilite {`
	`    background-color: #FFFF00 }`
	Apply in HTML:
	`<P>Highlight in`
	`<SPAN class=hilite>Yellow</SPAN>`
	`</P>`
		(Requires a style)

Hyperlink text	`A:LINK { color: #993300 }`
	`A:VISITED { color: #993333 }`
	`A:ACTIVE { color: #999933 }`
		`<BODY link="#993300"`
		`    vlink="#993333"`
		`    alink="#999933">`

Table or cell background	`.greenie {`
	`    background-color: #66CC66 }`
	Apply in HTML:
	`<TABLE class=greenie> <TR><TD>`
	`  On A Green Background`
	`</TD></TR></TABLE>`
		`<TABLE bgcolor="#66CC66">`
		`  <TR>`
		`    <TD>On Green</TD>`
		`  </TR>`
		`</TABLE>`

Table, paragraph, or image border	`.greenbox {`
	`    border-color: #00CC00 }`
	Apply in HTML:
	`<P class=greenbox>`
	`  This text has a green outline.`
	`</P>`
		(Requires a style)

Horizontal line	`HR { color: #993300 }`	(Requires a style)

My colors look wrong on 256-color computer systems

Source of the problem

Not all computer systems display all colors. In fact, depending on the video card and driver they use, many systems use a limited *palette* of just 256 colors. When the viewer's computer doesn't display the colors specified for your web pages and images, the browser must make do with the colors it has. The browser either shifts to the closest available color or *dithers* colors (approximates the specified color by alternating pixels of different colors).

For your web pages, this means that they might look great on your high-color screen, but not so great on another computer system. At the least, the colors may differ from what you intended. Fortunately, there are 216 colors designated as *web safe* because they are available to almost all viewers, regardless of operating system. (The remaining 40 colors out of 256 vary between systems.) The one way to avoid the color shift problem is to use only web-safe colors—both on your web pages and in your image files.

However, there is a catch. While web-safe colors are guaranteed to be displayed well, they aren't really the best set of colors. So what's a web designer to do? Follow these steps to provide the best overall look while usually avoiding color differences from system to system.

How to fix it

1. First, check the background and text colors of your web pages to make sure they are web safe. (Don't know how? See "Web color numbers" on page 67.) For these all-important colors, there's no sense using ones that might shift on you. ▶

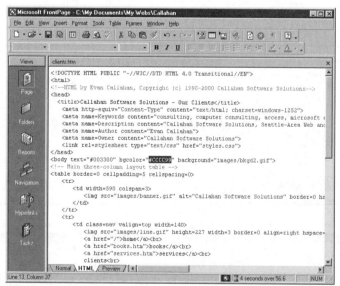

For background color and logos, play it web safe, *selecting only colors available on all systems.*

2. Open each of your image files in your graphics program, especially logos or graphical artwork with a lot of solid color; you'll want these colors to complement your background or text. Select colors in your image (use the eyedropper tool in Photoshop or Macromedia Fireworks) and check whether they are web safe. If they aren't, change them to web-safe colors and then resave the images as GIF files.

3. When you save GIF files, tell your graphics program to use an *adaptive palette* rather than the system palette or a web-safe palette. GIF images can have a maximum of 256 colors (fewer if you want a smaller image), and an adaptive palette selects colors that are actually in the image to make the best use of limited color. With an adaptive palette, your images will look great in high color. In 256 color, they won't be any worse than they would be with another palette.

4. Save photos in JPEG format—and don't worry about web-safe color. With JPEG format, you can't precisely control the colors you'll get. But web browsers always display JPEG images as best they can, with the available color depth.

5. Once you've fine-tuned your color, switch your display to 256-color mode to test your web pages. (In Windows 98, for example, open Control Panel, double-click Display, click the Settings tab, select 256 Colors, and then click OK.) Restart your web browser and take a look at your pages. Your images won't look quite as nice, of course. What you want to watch out for are areas of solid color that look wrong. Make note of any colors that you need to change, and then be sure to switch back to High Color mode.

Tip

Graphics programs such as Photoshop and Fireworks offer a Web Snap option when saving GIF files, which uses an adaptive palette but selects web-safe colors whenever the image colors are close to web safe. In addition, look for web-safe dithering, a handy feature for extending the web-safe color palette. To experiment with these additional colors, use the DitherBox filter (Photoshop 5.5) or the Web Dither fill option (Fireworks 3).

Note

Even when you use only web-safe colors, you might notice a color difference between systems. Each operating system has "gamma" settings that control the contrast and brightness of color, and every monitor can have its own settings as well. The best you can do is design graphics to look good on most systems; be aware they'll sometimes look wrong on others.

Colors in my images don't match other colors on the page

Source of the problem

Sometimes, the page just doesn't look right unless the colors match. If you have several images that are supposed to go together, you don't want each to have its own shade of blue. Still, even if you use the exact same color numbers on your web page and in your graphics software, the colors might not match in the viewer's web browser. What's going on?

The problem usually lies with web graphics formats. If you save images in JPEG format, solid colors are likely to change slightly because the image file is compressed and doesn't reproduce the image exactly. GIF format, on the other hand, uses a specific palette of colors for each image; however, if you save an image using a palette that doesn't include the color you want to match, your image will get the closest shade.

Regardless of graphics format, web browsers sometimes shift your choices to the nearest *web-safe* color—one of 216 colors that can be displayed on almost any computer screen. So the only way to guarantee a color match is to select web-safe colors and create images that use the same.

When your colors don't match exactly, follow these steps to get back on track.

How to fix it

1. If your web page or tables use background colors that you want to match with image colors, be sure to specify a web-safe color. (Don't know how? See "Web color numbers" on page 67.) Make note of the RGB values you've chosen.

2. In your graphics software, open the image file that needs to have matching color. Change the image colors to the web-safe RGB values. (In original artwork, you can change the color of objects in the image; in a GIF, you'll need to edit the image's color table or else substitute web-safe colors while saving. Search for *changing color* in your product documentation.)

3. Save the files in GIF format. If your software allows you to see the color palette you are using, make sure it includes the exact color value you want to match. Otherwise, save with an *exact* or *web-safe* palette to make sure the colors won't shift in the web browser.

> **Tip**
> The most noticeable color problems occur when the background of an image doesn't match the background page color. You can often avoid this problem altogether by saving "transparent" GIF images so the page background shows through. For information, see "The background doesn't appear around the edges of an image" on page 24.

Solid colors in my JPEG images look bad

Source of the problem

The JPEG image format is designed to compress and display photographs efficiently. When you save a JPEG, you decide how much detail you want to preserve. You can create big JPEG files that look just like the original image or small JPEG files that look—well, messy.

The process of compressing and then displaying a JPEG always causes some loss of clarity. In photos, as fortune would have it, this isn't too noticeable. In graphics, especially those with solid color or text, you'll notice blurring or specks of unwanted color.

If your image is primarily a logo, graphic, or a composite of text and graphics, consider using GIF format rather than JPEG to avoid the speckled appearance of solid color. However, if you do want to stick with JPEG—by far the best way to store photos or other images with subtle color gradation—follow these steps to improve image quality.

How to fix it

1. Locate the original high-resolution image file and open it in your graphics software. Or, rescan the image. (If you don't have a high-resolution version, you might still be able to improve your image somewhat using these steps. Unfortunately, you can't regain the image detail lost in JPEG compression. If the image is big enough, you can probably improve its appearance somewhat by reducing its size.)

2. Save or export as JPEG. Start by selecting high or maximum image quality, which creates the largest file size. If your software allows you to preview the file, reduce the quality gradually without creating too much grainy or speckled color.

3. Some graphics software allows you to introduce blurring or *lossy* compression. Experiment with this option to minimize the speckling effect, but use it sparingly to avoid images that appear out of focus.

4. Save the image and preview it in your web browser.

> **Note**
>
> When a JPEG looks bad, you'll usually need to go back to a higher resolution version in order to create a better image file. For this reason, it's important to save original graphics files and photos on your hard disk, even though you create smaller versions of the graphics for your web site. Otherwise, you might need to start over by scanning or recreating your images.

Colors in my GIF images are dithered or grainy

Source of the problem

Images look grainy on the computer screen for two primary reasons—either the computer can't display color well, or the image file doesn't contain good color. If your computer has only 256-color video, your images will naturally look grainy, unless they use only simple color. (See "My colors look wrong on 256-color computer systems" on page 70.) If your images look bad on a high-color system, however, it's probably because they weren't saved properly.

GIF images can have a maximum of 256 colors, and you can use even fewer colors to create a smaller image. The set of colors the GIF uses is called a *palette*. When the color palette you use to save your GIF file is inadequate, it causes *color shift* (you get different shades than you intended), *color banding* (colors don't transition well and show as bands), or *dithering* (areas that should be a solid color have jagged edges).

The trick is to save your image with an adequate color palette to reproduce it accurately, without wasting space with colors you don't need. Newer graphics programs, such as Photoshop 5.5 and Fireworks 3, make this process easy because they allow you to preview your images before you save them.

Follow these steps to resave your problem GIF files with the best possible color.

How to fix it

1. Open the original artwork file, such as a Fireworks, Photoshop, or Adobe Illustrator file, or scan a high-resolution image in your graphics software. If you don't have your original artwork—you have only a GIF or JPEG file, for example—you might be able to minimize graininess using a filter or effect, such as Blur or Despeckle, in your graphics program. However, you'll never be able to regain image information that is lost in the process of saving the image in GIF or JPEG format. If the image is big enough, one way to improve resolution is to reduce the size of the image.

> **Tip**
> If your image is a photo or has subtle gradations of color, you'll probably be better off saving in JPEG format rather than GIF. Designed for photo compression, JPEG handles color changes more gracefully and creates much smaller files. Beware, however: in JPEG images, solid colors aren't as consistent and fonts may look blurry.

> **Tip**
> If you have a large image with different colored sections, consider breaking it up into smaller pieces and "reassembling" them on your web page. This way, each part of the image can have its own optimal color settings. If you use Fireworks 3 or Adobe Image-Ready, your software can "slice" images for you and export separate files from a single graphic; alternatively, you can split the graphics yourself.

2. Once your image is ready, save or export it as a GIF file. Newer versions of graphics software, such as Photoshop 5.5 and Fireworks 3, allow you to preview the result with different settings so that you can pick the optimal settings for your image.

3. Select an adaptive palette, which uses colors that are actually in the image to make the best use of limited color. If you use the web-safe or system palette, your image uses a specific set of colors and can't represent gradual color changes.

4. Save your GIF with as many colors as needed to reproduce your image well—but no more. For composite artwork with lots of color, you might need a full complement of 256 colors to make it look just right. For a logo that has only 4 colors, on the other hand, save just 4 colors to produce the smallest file possible. (However, be aware that in images that include text, smooth font appearance depends on additional colors in the image.) ▶

5. Some graphics programs offer the option to dither colors as needed to produce smoother color transitions. If your image still displays some color banding, try specifying dithering.

6. When you're happy with the results, save the image and preview it in your web browser. Notice the size of your GIF files. If you saved a large image with lots of color, your file might be large and take a longer time to load.

Note

In some older graphics software versions, you might need to convert your image to *indexed color* before saving as GIF, selecting a number of colors or color "bits" (8-bit color is 256 colors, 7-bit is 128 colors, and so on).

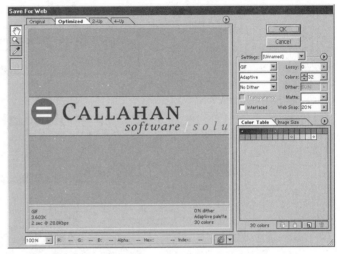

This logo has mostly web-safe color, but an adaptive palette with 32 colors ensures smooth font edges and color transitions.

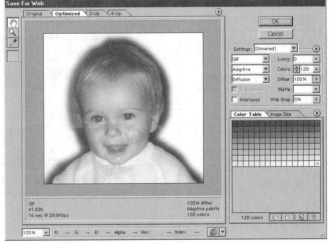

The baby picture, on the other hand, needs at least 128 colors, and benefits from dithering.

If fancy design and multimedia are the icing on the cake, editing web pages is the meat and potatoes. Like it or not, you're going to have to spend some time in a web page editor or design program if you're going to build a web site.

The topics in this chapter focus on two popular page design programs, Microsoft FrontPage and Allaire HomeSite. While these programs are very different, they share many of the same web page editing problems.

Whether you're having trouble getting out of the starting gate or running into HTML issues a good way down the road, follow this flowchart to find a solution.

Are you having trouble with features of FrontPage or HomeSite?

yes

no

Are you staring at a blank web page?

yes → **Go to...** There's nothing on my new page, page 78

no

Is your HTML code difficult to read and understand?

yes → **Go to...** My HTML is messy and hard to read, page 80

no

Does an HTML validation tool report errors on your page?

yes → **Go to...** An HTML validation tool reports errors in my code, page 86

no

Do you need to change something in all your files?

yes

no

Are you having trouble saving a file that someone else is working on?

yes → **Go to...** I got an error because someone else was working on the same page, page 85

If your solution isn't here

Check these related chapters:

Browsers, page 42
FrontPage, page 154
Office web features, page 244
Publishing & servers, page 262

Or see the general troubleshooting tips on page xvii

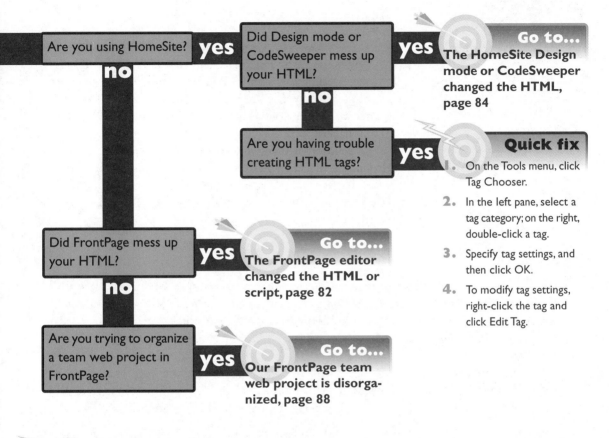

Are you using HomeSite? **yes** → **Did Design mode or CodeSweeper mess up your HTML?** **yes** →

Go to...
The HomeSite Design mode or CodeSweeper changed the HTML, page 84

no ↓ (under "Did Design mode...")

Are you having trouble creating HTML tags? **yes** →

Quick fix

1. On the Tools menu, click Tag Chooser.
2. In the left pane, select a tag category; on the right, double-click a tag.
3. Specify tag settings, and then click OK.
4. To modify tag settings, right-click the tag and click Edit Tag.

no ↓ (under "Are you using HomeSite?")

Did FrontPage mess up your HTML? **yes** →

Go to...
The FrontPage editor changed the HTML or script, page 82

no ↓

Are you trying to organize a team web project in FrontPage? **yes** →

Go to...
Our FrontPage team web project is disorganized, page 88

Quick fix

Like most editors, HomeSite and FrontPage allow you to change HTML in more than one file with a single command.

In HomeSite:

1. On the Search menu, click Extended Replace.
2. Enter text in the Find What and Replace With boxes.
3. Click In Folder, specify a folder, and click Replace.

In FrontPage:

1. On the Edit menu, click Replace.
2. Enter text in the Find What and Replace With boxes.
3. Select All Pages, select Find In HTML, and click Find In Web.
4. Double-click the first document in the list.
5. For each document, click Replace All and click Next Document.

There's nothing on my new page

Source of the problem

You're staring at a blank page in your HTML editor or page design program. It's tough to figure out where to begin, especially if you're new to web authoring. What you need is a jump start—something to get you rolling on your web page.

Your software might offer templates, samples, or wizards to help out. Or, you can pattern your page on someone else's existing page. Then, once you establish a basic layout for your page, you can include any text or images that you want, and you'll be off and running. To get past the blank page, follow these steps.

How to fix it

1. If you're using an HTML editor or page designer that offers templates or wizards, check what's available. In FrontPage, for example, you can use templates for individual pages or for entire webs—such as a personal or project web site. Web templates offer the fastest start, but creating individual pages from templates offers more flexibility. On the File menu, point to New and then click Page or Web.

   Or, if you know you want the same page structure as an existing web page, import the page and modify it to meet your needs. To import a page in HomeSite, on the File menu, click Open From Web. In FrontPage, on the File menu, click Import and then click From Web.

2. Set a title and other properties for your page. In FrontPage, for example, right-click your page and click Page Properties. In HTML, add a **<TITLE>** tag to the **<HEAD>** section and set attributes of the **<BODY>** tag, such as background and text color:

   ```
   <head>
     <title>Evan's Home Page - Photos, Family News, and More</title>
   </head>
   <body bgcolor="#cccc99" background="images/bkgd2.gif">
   ```

3. To apply consistent formatting on your page, consider linking to a style sheet using a **<LINK>** tag. In FrontPage, try a theme by clicking Theme on the Format menu. (Or, if you have a style sheet, click Style Sheet Links on the Format menu.)

4. Decide on a strategy for page layout. Most pages have a title at the top, main links at the top or left, and contact information and other details or links at the bottom. The center of the page generally contains text or graphics—the main content you're presenting. (You don't have

to design your web page in this way, of course, but this is what most people are used to seeing.) Create a large table that provides the general layout for the whole page. For more information, see "Page layout strategies" on page 212. ▶

Or, if you're using FrontPage, you might want to use shared borders to provide consistent border areas on all your pages. For information, see "Sharing page borders across an entire web site" on page 39.

5. If you have any logos or other image files for your web, insert them into the page. Most HTML editors and design programs, including FrontPage and HomeSite, add **<IMG>** tags automatically when you drag image files from a file list onto your page. For more information, see "Images" on page 188. ▶

6. Type your text. Or, if you have text on your computer that you want to include, copy and paste it into your page.

7. As you refine your design, preview and save your page frequently. Get feedback from friends or coworkers as you work—they might have ideas that otherwise wouldn't occur to you.

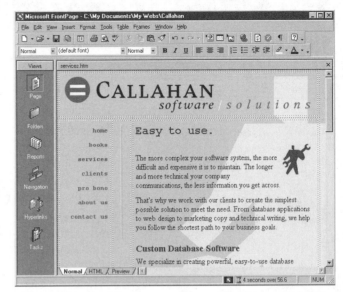

A large table provides the overall layout for my page, with the logo banner in a cell at the top and hyperlinks to other pages in a cell at the left.

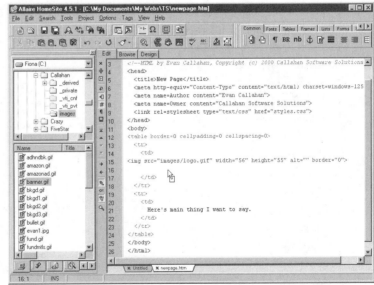

Adding images is the fastest way to get beyond the blank page. In HomeSite, drag image files from the file list and drop them in the appropriate place in your HTML.

My HTML is messy and hard to read

Source of the problem

When your HTML is disorganized or formatted inconsistently, it can be difficult to read it and to diagnose problems. If you share HTML files with coworkers, it's even more critical to keep your code in order, since each person needs to read and understand changes made by the others.

Follow these steps to reformat your HTML, either manually or with an HTML formatting tool.

> **Tip**
> If your software doesn't offer automatic HTML formatting, you can download a formatting tool from the web. HTML Tidy is available from the World Wide Web Consortium at *www.w3.org*, or see Appendix C on page 361 for other options.

How to fix it

1. If you don't have an HTML formatting tool, you can reformat code manually. First, insert line breaks to move each major tag to its own line. Indent tags inside tables and other blocks with tabs. Use consistent capitalization for tags and attributes. ▶

2. Use comments to explain what's going on in your HTML code—identifying sections of the page and clarifying the purpose of tags, for example. Browsers ignore these lines, but they help make your HTML easier to understand:

```
<!-- Navigation bar hyperlinks belong in this cell -->
```

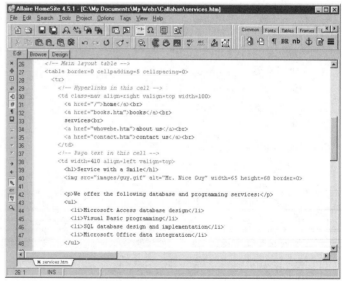

Well-formatted HTML is easier to read and understand.

3. If you're using FrontPage, you can tell it to re-format HTML whenever you switch to Normal view or save your page. On the Tools menu, click Page Options, click the HTML Source tab, and click Reformat Using The Rules Below. Set HTML format options and click OK. ▶

4. If you're using HomeSite, the CodeSweeper feature can format code for you. Save your page, and then click the CodeSweeper button on the toolbar.

To customize CodeSweeper options, click Settings on the Options menu and click CodeSweeper. To use the HTML Tidy formatter—which often produces the best results—select Allaire Default HTML Tidy Settings and then click Set As Default. Or, double-click any CodeSweeper entry to change settings, such as whether to capitalize the names of tags and attributes. ▶

5. After reformatting, preview your page in your browser. Look for any new spacing or layout problems, especially around hyperlinks and text formatting tags, such as **<B>** or **<I>**. Make adjustments to HTML as needed. As you edit or change your HTML later, follow the same rules for consistent, readable code.

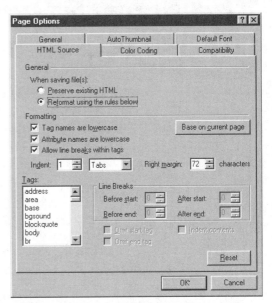

Front Page formats HTML according to rules you set.

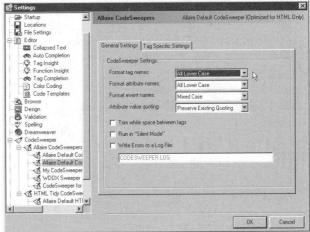

HomeSite's CodeSweeper is highly customizable, so you can format your code the way you like it.

The FrontPage editor changed the HTML or script

Source of the problem

You can use FrontPage as both a page designer and an HTML editor. Generally speaking, FrontPage preserves the HTML you've written in its original format—even when you switch to and from Normal view.

Whenever you change your page in Normal view, FrontPage has to write HTML—and it might not do what you want or expect. When you adjust columns in a table, for example, FrontPage sets or changes the width attribute in every cell and the table tag, which might change the layout of more than just the cells you wanted to change. If you use themes, shared borders, or other advanced FrontPage features, you'll see all sorts of special tags and scripts added by FrontPage behind the scenes. ▶

If FrontPage goofed up your HTML, follow these steps.

Note

If you're using FrontPage 98 or earlier, you'll see many potentially unwelcome changes to HTML. In FrontPage 97, in fact, you shouldn't open HTML files unless you don't care about the format of your code. FrontPage 2000 is much kinder to your HTML.

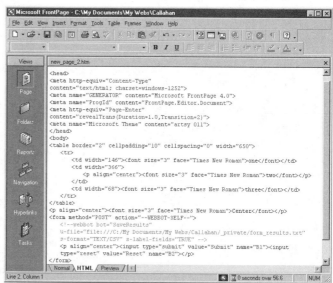

When you make changes in Normal view and then switch back to HTML view, your code might not be just how you left it. It could be cluttered and hard to read, and might even work differently.

How to fix it

1. Finish any changes you want to make in Normal view—this way, you won't have to fix your HTML code more than once.

2. Click the HTML tab and survey the damage. If the code isn't formatted the way you'd like, go ahead and fix it manually—FrontPage will generally leave your code alone once you do (although it might still make minor changes when you save the file). But don't change or remove HTML or any scripts that FrontPage added for features such as forms or dynamic effects; these are necessary to make the page work properly.

3. To change the way FrontPage formats HTML—telling it to use uppercase or lowercase tags, for example—click Page Options on the Tools menu, click the HTML Source tab, and set options. If you want FrontPage to reformat existing HTML based on these options, select Reformat Using The Rules Below.

4. When you change font settings in Normal view, FrontPage adds **<FONT>** tags that can clutter your page. You may prefer to set fonts using styles. To change the font in all tables in your page, for example, add a style block to the head section of your page:

```
<style>
  TD { font:10pt arial }
</style>
```

You can then remove unwanted **<FONT>** tags by hand, or by switching to Normal view, selecting the area you want to affect, and then clicking Remove Formatting on the Format menu.

5. If you've made adjustments to a table in Normal view, use HTML view to check the width, height, and alignment settings for cells in the table. FrontPage may have added unwanted attribute settings—overwriting your percentages with fixed width settings, for example. You can fix all the attributes in HTML view. To let FrontPage change them, switch to Normal view, select the cells you want, right-click the selection, and click Cell Properties.

Note

If you view the HTML source of your page in another editor or in the web browser, you may see tags and comments that aren't visible in FrontPage, even in HTML view. FrontPage adds these tags whenever you save a page that uses advanced features, such as themes, forms, or dynamic effects. If you edit or remove these tags, the features might cease to work.

6. Preview your page in a web browser. If FrontPage is still making changes that cause your page to work incorrectly, you might need to instruct it not to touch any part of your HTML. In HTML view, select the HTML that needs to remain intact, and click the Cut button on the toolbar. Switch to Normal view, point to Advanced on the Insert menu, click HTML, and type your code or press Ctrl+V to paste it. FrontPage adds special comment tags around this code that instruct the program not to interpret or change this code. ▶

You can tell FrontPage not to interpret or change a block of code.

7. If you don't like FrontPage's HTML or can't fix the problems it causes, don't edit in Normal view anymore. Use only HTML view, or use another editor such as HomeSite. Then, if you need a FrontPage feature on your site—a form that sends e-mail, for example—add it to your page once everything else is complete.

The HomeSite Design mode or CodeSweeper changed the HTML

Source of the problem

HomeSite's Design mode helps you lay out tables and text without writing HTML. You switch to this mode using the Design tab at the top of the editing window. When you do, HomeSite warns you—with good reason—that this mode could cause problems in your HTML. ▶ HomeSite's code formatting feature, CodeSweeper, is also not without its problems—it might not format code as you'd like and can occasionally cause layout problems on your page.

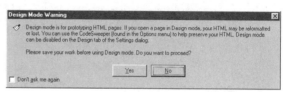

HomeSite warns you that using Design mode can be problematic.

After you make changes using Design mode or CodeSweeper, you won't be able to use the Undo command. Instead, follow these steps to solve the problem and avoid it in the future.

How to fix it

1. If you saved your page just before using Design mode or CodeSweeper, it's best to discard the changes you made and revert to the previous version of the file. Click Close on the File menu, and click No when HomeSite asks if you want to save changes.

2. If you inserted tags in Design mode, HomeSite might have inserted them in the wrong place. Click the Edit tab and look over your HTML carefully, moving or deleting elements as necessary. Once you have the page working, you may want to reformat the code that Design mode produced. To do this, click the CodeSweeper button on the toolbar.

3. After using CodeSweeper, preview your page in a browser. Look for problems in spacing or layout, especially around text-formatting tags such as **<B>** or **<I>**. Click the Edit tab and make adjustments to the HTML as needed.

Tip

CodeSweeper is customizable, and you can adjust its HTML output to suit your taste. To set options, click Settings on the Options menu, and then click CodeSweeper. To change the default CodeSweeper HomeSite uses—using HTML Tidy often produces the best results—select an entry in the list and click Set As Default. Double-click an entry to change settings. After you update settings, click the Code-Sweeper button to try them.

Tip

To avoid this problem in the future, use Design mode and CodeSweeper judiciously, saving your page beforehand and making your own code and format adjustments immediately afterward.

I got an error because someone else was working on the same page

Source of the problem

When you work with others on a web project, it's not uncommon to end up editing the same file at the same time over the network.

Unless you use special software that helps combine changes in the two files, only one person's changes will be saved in the file. ▶

When you see this error, follow these steps to resolve the issue.

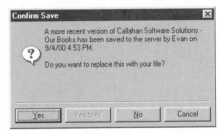

Only one person should edit a page at any given time.

How to fix it

1. Save a temporary version of your page with a different name.

   In HomeSite, for example, when asked if you want to reload the file, click No. Then click Save As on the File menu, type a new name for the page, and click OK.

   In FrontPage, when asked if you want to replace the other person's changes, click No. In the Save As box, type a new name for the page, and then click OK.

2. Later, once you've made sure the other user has closed the page, open it again. Switching between your version and the original, copy and paste your changes into the original file.

3. Save the original page, which now has your changes as well as the other person's. Close your temporary version, and then delete it.

Tip

To avoid this problem in the future, install a source control program, such as Microsoft Visual SourceSafe. If you're using FrontPage, basic source control is built in. On the Tools menu, click Web Settings, select Use Document Check-In And Check-Out, and then click OK. When you edit files, FrontPage allows you to check them out and indicates to other users that they are being edited.

An HTML validation tool reports errors in my code

Source of the problem

It's a good idea to check the correctness of your HTML with a validation tool, such as the Validate HTML feature in HomeSite. If your HTML follows the rules, you're less likely to have problems in different browser versions. But validation tools often turn up errors that are difficult to solve, and report others that aren't important.

There are three types of issues that your validation tool will turn up. First, it might warn you about tags you've used that don't conform to the current standard. Second, it might tell you about attributes that are missing or incorrect. Third, it will warn you about poorly formed HTML, such as missing end tags. ▶

In some cases, you can ignore the validation tool's complaints. To identify problems that really do matter, however, follow these steps.

How to fix it

1. Review each issue the validation tool brings up, locating it by its line number in your file. If you're using HomeSite, double-click each line in the results pane to jump to that line.

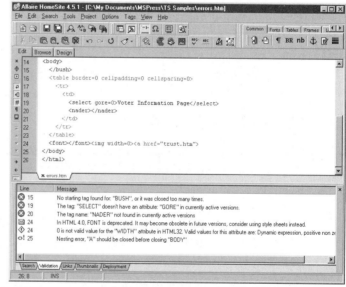

HTML validation tools are helpful, but their messages are sometimes difficult to decipher.

2. Fix typos and other obvious errors in HTML tags or attributes.

3. If you've failed to supply required attributes, such as the **src** attribute in an **<IMG>** tag, add them. Other attributes, such as **alt**, are recommended but not required. Unless you have a good reason to leave them out, add the attributes that the validation tool recommends.

4. If end tags are missing, add them. For example, if you start a hyperlink with **<A>**, you must finish it with an **</A>** end tag. On the other hand, the validation tool might also warn you about tags that don't necessarily need end tags to work properly. For example, **</P>** and **</LI>** end tags are not required.

5. If tags are out of proper order—the validation report might say "nesting error"—copy and paste to reorder them. Some browsers, for example, might not react well to the following HTML, because the **<A>** tag is still open when the **</B>** end tag arrives:

```
This is a <b><a href="big.htm">BIG</b> link.</a>
```

To fix the problem, place the **<A>** tag before the **<B>** tag.

6. If you've used tags that are for one particular browser, the validation tool will probably complain about them. You can ignore these warnings as long as you've made sure the errors don't adversely affect your page in other browsers.

7. If you've used tags such as **<FONT>** that are *deprecated*—no longer the preferred method in current standards—you'll see warnings. You can ignore these warnings, or replace the tags with their current equivalents. For example, if you don't anticipate anyone using an older browser version to view your page, you can replace **<FONT>** tags with styles. Ignore warnings about older standards, such as HTML 2.0, unless the warnings also apply to more recent versions.

8. If you're using HomeSite, you can customize the validation feature. For example, if your validation report includes errors for tags that work only in Netscape or Internet Explorer, you may want to change the options to allow these tags. On the Options menu, click Settings, and then click Validation. Select the HTML versions you want the validation tool to consider. To change other options, such as what level of errors to report, click Validator Settings. ▶

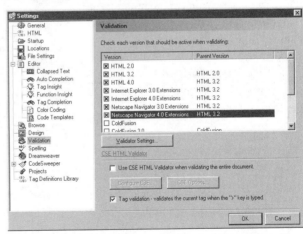

You can adjust validator settings to avoid warnings that don't apply or aren't helpful.

9. Once you've solved most of the problems, validate the page again and review any remaining warnings. If you can't figure out how to resolve an issue—but your page looks fine when you preview it—ignore the validation message.

Tip
There are many HTML validation tools available—some are software that you download and install, while others are available online for pages you've published on the Internet. When in doubt, get a second opinion on your page. For example, after your code is in good shape, try the online validation service of the World Wide Web Consortium at *validator.w3.org*. For a list of other options, see Appendix C.

Our FrontPage team web project is disorganized

Source of the problem

If your workgroup maintains a FrontPage web on your intranet—to share project information with other groups, for example—there's a lot to keep track of. What are the plans for the web site, and what is the schedule? Who is working on which pages? What should new pages or documents look like? As your web grows with input from different team members, it's easy to become disorganized.

Fortunately, FrontPage has features to help organize your team. For example, you can keep track of tasks and assign them to team members. You can enable source control so that you'll know which files are currently in use. Most important, you can create templates and standards so that your web pages will display some consistency. ▶

If your team web project is getting out of hand, follow these steps to get back on track.

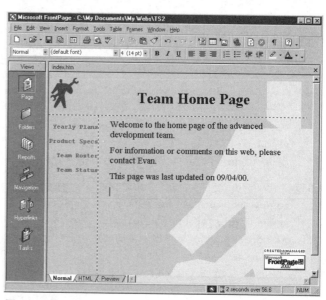

To encourage consistency, you need a solid template.

How to fix it

1. Take charge of the web project. While everyone on your team might work on web pages, it's best if one person manages the web plan, structure, and navigation. Formulate goals for the web and for your reorganization.

2. One likely problem in your team web is that individual pages don't fit into the big picture—either because they are not organized, or because they are too dissimilar from the rest. The first step is to create a *template*—a prototype web page—to help your team produce similar, compatible web pages. Include space for the common content your coworkers need to publish. Use the FrontPage formatting options you want everyone to adopt. For example, you might want to use shared borders to provide consistent navigation options. For formatting, you might want to select and apply a style sheet or theme.

Save your prototype page as a template. Click Save on the File menu, select FrontPage Template in the Save As Type list, and click OK. Specify a name for the template and select Save Template In Current Web. ▶

Now, when any team member clicks New on the File menu, the template will be available for creating a new page.

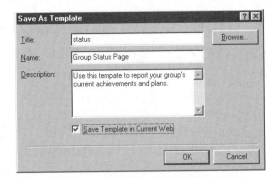

3. Next you'll want to organize existing web pages into a structure. For example, you might create a main page for each team or part of the project, and then use Navigation view to organize all related pages under the main pages. ▶

4. If necessary, set security options to ensure that no unauthorized users goof up your plan for the web. On the Tools menu, point to Security and click Permissions. Remove Author and Administer privileges for the team and assign them only to trusted users.

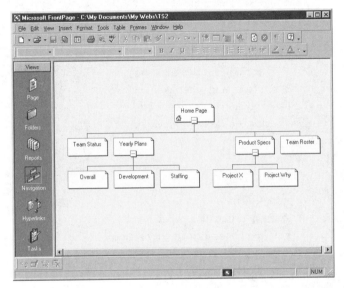

Tip

If users are stepping on each other's toes—trying to edit the same files at the same time—enable FrontPage source control. On the Tools menu, click Web Settings, select Use Document Check-In And Check-Out, and click OK. From this point on, a user will have to check out a page in order to change it.

To continue with this solution, go to the next page.

Our FrontPage team web project is disorganized

(continued from page 89)

5. FrontPage can help you track and manage tasks and assignments. First assign existing files in the web to the users who should own and maintain them. Right-click a file and click Properties, click the Workgroup tab, and select or type a name in the Assigned To box.

To manage tasks, click the Tasks button. And when you want to create and assign a general task, right-click the Tasks window and click Add Task. ▶

6. Announce your new web templates and direct your coworkers to their web tasks. Then, when people finish creating and updating pages, incorporate the pages into the navigation structure of your web.

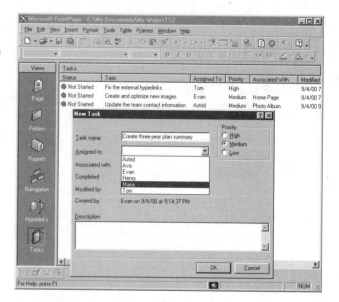

Creating a <HEAD> section

The first lines of a web page—most of which are enclosed inside the **<HEAD>** block—should provide general information about the page, such as its document type and description. The title of your page, as well as **<META>** tags that help search engines to index and display your site, belong in the **<HEAD>** block.

Here's a sample **<HEAD>** section with the most important elements:

```
<!DOCTYPE HTML PUBLIC "-//W3C//DTD HTML 4.0 Transitional//EN">
<html>
<!-- HTML by Evan Callahan, Copyright (c) 2000 -->
<head>
  <title>Personal Page</title>
  <meta name="Keywords" content="Callahan family, baby photos, sailing">
  <meta name="Description" content="My personal page, mostly nonsense.">
  <meta name="Author" content="Evan Callahan">
  <meta name="Owner" content="Callahan Software Solutions">
  <link rel="stylesheet" type="text/css" href="styles.css">
</head>
```

In the head section, you may also want to include scripts or styles—or links to external files that contain them. Your design software, such as FrontPage, might include its own tags here as well. Some of these, such as the **<META>** tag identifying FrontPage as the "generator" of the file, are optional. Others, such as tags that specify themes, borders, and page transitions, are required to make your page work properly.

Connecting to data stored in a database management system (DBMS) has long been a source of difficulty in web page development. Thanks to improved web standards, with the right tools it's now possible to bring data from nearly any source to your pages.

Microsoft FrontPage offers perhaps the easiest path to database connectivity—if your web server supports it. (See "FrontPage database system requirements" on page 101.) But complex features are bound to cause problems, and much of this chapter is devoted to FrontPage solutions.

If you're having trouble connecting to a database, follow this flowchart to find a solution. For general information, see "Using databases with your web site" on page 99, and "Connecting to a database using a script" on page 98.

If your solution isn't here

Check these related chapters:

Forms, page 122
FrontPage, page 154
Publishing & servers, page 262
Scripting, page 280

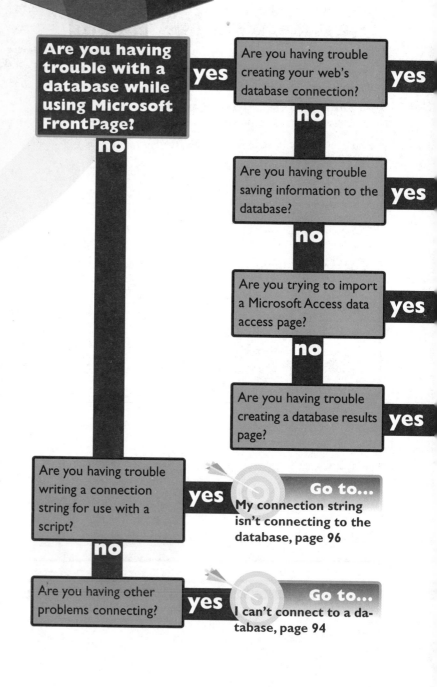

Are you having trouble with a database while using Microsoft FrontPage?

yes → Are you having trouble creating your web's database connection? **yes**

no → Are you having trouble saving information to the database? **yes**

no → Are you trying to import a Microsoft Access data access page? **yes**

no → Are you having trouble creating a database results page? **yes**

no ↓

Are you having trouble writing a connection string for use with a script? **yes** →

Go to...
My connection string isn't connecting to the database, page 96

no ↓

Are you having other problems connecting? **yes** →

Go to...
I can't connect to a database, page 94

Databases

Are database features dimmed on menus and in dialog boxes?

yes

Go to...
FrontPage database features are unavailable, page 100

no

Go to...
I can't create a FrontPage database connection, page 102

Go to...
FrontPage doesn't save the data in my form to the database, page 108

Quick fix

Data access pages are powerful and easy to create, but displaying them requires Microsoft Internet Explorer *and* Microsoft Office 2000.

1. Open the Microsoft Access database in its network location (the same location your web connects to).

2. Select a table or query, click Page on the Insert menu, and double-click Page Wizard.

3. Save the page into your FrontPage web (or save elsewhere, and then import into FrontPage).

Do you see an error message?

yes

Go to...
I get an error on my FrontPage database results page, page 104

no

Are you having trouble displaying results?

yes

Go to...
My FrontPage database results page doesn't display results, page 106

no

Are you having trouble displaying hyperlinks from a database?

yes

Go to...
Hyperlinks in my database don't appear as links on the page, page 107

I can't connect to a database

Source of the problem

In order to display data on your web pages—or update a database—your web server has to communicate with the database management system. (Not familiar with databases? See "Using databases with your web site" on the next page.)

If the database software isn't properly configured or if you provide incorrect information when connecting, you'll see errors or your page won't be displayed or won't update data. ▶

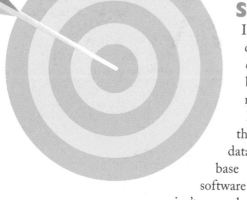

Many factors can cause your database connection not to work, and you might need to consult a database or network expert for assistance. But to diagnose and solve common problems, follow these steps.

For the database to work, your driver configuration and connection information have to be just right.

How to fix it

1. If possible, test the database using a method that doesn't rely on your web page or design program. For example, for an Access database, try to open the database in Access itself. For a SQL database, use another program to connect to the server and retrieve data. If you can't connect, there might be something wrong with the SQL server or database file. Verify your database configuration and, if needed, repair or replace the database file on the network.

2. Check the connection information you've provided. If you supply incorrect connection information on your page—and the web server and database driver are working properly—you'll see an error in the browser.

   For a SQL server database, for example, verify that you've specified the correct server name, database name, user ID, and password. For a file-based database, such as Microsoft Access, you usually need only a file name. Verify that you have the correct path, and if it is a network address, use a complete network path name, such as \\server\share\data\dbname.mdb.

3. If you are connecting through Open Database Connectivity (ODBC) drivers, check to make sure you have a *data source*—a predefined database connection—on your web server and check its configuration settings. To configure a system data source, open ODBC Data Sources in Windows Control Panel and click the System DSN tab. Click Add, or select an existing data source and click Configure. ▶

    If you have trouble with ODBC, you might not have the proper drivers installed on the web server. Search the Web for updated drivers from Microsoft or your database vendor.

4. If you don't control the web or database server—if the server is located at an Internet service provider (ISP) or on your corporate network, for example—contact your ISP or network administrator for assistance.

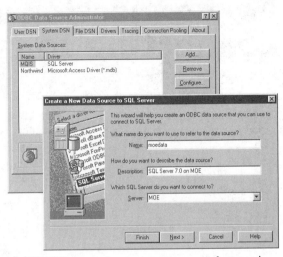

An ODBC system data source on your web server is usually the most foolproof method of providing connection information.

My connection string isn't connecting to the database

Source of the problem

When you use a script to connect to an Open Database Connectivity (ODBC) database, you supply a connection string that tells the database driver how to locate and open your database. For example, to open a database connection in an Active Server Pages (ASP) script, you might use a connection string such as the following with the Open method of the Connection object.

```
Provider=Microsoft.Jet.OLEDB.4.0;Data Source=C:\data\moe.mdb
```

If your connection string is invalid or incomplete, you'll get an error from the database driver when you view your page. Connection strings come in many flavors. For example, they can specify a predefined ODBC data source (created using tools on the web server system), use an ODBC driver without a data source, or bypass ODBC to connect directly with the database provider.

The following steps will help you overcome common errors and establish your connection to common databases.

How to fix it

1. Verify that the connection string is the problem by previewing your page. If your connection string is invalid, you will get an error when the server executes the line of script code that tries to open the connection. For example: *Microsoft OLE DB Provider for ODBC Drivers error '80004005' [Microsoft][ODBC Driver Manager] Data source name not found and no default driver specified. /ts/connect.asp, line 33*

2. Check the connection information you've provided. Connection properties, such as driver and provider names, must be spelled correctly for the connection to work. If you misspell property names or include properties that don't exist, they are ignored.

3. If you are connecting through an ODBC driver, the most foolproof connection method is to use a system data source on your web server, referring to the data source name (DSN):

    ```
    DSN=moedata
    ```

    For a SQL server, you'll probably need to specify a few options, such as user ID, password, and database:

    ```
    DSN=moedata;UID=curly;PWD=password;DB=contacts
    ```

4. If you don't have an ODBC system data source on your server and don't have access to the server, you can connect without a data source. The following connection string demonstrates how to connect to a SQL server named "moe":

```
DRIVER={SQL Server};SERVER=moe;DB=contacts;UID=curly;PWD=password
```

With the Microsoft Access driver, you use the **DBQ** property to select the database file:

```
DRIVER={Microsoft Access Driver (*.mdb)};DBQ=C:\data\moe.mdb
```

For the text file driver or other drivers where each table is a single file, you specify a folder with the **DBQ** property:

```
Driver={Microsoft Text Driver (*.txt; *.csv)};DBQ=C:\moetext
```

5. Microsoft servers with recent data access software (Data Access Components 2.5 or later) offer faster, more direct connections to your database through the OLE DB interface. Connect to a SQL database using the following string:

```
Provider=SQLOLEDB; Server=moe; User ID=curly; Password=password;
   Database=contacts
```

For an Access database, specify the file name using the Data Source property:

```
Provider=Microsoft.Jet.OLEDB.4.0; Data Source=C:\data\moe.mdb
```

If your Access database is password-protected, you might need to specify additional properties, such as **Jet OLEDB:Database Password** or **Jet OLEDB:System Database**:

```
Provider=Microsoft.Jet.OLEDB.4.0; Data Source=C:\data\moe.mdb;
   Jet OLEDB:System Database=C:\data\system.mdw; User ID=curly;
   Password=password
```

6. If you still can't connect, consult your database driver documentation.

Connecting to a database using a script

To connect to a database, most web pages use scripts on the web server. These scripts send requests to the database in the form of Structured Query Language (SQL). If you use a page design program with database features, you might not need to write scripts or SQL queries; the program writes them for you. For more flexibility, though, use your server's scripting language to work with a database.

With Active Server Pages (ASP) on a Windows web server, for example, you can include VBScript code in your page to connect to an Access database and run a query:

```
<%
Set Conn = Server.CreateObject("ADODB.Connection")
Conn.Open "Provider=Microsoft.Jet.OLEDB.4.0;Data Source=C:\data\moe.mdb"
Set RS = Conn.Execute("SELECT * FROM contacts WHERE city='Seattle'")
Response.Write "Contact Name: " & RS("name")
%>
```

> **To continue with this solution, go to the next page.**

My connection string isn't connecting to the database

(continued from page 97)

If your server has Allaire ColdFusion installed, you use its tag-like syntax to accomplish the same thing (the sample assumes you've defined a ColdFusion data source called "moe"):

```
<cfquery name="cq" datasource="moe">
  SELECT * FROM contacts WHERE city='Seattle'
</cfquery>
<cfoutput query="cq">
  Contact Name: #Name#
</cfoutput>
```

If you use a UNIX or Linux web server, you might want to use a PHP script such as the following, which connects to a MySQL database:

```
<?php
$db = mysql_connect("localhost", "root", "passwd");
mysql_select_db("moe",$db);
$result = mysql_query("SELECT * FROM contacts WHERE city='Seattle'",$db);
printf("Contact Name: %s\n", mysql_result($result,0,"name"));
?>
```

Other configurations

You might be able to use database features with other web server configurations—as long as they support both ODBC and ASP. If your web server doesn't have FrontPage server extensions, for example, you can't create database pages on the server or publish them to the server—but you might be able to run them. Create and test the pages on your own computer or a local FrontPage-extended web server. Then close the web and use a File Transfer Protocol (FTP) program to copy all files to the non-FrontPage web server.

Some non-Microsoft web servers, such as the Apache web server running on Solaris, Linux, or HP-UX, can run ASP through an add-on called Chili!ASP. If your web server has Chili!ASP, FrontPage server extensions, and a SQL database that you want to access, you're in business. First create database pages in a FrontPage web, either on your own computer or on a Microsoft web server such as PWS. Then publish the pages to the web server. To avoid connection problems, use an ODBC data source (DSN) with the same name on your local server as on the Apache (or other) web server. Note that you can't use a Microsoft Access database on these web servers. Also, remember that UNIX connection information and file names are case-sensitive; you must use the proper capitalization.

Using databases with your web site

Ordinary HTML pages are static; each time people view your pages, they see the same thing (unless you've published new pages). If you want to provide dynamic content or keep track of information the viewer enters, you need to connect to a database management system (DBMS). For example, if you are developing a web-based storefront, you'll need to display information about products and pricing, and also save information about orders.

When a web page displays data or updates a database, several software components are at work. First, the web page contains script code—mixed in with standard HTML—that runs on the server and tells it how to connect to the database and display data. Next, the web server needs a database connector, or driver, through which it sends queries and instructions to the DBMS. Finally, there is the DBMS itself, which stores information on disk and retrieves it. It can be either a file-based database, such as Microsoft Access, or a powerful database server, such as Microsoft SQL Server or Oracle DBMS.

The set of database tools you use depends primarily on the web server you've selected:

- If you use a Microsoft web server, such as Internet Information Server (IIS) or Personal Web Server, your best bet is an Access database or—for high-traffic web sites—a SQL Server database. To design dynamic pages, you're best off using Active Server Pages (ASP) scripts, which you can write yourself in an editor such as HomeSite. Or, you can create dynamic pages without programming using the Database Results Wizard in FrontPage.

- If your web server is extended with Allaire ColdFusion Server, you can use ColdFusion Markup Language to design web pages that work with nearly any database. Like HTML, ColdFusion is tag-based, making it an easy step up for web designers not familiar with programming languages.

- If you use an Apache web server—on a UNIX or Linux system, for example—many DBMS options are available, including Sybase SQL Server, Oracle DBMS, PostgreSQL, and MySQL. To create scripted pages, you might want to use the PHP scripting language, or you might integrate the database through Common Gateway Interface (CGI) programs written in Perl or C++.

Note

Most FrontPage features work with non-Microsoft web servers, such as Apache. However, the program's database features work only on servers that support ASP, such as Microsoft IIS. For more information, see "FrontPage database system requirements" on page 101.

FrontPage database features are unavailable

Source of the problem

The database features of FrontPage require that specific software be configured on your web server. If FrontPage detects that you can't use these features, it disables them on menus. For example, when database features are unavailable, the Database submenu on the Insert menu is dimmed.

If you do have the necessary software, follow these steps to make database features available.

Note

Even if the Database menu is available, it doesn't necessarily mean that your FrontPage web can use a database. For information on the software you need in order to connect to a database, see "FrontPage database system requirements" on the facing page.

How to fix it

1. Database features aren't available unless a web is open. If you are working on a single page that isn't in a web—or don't have a page open at all—FrontPage can't create or use database connections. To open a web, click Open Web on the File menu, locate the folder that contains the web, and click Open.

2. FrontPage allows you to specify the browsers and servers with which you want your web to be compatible. If you've told FrontPage that your web server doesn't have Active Server Pages (ASP) available, it disables database features. If your server does have Active Server Pages capability, turn the feature on. On the Tools menu, click Page Options, click the Compatibility tab, select Enabled With Microsoft FrontPage Server Extensions, select Active Server Pages, and then click OK. ▶

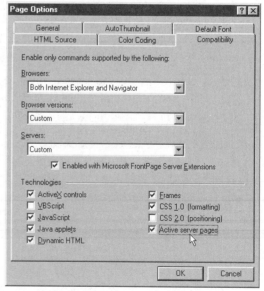

FrontPage database features require Active Server Pages (ASP) capability.

3. Create your database pages using either the Database Results Wizard or the Save Form Results component. To use the Database Results Wizard, point to Database on the Insert menu and click Results. For the Save Form Results component, right-click a form and click Form Properties, click Send To Database, and then click Options.

Authoring pages in a disk-based web

Although the inclusion of database pages in your web site requires a web server, FrontPage 2000 lets you create them in a disk-based web on your own computer. If you don't have a local web server and you don't want to tie up the server for which your web is destined, you might want to use this strategy. Although you develop the pages, you won't be able to see a preview that includes data—but once you publish them, the ASP pages will retrieve and display data. ▶

FrontPage database system requirements

The database features in FrontPage 2000 are designed to work best with Microsoft's web server, Internet Information Server (IIS), running on Windows NT or Windows 2000 Server. These features require Active Server Pages (ASP) scripting and Open Database Connectivity (ODBC) drivers.

For full FrontPage database support, your web server requires:

- Microsoft Windows 95, 98, NT, or 2000

- Microsoft IIS, Peer Web Services 3 or later, or Personal Web Server with ASP installed

- FrontPage 2000 Server Extensions, version 4.0.2.2717 or later (included in recent versions of IIS or available from Microsoft at *officeupdate.microsoft.com/frontpage/wpp/serk*)

- Microsoft Data Access Components 2.1 or later, which includes ODBC drivers (installed with Windows 2000 and Office 2000, or available at *www.microsoft.com/data*)

- For SQL database support: Microsoft SQL Server or other ODBC-compliant database server

- For file-based data access: Microsoft Access, dBASE, FoxPro, Excel, Paradox, or comma-delimited text files are supported

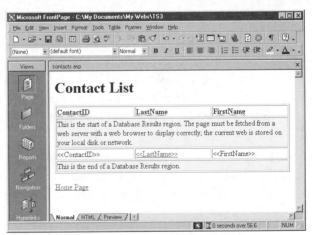

If you're working in a disk-based web, the Database Results region reminds you that it requires a web server.

I can't create a FrontPage database connection

Source of the problem

To connect with a database, FrontPage uses Open Database Connectivity (ODBC) drivers. Once you create a database connection for your web, the FrontPage Database Results Wizard and Save Results component help you create pages that retrieve or update data.

If there's something wrong with your database configuration, or if you provide incorrect information when connecting, FrontPage won't be able to create the database connection. ▶

There are many factors that can cause your database connection not to work, and you might need to consult a database or network expert for assistance. But to diagnose and solve common problems, follow these steps.

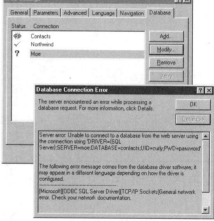

How to fix it

Preparing to connect

1. If you're having trouble connecting to a database file—a Microsoft Access (.mdb) file, for example—the easiest solution is to import or copy the database file into your web. (However, if the database is used by other people or programs from a location outside your web, skip to step 2.) On the File menu, click Import, click Add File, select the database file or files, click Open, and then click OK. If the file is a Microsoft Access database, FrontPage offers to create a database connection for you and move the file to its own secure folder.

When FrontPage can't connect to a database, it might pass on error information from the database driver.

2. To use a database file that isn't actually in your FrontPage web—a SQL or server database file on the network, for example—your best bet is to create an ODBC data source that tells the server how to connect to the database. On the web server, open the Windows Control Panel, double-click ODBC Data Sources, and click the System DSN tab. Click Add, select a driver, and specify options.

If you don't have access to the web server, you can't create a system data source. Instead, you'll need to connect directly to the file or database server.

3. If you receive ODBC errors or can't use your database outside FrontPage, there might be something wrong with your database server, files, or ODBC drivers. Contact your network administrator or ISP, or consult your driver or database documentation.

Creating or fixing the connection

1. On the Tools menu, click Web Settings, and then click the Database tab.

2. If your connection is already in the list, select it and click Verify. If you get an error, click Details to read more. To fix your connection, click Modify. If you don't have a connection yet, click Add, and then type a descriptive name for the connection. ▶

3. If you created an ODBC data source, click System Data Source On Web Server, click Browse, select your data source, and click OK. (If you see the error "This web server does not allow a client to list the server's data sources," click Custom Definition, click Advanced, type **dsn=*name***, and click OK.)

FrontPage can connect through an ODBC data source or directly to a server or file you specify.

If your database is on a SQL server (and you don't have a system data source), click Network Connection To Database Server, click Browse, specify the server type and name, and click OK.

For a file-based database, click File Or Folder In Current Web, click Browse, select the file, and click OK. If your file is not in the web, you can type its full path and file name in the URL box.

4. If your database requires a user name or password, click Advanced, and type your user name and password in the boxes provided. You can also enter additional parameters here. For example, if your Access database requires a workgroup security (.mdw or .mda) file, click Add, type **SystemDB** in the Name box, type the full path to the file in the Value box, and click OK.

5. Click OK, and then click Verify. If you still see an error, recheck the connection information you've provided, such as the server and database names, user ID, and password, or consult your network administrator or ISP.

> **Tip**
> Are you creating a web on your own computer but planning to publish it to another server? Both computers need to connect to the database for your database pages to work. If you are connected to the web server through a network, you can use the same database from both copies of the web. If you aren't on the same network— your web site is located at an ISP, for example—create a copy of the database on your own machine.

I get an error on my FrontPage database results page

Source of the problem

When you include database results on a page using the Database Results Wizard, FrontPage writes an Active Server Pages (ASP) script for you. For the script to display data in a browser, a number of software components must be working together: the web server running the ASP script, the Open Database Connectivity (ODBC) connection to the database, and the SQL query you've submitted. If you've taken advantage of the flexibility built into these FrontPage features—specifying your own queries or connection strings, for example—you're even more likely to run into problems. ▶

When an error message appears, it might give a clue as to what is going on behind the scenes. To diagnose and solve the problem, follow these steps.

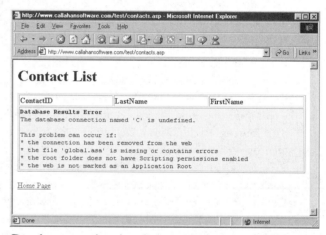

Database operations involve many software components and are prone to errors.

How to fix it

1. If the FrontPage database connection for your web isn't working, you'll receive this message: *The database connection named 'Contacts' is undefined.*

   This could indicate several problems; to solve most of them, refresh your database connection. Open the FrontPage web on the server (not your local copy of the web, if you have one). On the Tools menu, click Web Settings, and then click the Database tab. Click Modify, click OK, and then click Verify. ▶

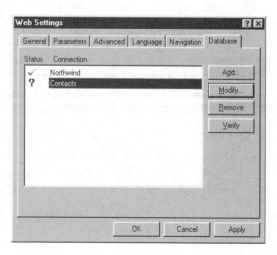

2. If FrontPage displays an error message when verifying the connection, click Details to read the messages it received from the ODBC driver. There might be something wrong with your ODBC configuration, connection information, or the database itself. For ideas on solving the problem, see "I can't create a FrontPage database connection" on page 102.

3. If FrontPage is able to make a connection but can't run the query you've requested, you'll see an error in the results region of your page. For example, if your database file has been moved, deleted, or is unavailable on the network, you'll see the following message: *Database Results Error. [Microsoft][ODBC Microsoft Access Driver] '(unknown)' is not a valid path. Make sure that the path name is spelled correctly and that you are connected to the server on which the file resides.*

Try to address the problem indicated by the message. In this case, verify the location and network availability of the Access database file. Modify connection properties, if necessary (see step 1), or contact your network or database administrator for assistance.

4. If you specified query criteria in the Database Results Wizard, you might see a database error followed by this message: *One or more form fields were empty. You should provide default values for all form fields that are used in the query.*

To fix the problem, provide default values for all criteria fields. Double-click the database results region, click Next, click Next again, click More Options, click Defaults, and then click each entry in the list and type a default value. ▶

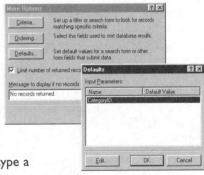

Tip

You might want to change the formatting of a database results region using FrontPage design tools. However, if you later make any change to the properties of the region using the Database Results Wizard, your formatting is lost. To work around the problem, create styles for your page and apply them to the elements of the results area. This way, you won't lose the style information when FrontPage updates the results region.

5. If you entered a custom SQL query using the Database Results Wizard, your query might be invalid. To verify your query, double-click the database region, click Next, click Custom Query, and click Edit. Update the query if necessary and test it. If possible, test your query outside of FrontPage—in Microsoft Access, for example.

If you use *parameters* in your query—values passed to the query from form fields—make sure their data types match the data in the field. And if a database field contains text, enclose the query parameter with single quotation marks:

```
SELECT * FROM Contacts WHERE (LastName =
'::LastName::')
```

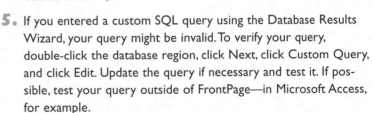

My FrontPage database results page doesn't display results

Source of the problem

When you include database results on a page using the Database Results Wizard, FrontPage writes an Active Server Pages (ASP) script for you. For the script to display data in a browser, ASP must be working properly, and the query you run must result in data from the database.

For some problems, however, no error is displayed —but you won't see any data from the database, either. To diagnose and solve the problem, follow these steps.

How to fix it

1. If your page doesn't have the correct file name extension, the script won't run. If its extension is .htm, right-click the file in the folders list, click Rename, and change the extension to **.asp**.

2. If you are working on a disk-based copy of your web—where ASP isn't installed—your preview of the page won't include data. Publish the web, and then preview the page on the server. ▶

3. If you're using Personal Web Server and you installed ASP *after* creating your pages, ASP might not run. To fix the problem, refresh the database connection. On the Tools menu, click Web Settings, and then click the Database tab. Click Modify, click OK, and then click Verify.

4. If your data table is empty, or if you've specified criteria and no records fit your criteria, the database results region displays the following message: *No records returned.*

   To display records, change your criteria settings or add records that meet the criteria.

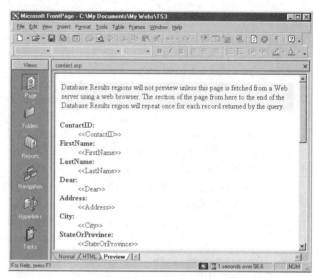

If ASP isn't enabled—if you preview your page in a disk-based web, for example—you won't see database results.

> **Tip**
>
> The Database Results Wizard allows you to change the message it displays when no records meet your criteria. Double-click the database results region, click Next, click Next again, click More Options, and enter text in the Message To Display If No Records Are Returned box.

Hyperlinks in my database don't appear as links on the page

Source of the problem

If your web page displays a large number of hyperlinks—perhaps even a list that changes frequently—you might want to store the links in a database. But when you display the links in a FrontPage database results region, they don't appear as hyperlinks. Even if you've used the Hyperlink data type in a Microsoft Access database, the database drivers that FrontPage uses don't recognize the data as a list of web links.

To get your hyperlinks working, the trick is to include HTML in the data itself. Follow these steps.

How to fix it

1. Open the table in your database.

2. If the field that currently stores hyperlinks doesn't use the Text data type—for example, if it is a Microsoft Access database and the field uses the Hyperlink data type—add a new text field to store link information.

3. In each record, enter an HTML **<A>** tag for the hyperlink you want, including the text you want to display and specifying a web address in the **href** attribute. For example, if you want to include a link to Microsoft's web site, set the data field to one of the following:

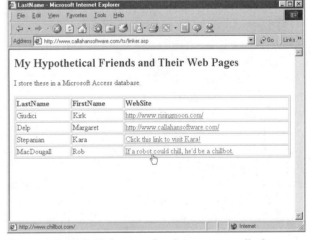

By storing HTML in your database, you can display hyperlinks or other web elements inside database results.

```
<a href="http://www.microsoft.com/">www.microsoft.com</a>
<a href="http://www.microsoft.com/">Microsoft Corporation</a>
```

4. Open your database page in FrontPage. In the database results region, double-click the field that contains the links, click Column Value Contains HTML, and click OK. Save and preview the page.

FrontPage doesn't save the data in my form to the database

Source of the problem

With the Save Results component, FrontPage can help you create the forms needed to add records to a database. Once you create a form and add text boxes or other controls for viewers to enter data, you can tell FrontPage to save form results to a database. If you don't already have a database connected to your web, FrontPage can create a Microsoft Access database to store the results for you.

To save results, FrontPage uses an Active Server Pages (ASP) script and connects to the database using Open Database Connectivity (ODBC) drivers. If ASP isn't working, or if something is wrong with your connection, your form page won't work. In addition, if you didn't specify proper settings for your form, you might not get the results you want.

To track down the problem and get the data flowing into your database, follow these steps.

If you create a form on your page, FrontPage will write an ASP script to add data to your database.

How to fix it

1. Make sure you correctly set form properties by specifying a database location and the fields to store data. By default, FrontPage sends form results to a file. To tell it to send results to the database, right-click the form, click Form Properties, click Send To Database, click Options, and select a database connection and table for your form results. (If you don't have a database, click Create Database to create an Access 2000 database. If you have a database but haven't created a connection, click Add Connection.)

Tip

To make it easier to identify the data contained in the fields of the form, specify descriptive names for the fields before setting up the database connection. Double-click each field and type a name, such as LastName or E-mail.

To specify which fields should store each value from the form, click the Saved Fields tab, and then double-click each field in the list to specify a destination field in the database. ▶

By setting form properties, you tell FrontPage how to store the information into database fields.

2. If your page doesn't have the correct file name extension, the script won't run. If its extension is .htm, right-click the file in the folders list, click Rename, and change the extension to **.asp**.

3. If you are working on a disk-based copy of your web—where ASP isn't installed—you can't preview your form page in a browser. (You can use the Preview tab in FrontPage, but the form won't appear as it will when the page gets published.) To use the form, publish the web and then preview the page on the server.

4. If FrontPage displays an error message when verifying your database connection, click Details to read the messages it received from the ODBC driver. There might be something wrong with your ODBC configuration, connection information, or the database itself. For ideas on solving the problem, see "I can't create a FrontPage database connection" on page 102.

5. If you see an error message when your form runs, it might indicate a problem you can solve by changing the form or the database. For example, if your database expects a number and you try to enter text, you'll see an error message such as: Cannot save value "This is a sentence." to database field "Number." Error Description: Type mismatch.

Or, if your database requires a value for a specific field and you omit it on your form, you'll see an error message like this: Cannot update the database. Error Description: [Microsoft][ODBC Microsoft Access Driver]Error in row.

Make sure all required fields are on the form, and use validation—a method ensuring that viewers enter appropriate values. First double-click each field and, if appropriate, enter a default for the field in the Initial Value box. Then click Validate, select a value in the Data Type box, click Required (if appropriate), and click OK twice. If you don't want to include a field on the form but the database requires it, modify your database to supply a default value, or add a hidden field to the form with a valid value. (In the Form Properties box, click Advanced.)

6. If your form still doesn't submit data even after you've made the above changes, you might need to let FrontPage re-create the database script. To do this, right-click the Form and click Form Properties, click Send To Other, and click OK. Then repeat step 1 above.

To get your message across effectively, you'll want to choose an appropriate font, or typeface. If you don't specify otherwise, web browsers use a default font and text size.

But getting the font you want can be a tricky process. There are several HTML tags and methods to choose from, and font support varies among computer systems. If you're not careful, some viewers might not see the page as you intend.

For a list of suggested sets of fonts that most browsers support, see "Specifying font families" on page 119.

For solutions to common font difficulties, follow this flowchart.

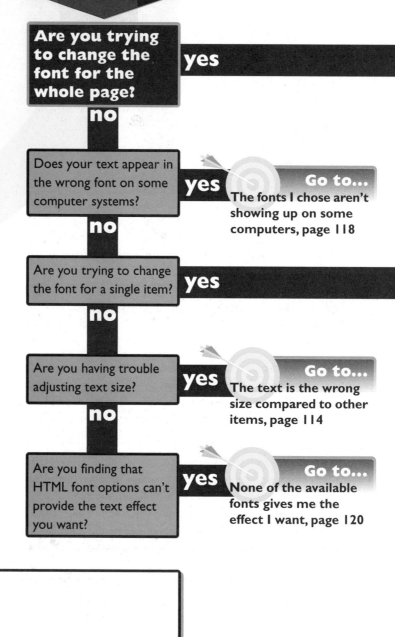

Are you trying to change the font for the whole page?

yes

no

Does your text appear in the wrong font on some computer systems?

yes

Go to...
The fonts I chose aren't showing up on some computers, page 118

no

Are you trying to change the font for a single item?

yes

no

Are you having trouble adjusting text size?

yes

Go to...
The text is the wrong size compared to other items, page 114

no

Are you finding that HTML font options can't provide the text effect you want?

yes

Go to...
None of the available fonts gives me the effect I want, page 120

If your solution isn't here
Check these related chapters:
   Browsers, page 42
   Hyperlinks, page 174
   Styles, page 296
   Text formatting, page 322
Or see the general troubleshooting tips on page xvii

Are you using a FrontPage theme?

yes

no

Go to...

The default font doesn't look right, page 112

Quick fix

A theme defines the colors and default fonts for your page or entire web. If you modify the theme, all pages based on it will change.

1. Click Theme on the Format menu, click Modify, and click Text.

2. Select a font from the Font list.

3. To change heading text, select each heading name in the Item list and select a font for each one.

4. Click OK twice.

Quick fix

To set the font of an item, you can either use a cascading style sheet (CSS) **style** property or the HTML **<FONT>** tag. A style is more flexible, but your font change won't show in some browsers (such as Netscape 3).

In HTML+CSS:

1. In the tag that contains the text you want to change, use the **style** attribute to set the CSS **font** property.

2. In the **font** setting, specify italic or bold (if desired), followed by font size, followed by a list of font names. For example:

```
<td style=
    "font:bold 24pt 'courier new', monospace">
    This is big typewriter-style text.
</td>
```

In HTML only:

1. Enclose the text you want to change inside a **<FONT>** tag, setting the **size** attribute from 1 to 7 and the **face** attribute to a list of font names.

2. If you want italic or bold text, use **<I>** and **<B>** tags. For example:

```
<font size=6 face="'courier new', monospace">
    <b>This is big typewriter-style text.</b>
</font>
```

In FrontPage:

1. Select the text you want to change.

2. Click Font on the Format menu.

3. Select a font name (or type a list of fonts), point size, and other font formatting options, and then click OK.

The default font doesn't look right

Source of the problem

Unless you specify otherwise, most browsers display text on the page in a Times Roman-style typeface, similar to the text in many newspapers and books. (The text in this paragraph is an example.) If this font isn't appropriate for your page, you've probably tried to change it—whether in HTML or using your page design program—and you might have run into some trouble. ▶

In FrontPage, for example, you can select text in your page and change the font using the toolbar. This changes the font of your selection, but doesn't change the default font for the whole page. Or, in HTML, you might have tried the equivalent—adding <FONT> tags around text. In either case, you'll clutter your page with font settings, but you still won't have changed the default font. Worse, if you later decide to change fonts, you'll have to change them in many different places.

To set the default font style, follow these steps.

Setting a default font is easier and more effective than setting the font of each block of text individually.

How to fix it

1. If you've set fonts using **<FONT>** tags, find all those that indicate your desired default font—the font you want for most of the text on the page—and remove them. This will reduce clutter on your page and ensure that your font isn't applied inconsistently. (For now, you can leave tags that set occasional font accents. However, you might want to use styles to replace them as well.)

2. Using a **<STYLE>** section or external style sheet, set the **font-family** property for the **<BODY>** and **<TD>** tags.

Note
If you've used Internet Explorer's **<BASEFONT>** tag to set a font, remove it. A default style produces more consistent results and works in more browsers.

For example, to set the default font to Verdana (or Geneva or another sans-serif font, if Verdana is not available), add the following lines to the **<HEAD>** section of your page:

```
<style>
  BODY, TD
  { font-family:Verdana,Geneva,sans-serif }
</style>
```

3. If you want a different font for other page elements, such as headings, add additional style declarations. For example, add the following line in the **<STYLE>** section to change the heading font to Comic Sans MS.

```
H1, H2, H3 { font-family:'Comic Sans MS',
Helvetica,sans-serif }
```

Then use **<H1>**, **<H2>**, and **<H3>** tags to mark heading text throughout your HTML (rather than formatting each head with its own **<FONT>** tag).

Setting default font styles in FrontPage

1. To remove all existing font formatting, click Select All on the Edit menu, and then click Remove Formatting on the Format menu.

If your page already has specific font accents, however, you may want to preserve them. Instead of selecting the whole page, select each section of the page that *doesn't* use a special font setting and click Remove Formatting on the Format menu.

2. Right-click the page and click Page Properties, click Style, click Format, and click Font. Select a font from the Font list—preferably a font that's likely to be available on most systems, such as Arial or Verdana—and then click OK three times.

3. To make your default work in Netscape 4 tables, you must specify the same font for **<TD>** tags as for normal text. Click Style on the Format menu, select td in the Styles list (if td isn't shown, select All HTML Tags in the List box), click Modify, click Format, and click Font. Select a font, and then click OK three times.

4. To format headings, use heading styles rather than font formatting. Click the text of each heading on your page and select a style, such as Heading 1 or Heading 2, in the Style box at the left side of the toolbar.

Note

To set the default font, you must use a style. This means that your font setting will appear only in browsers that support cascading style sheets (CSS), such as Internet Explorer 3 and later or Netscape 4 and later. Fortunately, this covers the vast majority of viewers—and browsers that don't understand the style setting will simply display the text in the browser's default font.

Tip

To set consistent font styles for your entire FrontPage web, you can apply an external style sheet or a theme. (See "Styles" on page 296.) If you do use a style sheet or theme, however, you should make default font changes there, rather than in individual web pages.

The text is the wrong size compared to other items

Source of the problem

Different strokes for different folks. That's the theory behind text size on the web, where your text is guaranteed to vary depending on the viewer's browser and system. Windows, for example, displays text about 20 percent larger than does the Macintosh operating system. Different fonts vary in the space they take up, even at the same point size. What's more, viewers can change text size settings in their browsers if they find your text hard to read. ▶

Generally, it's best to design your page so that any font size works—and so that the relative text size on your page is preserved regardless of the actual size. However, using cascading style sheets (CSS), you can also set fonts to precise sizes where necessary.

If your font sizes aren't right, follow these steps.

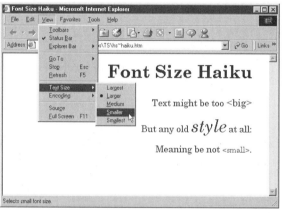

Design your page to look good at any text size, even if the viewer changes sizes.

How to fix it

1. If you've set fonts using **<FONT>** tags, you might want to replace them with other options; HTML standards now recommend using styles instead. If you do want to use them, do so consistently, setting the **size** attribute to a value of 1 to 7. (Size 3 is the default.)

```
<font size="4">Larger than average.</font>
```

Use a separate **<FONT>** tag for each block of text and each table cell.

Note

Browsers might interpret your font size settings differently, especially when viewers try to enlarge or reduce text size. In Netscape, viewers can always adjust text size. In Internet Explorer, fonts for which you've specified an exact height using CSS don't ever change (unless browser accessibility options are set to ignore font sizes). If you want to let users decide the size, don't use exact font size settings.

2. For bold headings on your page, use heading tags—**<H1>** for very large text through **<H6>** for text smaller than the page text.

3. To change the default text size for your page, use a CSS style. In a **<STYLE>** section or external style sheet, set the **font-size** property for the **<BODY>** and **<TD>** tags. For example, to increase the size of the default font, add the following lines to the **<HEAD>** section of your page:

```
<style>
  BODY, TD { font-size:larger }
</style>
```

Font size settings are very flexible. You can specify:

- Relative sizes: smaller or larger

- Named sizes: xx-small, x-small, small, medium, large, x-large, xx-large

- Percentage sizes, such as 125%

- Exact font heights in inches, points, or pixels, such as .18in, 11pt, or 14px

4. To change individual text sizes, create a style and apply it to appropriate tags. If you need to size text precisely, use pixels, which are less likely to vary among computer systems. For example, this style section creates a style called small:

```
<style>
  .small { font-size:12px }
</style>
```

To use the style, set the **class** attribute of any tag containing text that you want changed.

```
<p class="small">This paragraph is exactly 12 pixels tall.</p>
```

Tip

Very small or large font sizes can be hard to read, and often aren't the exact size you want. If you want text or hyperlinks to fit in a small space on your page—or appear in a specific large size—you might want to create an image using a graphics program such as Fireworks or Photoshop. For information, see "None of the available fonts gives me the effect I want" on page 120.

To continue with this solution, go to the next page.

The text is the wrong size compared to other items

(continued from page 115)

Source of the problem

Text you type on pages in FrontPage appears in the default size for Internet Explorer. When viewers open your page, they might see a different text size based on their system or browser settings.

Generally, it's best to design your page so that any font size works. However, if you want most viewers to see smaller or larger type, FrontPage makes it easy to change font size for part or all of your page. And if you want to set font size precisely—so it won't change between browsers—you can use a style.

If your font sizes aren't right, follow these steps.

How to fix it

Changing font sizes in FrontPage

The simplest way to change font size in FrontPage is to select text and change font size on the Formatting toolbar. For a larger than average font, select size 4–7; for smaller than average, select size 1 or 2. FrontPage adds <FONT> tags throughout your page. When you add new paragraphs or table cells, be sure to select a font size for them. ▶

Styles offer more flexible overall formatting and allow you to specify exact font heights where necessary. To specify font styles, follow these steps.

1. Remove all existing font formatting. Click Select All on the Edit menu, and then click Remove Formatting on the Format menu.

2. If the text size associated with an HTML tag is not what you want, change it using styles. For example, you can change the default text size using styles for the **<BODY>** and **<TD>** tags, or the heading text size using styles for tags such as **<H1>**. Click Style on the Format menu, select a tag name (such as **body**, **td**, or **h1**) in the Styles list, click Modify, click Format, and click Font. Enter a font size in the size box, and then click OK three times. ▶

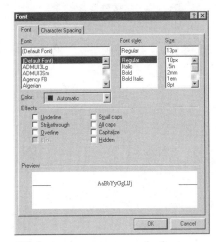

With a style, you can set the font height to a specific number of pixels.

Font size settings are very flexible. You can specify:

● Relative sizes: smaller or larger

● Named sizes: xx-small, x-small, small, medium, large, x-large, xx-large

● Percentage sizes, such as 125%

● Exact font heights in inches, points, or pixels, such as .18in, 11pt, or 14px

3. For special sizes—to define a text style that's exactly 12 pixels, for example—create a new style and then apply it to elements of your page. Click Style on the Format menu, click New, type a name beginning with a period (such as **.small**), click Format, click Font, enter a font size, and then click OK three times.

4. To apply styles—either a built-in style, such as Heading 1, or your custom styles—click any paragraph, cell, or other page element, and then select a style in the Style box at the left side of the Formatting toolbar.

The fonts I chose aren't showing up on some computers

Source of the problem

Selecting fonts for your page can be a tricky process. The problem is, not everyone has the same fonts installed—and for users of different systems, such as Macintosh or Windows, the same fonts aren't always available. When a browser can't display the font you've specified, it uses its default font, usually a standard typeface such as Times Roman.

Fortunately, you can specify alternate fonts that the browser should use if your first choice isn't available. This way, you can select one font that's likely to be available in Windows, another for Macintosh, and fallback positions in case users don't have your fonts installed.

If your page displays text in the wrong font, follow these steps.

> **Tip**
> If it's important that text appear the same for all viewers, you can create an image containing the text using a graphics program such as Fireworks or Photoshop. This allows you to use effects, and guarantees that your text will be the same size—but it might make your pages load more slowly. For information, see "None of the available fonts gives me the effect I want" on page 120.

How to fix it

1. In your HTML and style sheets, replace each font specification with an appropriate list of font names. Browsers will display text using the first listed font that is installed on the viewer's system. (For ideas on what to include in your font lists, see "Specifying font families" on the next page.)

In HomeSite, for example, click Extended Replace on the Search menu. In FrontPage, click the HTML tab, and then click Replace on the Edit menu. In the Find What box, type the font for which you want to specify alternates, such as **Arial**. In the Replace With box, type a list of fonts separated by commas, such as **Arial, Helvetica, sans-serif**. Repeat this step for each font you use on the page. ▶

When you're finished, each **<FONT>** tag or style declaration in your HTML should look something like this:

```
<font face="Arial,
Helvetica, sans-serif">Arial
text, if possible.</font>
```

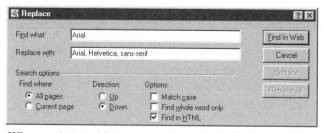

Where you've specified one font in your HTML, replace it with a list of fonts to provide alternates.

```
<style>
  BODY, TD {
    font-family: Arial, Helvetica, sans-serif
  }
</style>
```

2. Thereafter, use a font list rather than a single font name when specifying fonts—whether in the **face** attribute of the **<FONT>** tag or using the CSS **font-family** property.

In FrontPage, type a list of fonts into the Font box in a dialog box or on the toolbar rather than selecting just one font from the list.

3. If possible, test your page on other systems to make sure that the fonts look right.

Specifying font families

The key to displaying the fonts you want—or at least similar alternatives—is to specify fonts commonly installed on different computer systems. At the end of each font specification, include a generic font type, such as **serif**, **sans-serif**, or **monospace**.

Here are a few common serif font families—proportionally spaced typefaces you're used to seeing in newspapers and books (names with spaces are quoted, as required in HTML):

- 'Times New Roman', Times, serif
- Georgia, 'New York', 'Times New Roman', Times, serif
- Garamond, Palatino, serif

These are sans-serif font families—also proportionally spaced but plainer typefaces:

- Arial, Helvetica, sans-serif
- 'Arial Narrow', Helvetica, sans-serif
- Verdana, Geneva, Helvetica, sans-serif
- 'Comic Sans MS', Helvetica, sans-serif
- System, Chicago, sans-serif

Finally, use this declaration for a monospace, typewriter-style font:

- 'Courier New', Courier, monospace

None of the available fonts gives me the effect I want

Source of the problem

Typography isn't the strong point of the web. Things we take for granted in printed materials—clear type at any size, fancy effects, and rich color—aren't easy to achieve on a web page.

Perhaps you have a specific effect in mind, such as glowing text or text with a shadow. Or maybe you have a perfect font on your system, but you know it won't be available in every browser. Or, you want to fit text into a specific space on your page, and the available font sizes aren't fitting properly—especially from one browser to another.

The solution lies with graphics programs—Macromedia Fireworks, Adobe Photoshop, or ImageReady, for example—that offer sophisticated text handling. By creating an image to display your text, you'll have much more control over its appearance. The downside is that your page will take longer to load, users won't be able to adjust the size of your text, and your site won't be as easy to search. Even so, much of the text you see on the web—headings, banners, buttons, and labels, in particular—is sent to you as an image rather than as HTML text. ▶

If ordinary web text isn't working on your page, follow these steps.

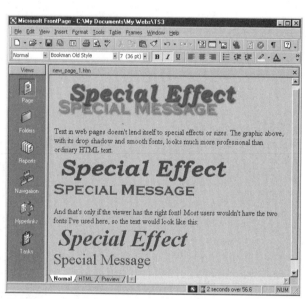

For banners, buttons, and other accent text, images offer much better control of text appearance.

How to fix it

1. Determine the exact size of the area you want your text to fill, in pixels. For example, if the text belongs in a table cell, check the width and height of the **<TD>** tag.

2. Open your graphics program and create a new document of this size, setting the canvas color for the image to the background color of your page. In Fireworks, for example, click New on the

File menu, enter values in the width and height boxes, and click Custom under Canvas Color to select the background color.

3. Click the text tool and click on your image where you want the text to begin. Select font, color, and other text options, such as bold and italic. Type the text you want—or, if there's a lot of text, switch back to your page and copy it—and then click OK. Repeat for each additional text item you want to add. ▶

4. Add effects to the text, if you want. In Fireworks, click the Effect palette, select an effect such as Drop Shadow or Glow, and then set options for the effect. You can see the results as you make changes.

In a graphics program, you can adjust font size and position precisely and apply snappy effects.

5. Export your image as a transparent GIF file. Use an adaptive palette with as few colors as necessary for smooth font edges (for plain text, you might need only 8 colors; with effects, you might need 128). In Fireworks, click Export Preview on the File menu, select options, click Export, and save the file in a folder accessible to your web page.

6. Switch back to your page-editing or design program and insert the image into your page. In FrontPage, for example, point to Picture on the Insert menu, click From File, select your image, and click OK.

Tip

One of the biggest disadvantages to using images to display text is that it makes the text on your page more difficult to update. Be sure to save the original artwork, such as a Fireworks or Photoshop file, whenever you create images for your pages. This way, you'll be able to make changes to the text more easily.

7. In the **<IMG>** tag, set the **alt** attribute to the very same text that the image includes. This way, your text will appear while the picture downloads, and search engines will be able to index the text.

```
<img src="text.gif" alt="This is the text." height=40 width=200 border=0>
```

If you're using FrontPage, right-click the image and click Picture Properties, enter the text in the Text box under Alternative Representations, and then click OK.

Most web pages present information to viewers. Now and again, however, you'll want to get information back. On the web, you do this with a form. Browsers can display text boxes, lists, and buttons to help you collect the information you need and submit it to a script or program on the server.

You might run into problems with your form's appearance, since there are minor differences among browsers. Or, your form might not work as you'd hoped, either because it doesn't collect the right information or because of a problem with the script or program it sends data to.

To track down common form issues, follow this flowchart. For general information about forms, see "Sending e-mail from a web page" on page 130, and "Using the GET and POST form methods" on page 138.

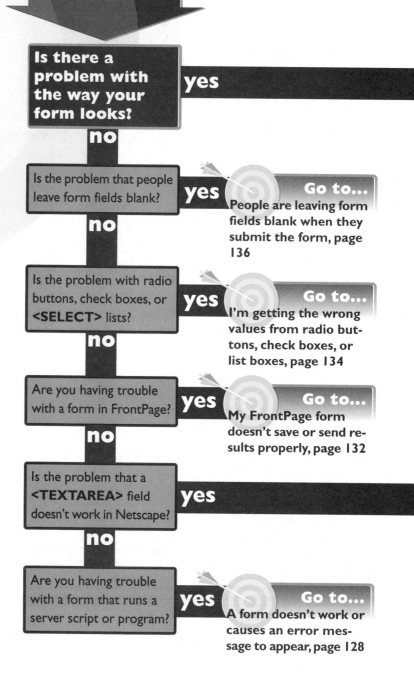

Is there a problem with the way your form looks? yes

no

Is the problem that people leave form fields blank? **yes**

Go to...
People are leaving form fields blank when they submit the form, page 136

no

Is the problem with radio buttons, check boxes, or **<SELECT>** lists? **yes**

Go to...
I'm getting the wrong values from radio buttons, check boxes, or list boxes, page 134

no

Are you having trouble with a form in FrontPage? **yes**

Go to...
My FrontPage form doesn't save or send results properly, page 132

no

Is the problem that a **<TEXTAREA>** field doesn't work in Netscape? **yes**

no

Are you having trouble with a form that runs a server script or program? **yes**

Go to...
A form doesn't work or causes an error message to appear, page 128

Are you having trouble fitting a form into a small space? **yes**

no

Is the problem with the size of your text fields? **yes**

Go to...
My text fields have different widths in different browsers, page 127

no

Is the problem with radio buttons? **yes**

Go to...
The radio buttons have a square background around them, page 131

no

Are you having trouble arranging form fields so that they look right? **yes**

Go to...
The layout of my form doesn't look right, page 124

Quick fix
Browsers always include a line break at the end of a form. If you're trying to place something directly under a form, or trying to fit a small form into a table cell, you won't want the extra line.

To remove the line, enclose the form contents in a cell, but place the **<FORM>** and **</FORM>** tags outside the cell. For example, the following HTML creates a search form just 30 pixels high, avoiding the extra line break:

```
<tr>
<form action=find.cgi>
<td height=30>
  <b>Find:</b>
  <input name=findtext
    size=14>
  <input type=image
    src=go.gif
    height=24 width=24
    align=absmiddle>
</td>
</form>
</tr>
```

Quick fix
By default, Netscape 4 doesn't wrap text in a text box, even if there are multiple lines. To make your form work the same in Netscape and Internet Explorer, set the **<TEXTAREA>** tag's **wrap** attribute to **soft**:

```
<textarea name="msg"
  rows=5 cols=30
  wrap=soft>
</textarea>
```

If your solution isn't here
Check these related chapters:
Databases, page 92
FrontPage, page 154
Publishing & servers, page 262
Scripting, page 280
Tables, page 310
Or see the general troubleshooting tips on page xvii

The layout of my form doesn't look right

Source of the problem

You're ready to get some information from viewers, and you've added fields—text boxes, for example—to a form. You might be using a design program, such as FrontPage, or perhaps you are creating the form in HTML using <FORM>, <INPUT>, and <SELECT> tags. But when you preview your form, the fields don't line up and they look messy.

To get your form into shape, you have two options. The first is to use *preformatted text*, which causes browsers to use a monospace font and display spacing and line breaks precisely as shown in your HTML. (Ordinarily, browsers collapse multiple spaces or line breaks into a single space.) The second option is to use a table to control your form layout. In either case, you'll want to adjust field sizes to make your form line up well. If your form doesn't look right, follow these steps.

Note

Because Internet Explorer and Netscape interpret the size of text fields differently, you should always test your forms in both browsers. If fields don't fit properly, see "My text fields have different widths in different browsers" on page 127.

How to fix it

1. To start, adjust the width of your text fields so that similar fields have the same size. In your **<INPUT>** tags, set the **size** attribute.

   ```
   <input type="text" name="realname" size="34">
   <input type="text" name="email" size="34">
   ```

   If you use FrontPage, click each field and drag the size handles to adjust its size.

2. Format your form using one of the following methods.

Using preformatted text

The simplest strategy for lining up text in a form takes advantage of the <PRE> tag to display the exact spacing you indicate in your HTML. The browser uses a monospace font, such as Courier, so that each character or space occupies the same width on the page. ▶

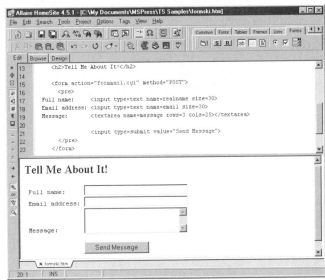

1. In HTML, enclose the contents of the form in a **<PRE>** block. (In FrontPage, select the contents of the form and then select Formatted in the Style box at the left side of the Formatting toolbar.)

2. Add spaces, tabs, and line breaks between text and **<INPUT>** tags to line up elements as you'd like.

Using a table

If you don't want to use a monospace font, or you have a specific design in mind for your form, use a table to align elements precisely. ▶

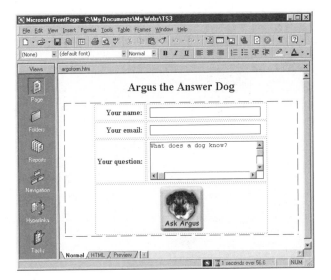

1. Inside the **<FORM>** block, create a table with at least two columns—one for field labels and a second for corresponding fields—and one row for each field.

2. Move your text and **<INPUT>** tags inside the **<TD>** tags. (In FrontPage, select and drag the text and fields into the appropriate cells.)

> *To continue with this solution, go to the next page.*

The layout of my form doesn't look right

(continued from page 125)

3. For each **\<TD\>** tag that contains a field label, use **align="right"** to align the labels next to the fields in the next column. (In FrontPage, select the cells and click the Align Right button on the Formatting toolbar.)

4. To adjust the spacing between fields, set the **cellpadding** attribute in the **\<TABLE\>** tag. (In FrontPage, right-click the table, click Table Properties, and enter a value in the Cell Padding box.) Here's what your HTML might look like:

```
<H2 align=center>Argus the Answer Dog</H2>
<form method="POST" action="argus.cgi">
  <table border=0 cellpadding=5>
    <tr>
      <td align=right><b>Your name:</b></td>
      <td><input type="text" name="name"
        size=34></td>
    </tr>
    <tr>
      <td align=right><b>Your email:</b></td>
      <td><input type="text" name="email"
        size=34></td>
    </tr>
    <tr>
      <td align=right><b>Your question:</b></td>
      <td><textarea name="question" rows=3 cols=29></textarea></td>
    </tr>
    <tr>
      <td align=center colspan=2>
      <input type="image" src="argusbtn.gif" width=94 height=94></td>
    </tr>
  </table>
</form>
```

Tip

If you don't like the way the standard Submit button looks on your form, use an image. In the **\<INPUT\>** tag, set **type="image"** and set the **src** attribute to the image file name. Or, in FrontPage, point to Form on the Insert menu and click Picture. Some graphics programs, such as Fireworks, include templates for creating button images.

My text fields have different widths in different browsers

Source of the problem

When you use the size attribute of an <INPUT> field to set the width of the field, Netscape and Internet Explorer interpret your setting differently. This happens because Internet Explorer uses a proportional font for text boxes, while Netscape uses a monospace font, which is wider. ▶

To make text boxes the same width in most cases, follow these steps.

Browsers set text box size differently.

How to fix it

1. If you want to use a monospace font in Internet Explorer—the simplest solution—specify the font in a style for the **<INPUT>** tag. Place this code in the **<HEAD>** section of your page:

```
<style>
  input { font-family:'courier new',
    courier, monospace }
</style>
```

2. If you'd rather keep the proportional font in Internet Explorer, use a style to set each text box's width:

```
<input type="text" name="email" size=32
  style="width:260px">
```

Because Netscape 4 ignores this style, you should first set the **size** attribute while previewing in Netscape 4 to make sure the box fits properly. Then adjust the **width** property setting in pixels so the width is the same in Internet Explorer.

3. Preview your page in both browsers, and on multiple computer systems if possible.

> **Note**
>
> Netscape adjusts text box sizes when a viewer adjusts the font size in his or her browser. For this reason, you can't be sure that your **<INPUT>** fields will fit in a given space—at least not in Netscape 4 or earlier, where setting the tag's **width** style has no effect.

A form doesn't work or causes an error message to appear

Source of the problem

Most forms are designed to gather information from the person viewing your page and send it to a script or program on the web server. In the <FORM> tag, you use the **action** attribute to specify which script or program file to run when the viewer submits the form. For example, if you create a form for viewers to send you e-mail, the viewer types a name, e-mail address, and whatever else you want to know. The form then passes that information to a Common Gateway Interface (CGI) program or a server script—such as an Active Server Pages (ASP) script—that sends the e-mail.

To work, your program must be configured properly on the server and have the necessary permissions to do its task. Also, the form must send the right information to the program, using <INPUT> tags with correct names and settings. In some cases, you'll need to send additional information to the program using *hidden fields*—<INPUT> tags with information that doesn't actually appear on the form, such as the e-mail address you want to send the information to. If any of these pieces isn't in place, your form might not work. ▶

To diagnose and solve form problems, follow these steps.

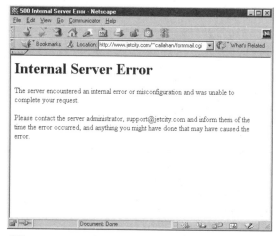

When you use a form to run a script or program on the server, it's easy to run into trouble.

How to fix it

Tip

Many ASP and Perl server scripts, as well as other CGI programs, are available for free on the web. If you control your web server or your ISP allows you to use scripts, you can add them to your web site. For a list of resources, see Appendix C.

1. If the browser displays an error such as "404 Page Not Found" or "Can't open Perl script" when you submit the form, you might not have the correct name or path in the **<FORM>** tag's **action** attribute. Check the path in your form, and recheck the script's location on the server.

2. If you see an error such as "Internal Server Error" or "The page cannot be displayed," you might not have the right permissions for CGI or ASP scripting. If you have access to the server, make sure that the folder containing the script allows script execution and that your script file is marked as executable. (In UNIX or Linux, you can change file permissions using the **chmod** command—type **chmod 755 filename.cgi** to allow your script to run.)

3. If your script requires parameters, such as an e-mail address or file you want to send information to, make sure you provide them. (If you're using someone else's script, look over the script or its documentation to find out what's required.) If information is missing, you might not get the right results. In some cases, you provide script parameters as variables by editing the script itself; in other cases, as hidden fields in your form. For example, this line of HTML sets the **recipient** parameter for an e-mail script:

```
<input type="hidden" name="recipient" value="mailme@callahansoftware.com">
```

4. If your script runs but doesn't do what it's supposed to—doesn't send an e-mail, for example—the problem could be difficult to track down. For an e-mail script, check to make sure the sendmail program (or SMTP server) is working. For a script that modifies files, make sure they are available and have the required permissions. If all else fails, look for bugs in the script itself, or contact your ISP or server administrator.

To continue with this solution, go to the next page.

A form doesn't work or causes an error message to appear

(continued from page 129)

Sending e-mail from a web page

Most web servers allow you to send e-mail from a web page. Many UNIX-based and Linux-based ISPs provide a free Perl script called formmail.pl or formmail.cgi that you can use to send mail. (Others allow you to post your own script to the server.) The following form, for example, collects information and uses formmail.cgi to send an e-mail message.

> **Note**
> If you use a UNIX-based or Linux-based web server, remember that file names are case sensitive—FormMail.cgi is not the same as formmail.cgi.

```
<form action="formmail.cgi" method="POST">
  <input type="hidden" name="recipient" value="mailme@callahansoftware.com">
  <input type="hidden" name="subject" value="Web Form Response">
  <p>Your name:<br>
  <input type="text" name="realname" size=24 maxlength=60></p>
  <p>Your email:<br>
  <input type="text" name="email" size=24 maxlength=60></p>
  <p>Your message:<br>
  <textarea name="message" cols=40 rows=8></textarea></p>
  <p><input type="submit" value="Send Message"></p>
</form>
```

If your web server uses Windows and Internet Information Server (IIS), you can write your own ASP script. The following script, for example, sends mail from the form above (you'd need to change the action to formmail.asp):

```
<% ' FormMail.asp - Sends e-mail using the CDONTS Newmail object.
Set objMail = CreateObject("CDONTS.Newmail")
objMail.From = Request("realname") & " <" & Request("email") & ">"
objMail.To = Request("recipient")
objMail.Subject = Request("subject")
objMail.Body = Request("message")
objMail.Send
%>
```

The radio buttons have a square background around them

Source of the problem

In Netscape 4, radio buttons always use the background color of the page. If the background color of your form—or the table or cell that contains it—is different from the background color of the page, your radio buttons will have boxes around them. Because Netscape 4 supports cascading style sheets (CSS), you can easily solve this problem. ▶

Just follow these steps.

How to fix it

1. Using the **style** attribute of the **<INPUT>** tag, set the CSS **background-color** property of all radio buttons to the background color of the form.

   For example, your HTML might look like this:

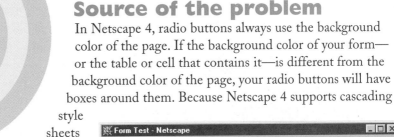

Netscape 4 uses the page background color for radio buttons.

```
<form>
<p>This is a test of:<br>
<input type="radio" name="ttype" value="nav"
   style="background-color:#cc3333" checked>
   Netscape Navigator<br>
<input type="radio" name="ttype" value="ie"
   style="background-color:#cc3333">
   Internet Explorer<br>
<input type="radio" name="ttype" value="ebs"
   style="background-color:#cc3333">
   The Emergency Broadcast System</p>
```

Note
This technique has a minor side effect in some browsers. Netscape 6, for example, uses the background color of a radio button on the *inside* of the button.

2. Preview in all browsers to make sure the colors are consistent.

My FrontPage form doesn't save or send results properly

Source of the problem

With the Save Results component, FrontPage can help you save information from your form to a file or send it to an e-mail address. Once you create a form and add text boxes or other controls for viewers to enter data, you can tell FrontPage where to save or send the information—and in what format you want it.

To save results, FrontPage uses a special program that's part of FrontPage Server Extensions. ▶ If your server doesn't have the extensions installed and properly configured, or if you didn't specify proper settings for your form, you might not get the results you want.

To track down the problem and get the information to its proper destination, follow these steps.

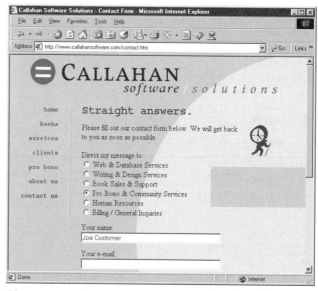

If you create a form on your page, FrontPage will save submitted information in a file or e-mail it to you.

How to fix it

1. If you are working on a disk-based copy of your web—where FrontPage Server Extensions aren't installed—your form won't work in a browser. (You can preview the page, but if you submit the form, you'll see an error page entitled "FrontPage Run-Time Component Page" and no information will be saved.) To use the form, publish the web to a server that uses FrontPage Server Extensions, and then preview the page on the server.

2. Did you set form properties, specifying a destination for form results? If you didn't, you might have trouble finding the information submitted through the form. Unless you specify otherwise, FrontPage saves form results in a text file. It names the file form_results.txt and saves it in the _private folder inside your web. You probably can't open this file in a browser, because FrontPage makes the _private folder unreadable for security reasons. To view it, click Folders under Views, double-click the _private folder, and double-click form_results.txt.

To change the file location FrontPage uses for form results, right-click the form, click Form Properties, and enter a path and file name in the File Name box. To change the file format to something other than plain text, click Options and select an option in the File Format box.

3. If you want FrontPage to send results to you by e-mail, right-click the form, click Form Properties, and enter your address in the E-mail Address box.

To set options for the e-mail, click Options and click the E-mail Results tab. For example, you might want to change the e-mail format to HTML or to a text database format, which you can more easily copy to a spreadsheet. And if your form has a field allowing visitors to enter an e-mail address, be sure to enter the field name in the Reply-To Line box, so that you can easily respond to messages that are sent to you. ▶

4. If your form still doesn't send e-mail—or if you see an error when submitting the form—there might be a problem with the server extensions, or with configuration of the mail or SMTP service on your web server. Contact your server administrator.

5. If the results file or e-mail displays short field names, such as T1 and S1, you need to specify descriptive names for the fields in your form. Double-click each field and type a name, such as **LastName** or **Email**.

6. If the results include fields you don't want, you can remove them. For example, FrontPage saves the "value" of the Submit button (usually named B1), which you don't need. To remove it, right-click the form, click Form Properties, click Options, click the Saved Fields tab, and delete the field name from the list.

7. If you don't like the Form Confirmation page that FrontPage displays when viewers submit a form, create and save a custom confirmation page. Then, right-click the form, click Form Properties, click Options, click the Confirmation Page tab, and type the file name.

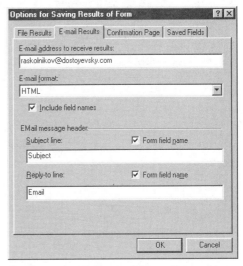

Set form properties to tell FrontPage where to send information that visitors enter. For example, you can specify a format for the e-mail sent by FrontPage.

Note

If you don't want to use FrontPage components to process form data, you can send results to an Active Server Pages (ASP) script or other program on the server. Right-click the form, click Form Properties, click Send To Other, click Options, and type the path and name of the program or script in the Action box. If you want the form to submit hidden field values—often required by a script—click the Advanced button in the Form Properties dialog box to specify them.

You can also send form results to a database. If you're having trouble doing this, see "FrontPage doesn't save the data in my form to the database" on page 108.

I'm getting the wrong values from radio buttons, check boxes, or list boxes

Source of the problem

To assist people in submitting information through your forms, you can use radio buttons, check boxes, and list boxes. This way, rather than typing their selections, viewers simply click options from the choices you provide. In HTML, you include these types of fields with <INPUT> tags—with the **type** attribute set to **"radio"** or **"checkbox"**—and <SELECT> blocks with <OPTION> tags that specify entries in a list. ▶

If you don't set up the tags properly, you might not get the values you expect—or your form might not work at all.

If your radio buttons, check boxes, or list boxes aren't working, follow these steps.

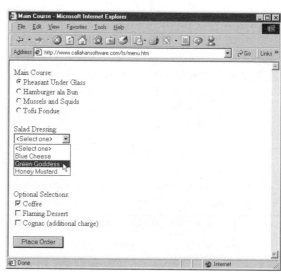

Unless your <INPUT> and <SELECT> tags have proper settings, your form won't submit the values you want.

How to fix it

1. If your form submits information to a script or database, check the field names and values the script or database expects. If the form submits information to a file or sends it via e-mail, decide on the field names and values that will best convey the viewer's selections. As you correct the problem, it's important to know what field name and value combinations you're aiming for.

2. For radio buttons—**<INPUT>** tags with the **type** attribute set to **"radio"**—be sure you've given each button in a group the same **name** attribute, but a different **value** attribute. (The name identifies the group of buttons, while the value tells the form what to submit when each button is selected.) Otherwise, your form won't treat the buttons as a group or won't submit a distinct value for the selected option. Remember that the text you display next to each button on the form is not necessarily the same as the submitted value—the value is often an abbreviation.

The following HTML creates a group of radio buttons, the first of which is checked by default, that submit one of four values for a field called Entree:

```
<p>Main Course:<br>
<input type="radio" name="Entree" value="Bird" checked>Pheasant<br>
<input type="radio" name="Entree"
   value="Burger">Hamburger ala Bun<br>
<input type="radio" name="Entree"
   value="Seafood">Mussels and Squids<br>
<input type="radio" name="Entree"
   value="Beancurd">Tofu Fondue</p>
```

Tip

If you use FrontPage to create a form, you'll notice that when you first insert fields on a form, they have short, non-descript names and values such as N1 and V1. Fortunately, FrontPage makes it easy to change field names and values: double-click each field on the form and enter values in the boxes provided.

3. For check boxes—**<INPUT>** tags with the **type** attribute set to **"checkbox"**—give each **<INPUT>** tag a different **name** attribute. Set the **value** attribute to **on** or **yes**, or to any value you want the form to submit when the box is checked. (When the box isn't checked, no value is submitted—neither **off** nor **no**, as you might expect. If you need to submit a value in either case, use two radio buttons in a group, one with a Yes value and the other with a No value.)

The following HTML creates two check boxes, the first of which is checked by default. For each check box that is selected, the form will submit the value **Please** for that field:

```
<p>Optional Selections:<br>
<input type="checkbox" name="Coffee" value="Please" checked>Coffee<br>
<input type="checkbox" name="Fire" value="Please">Flaming Dessert<br>
```

4. For list boxes—**<SELECT>** blocks with list entries defined by **<OPTION>** tags—you can either specify a value for each entry or omit them to submit the list entries themselves. For a drop-down list, set the **<SELECT>** tag's **size** attribute to **1**; for a list box, set it to the number of entries you want to see without scrolling.

The following HTML creates a drop-down list with four entries, the first of which is selected by default. The first option has no value specified, so the form submits **Vinaigrette** if it is selected. For the other options, it submits the specified value, i.e., **Blue, Green,** or **Yellow**:

```
<p>Salad Dressing:<br>
<select name="Salad" size=1>
   <option selected>Vinaigrette</option>
   <option value="Blue">Blue Cheese</option>
   <option value="Green">Green Goddess</option>
   <option value="Yellow">Honey Mustard</option>
</select></p>
```

People are leaving form fields blank when they submit the form

Source of the problem

Most people don't like to type. Given the opportunity, they'll leave things blank. But there is information you need—for example, if you want to respond to people, you'll need their contact information.

To get the information you want, you might need to give people some encouragement. One way to do this is on the form, providing default values and indicating required fields so viewers are less likely to leave fields blank. Another strategy is to add a *validation script*—JavaScript that runs when the user submits the form, checking the contents of each required field. If a validation script finds that fields are missing, it displays a message and doesn't submit the form. Finally, you can check the form information as it appears to the server script or program after the form is submitted, and display an error page or return to the form.

If viewers are submitting your form without the information you need, follow these steps to address the problem.

How to fix it

1. On your form, indicate fields that are required with a message or symbol. Or, indicate optional fields, leaving visitors to infer that the remaining fields are required. ▶

2. To minimize how much typing you ask visitors to do, use radio buttons, check boxes, and list boxes, where appropriate. For example, rather than asking people to type the reason for their interest, provide a list of options to select from. Then, set a default option—for radio buttons or check boxes,

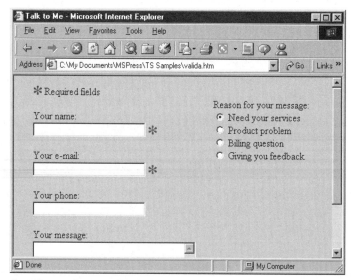

Let viewers know what information you need.

use the **checked** attribute in the **<INPUT>** tag; for list boxes, use the **selected** attribute in the **<OPTION>** tag.

3. To prevent the form from being submitted without key information, such as a person's name, use a custom validation script on your page. The following JavaScript function, for example, checks to make sure the **realname** and **email** fields are filled in. If a field is blank, the script displays a message from the browser and then sets the focus to the required field:

A script can check for valid values before your form is submitted to the server.

```
<script language="JavaScript">
<!--
function validate(form) {
  // Check for name and e-mail
    entries.
  if (form.realname.value == "") {
    alert("Please type your name.");
    form.realname.focus();
    return false;  // Don't submit the form
  } else if (form.email.value == "") {
    alert("Please type your e-mail address.");
    form.email.focus();
    return false;  // Don't submit the form
  }
  return true;     // Required fields are there - submit the form
}
//-->
</script>
```

To use the script, insert the code into the **<HEAD>** section of your page. Then attach the function to the **onSubmit** event of the form as follows, so that it will run in the browser before the information is submitted to the server script. (The **return** statement ensures that the form isn't submitted if the script discovers missing information.)

```
<form action="formmail.cgi" method=POST onSubmit="return validate(this)">
```

For other validation script ideas, search the web or see Appendix C.

4. If you don't want to display messages in the browser, you can handle missing information with your server script or program. When critical information is left out, the simplest solution is to display an error page, telling users to click the Back button in their browser and fill in the required fields. Or, your server script might be more sophisticated, displaying the form again with the existing information filled in and missing fields highlighted.

To continue with this solution, go to the next page.

People are leaving form fields blank when they submit the form

(continued from page 137)

Setting Validation in FrontPage

FrontPage can write a script that checks form entries in any field—you can simply require that a value be entered, or specify what type of data the field should contain.

1. Double-click the field you want FrontPage to validate.

2. Click Validate. Select the Required box, and set other options for the field as appropriate. ▶

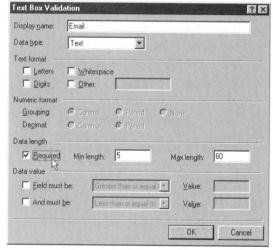

Design programs such as FrontPage can write validation scripts for you.

Using the GET and POST form methods

Browsers offer two ways to submit form information: GET and POST. With GET, the form values are appended to the end of the URL and separated from it by a question mark, like this:

```
http://www.risingmoon.com/order.asp?Entree=Bird&Salad=Blue&Coffee=Please
```

As you can see, if you have many fields on your form, the GET method gets pretty unruly. But GET has one interesting side effect. When viewers bookmark the page, the field values are saved along with it so that the same values get submitted when the viewer returns to the page. While this makes no sense for a one-time form submission, it might make sense for a product page (where the URL includes the product code, for example).

Although the default is GET, you'll specify POST for most types of forms. The form submits the same information, but instead of traveling in the URL, it is transmitted behind the scenes as a series of HTTP headers. To submit a form using POST, set the **method** attribute in the **<FORM>** tag:

```
<form method="POST" action="order.asp">
```

Unless you want viewers to see the values they are sending—and be able to use the same values again—use POST.

With frames, you can arrange two or more pages in the browser on a single frames page, and use links in one frame to load pages into another.

You might run into problems as you create a frames page, either with the way frames appear in a browser or the way they work. And because of the disadvantages of frames, you might choose to do without them.

If you use FrontPage, you'll enjoy easy frame editing, but you might have some trouble locating the frame editing features you need.

For general information on frames and whether you should use them, see "Deciding when to use frames" on page 143.

And for solutions to common difficulties with frames, follow this flowchart.

If your solution isn't here

Check these related chapters:

Browsers, page 42
Hyperlinks, page 174
Layout, page 206
Scripting, page 280
Tables, page 310
Or see the general troubleshooting tips on page xvii

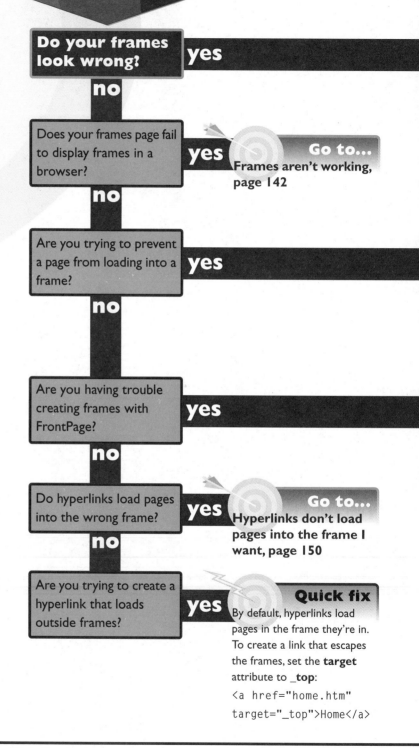

Do your frames look wrong? yes

no

Does your frames page fail to display frames in a browser? yes

Go to...
Frames aren't working, page 142

no

Are you trying to prevent a page from loading into a frame? yes

no

Are you having trouble creating frames with FrontPage? yes

no

Do hyperlinks load pages into the wrong frame? yes

Go to...
Hyperlinks don't load pages into the frame I want, page 150

no

Are you trying to create a hyperlink that loads outside frames? yes

Quick fix

By default, hyperlinks load pages in the frame they're in. To create a link that escapes the frames, set the **target** attribute to **_top**:

```
<a href="home.htm"
target="_top">Home</a>
```

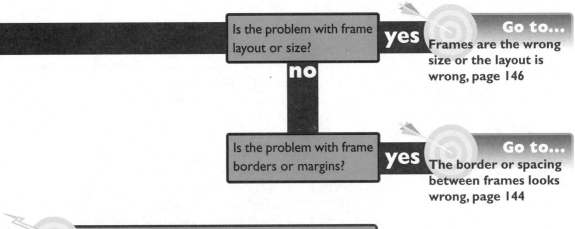

Is the problem with frame layout or size?

yes

Go to...
Frames are the wrong size or the layout is wrong, page 146

no

Is the problem with frame borders or margins?

yes

Go to...
The border or spacing between frames looks wrong, page 144

Quick fix
To frame-proof a page, use JavaScript in the **<BODY>** tag:
```
<body onload="if(top!=self) top.location=location">
```

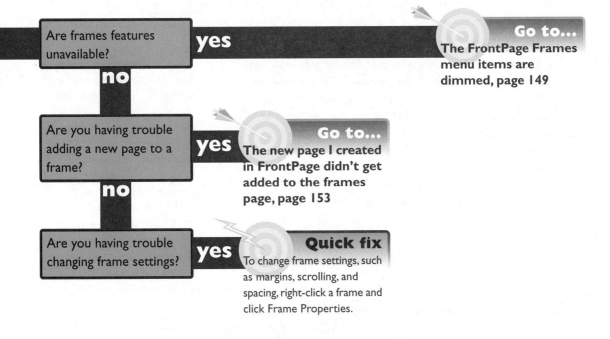

Are frames features unavailable?

yes

Go to...
The FrontPage Frames menu items are dimmed, page 149

no

Are you having trouble adding a new page to a frame?

yes

Go to...
The new page I created in FrontPage didn't get added to the frames page, page 153

no

Are you having trouble changing frame settings?

yes

Quick fix
To change frame settings, such as margins, scrolling, and spacing, right-click a frame and click Frame Properties.

Frames aren't working

Source of the problem

To display frames, you need three things: a page that defines a *frameset* (an overall page layout), separate pages to appear in the frames, and a browser that is capable of displaying frames. If any of these elements is missing, the browser will display a blank page, an error page, or just one page rather than the frames you intended.

Nowadays, browser support is no longer a likely culprit. Nearly all browsers can display frames—Netscape 2 and later, Internet Explorer 3 and later, as well as many others. For browsers that don't display frames, such as the text-only browser Lynx, you can provide an alternative page or special message in a <NOFRAMES> section.

If you don't see the frames in a browser, follow these steps.

How to fix it

1. If your frames page has a **<BODY>** section, delete it so that the **<FRAMESET>** tag immediately follows the **<HEAD>** section. A frames page should not have a **<BODY>** section. If it does, the browser displays the contents of that section, but ignores your **<FRAMESET>** and **<FRAME>** tags. (If you want to display the content that was in the **<BODY>** section, move it to another page that's displayed in one of your frames.)

2. In the **<FRAMESET>** tags on your frames page, you must specify row heights and column widths using the **rows** and **cols** attributes; otherwise, not all frames will appear. For each **<FRAME>** (or **<FRAMESET>**) tag the frameset contains, specify a width or height in pixels or percent, or specify an asterisk (*) to indicate that the browser should divide available space. For example, the following section defines a frameset with two side-by-side frames, the first 120 pixels wide and the other taking the remainder of the browser window:

```
<frameset cols="120,*">
  <frame src="navbar.htm">
  <frame src="main.htm">
</frameset>
```

> **Tip**
>
> Even if your viewers never see it, providing a **<NOFRAMES>** section for your document will have the additional advantage of making your site easier to find. Some search engines don't index frames pages because they don't contain text—but if you have text in your **<NOFRAMES>** section, search engines might find it. For this reason, it's a good idea to include some introductory information in this section.

3. Be sure that every **<FRAME>** tag specifies a file with the **src** attribute; otherwise, that frame will appear blank. In addition, make sure the pages you refer to all exist. If they don't, the browser will display an error message in that frame, such as "Page Not Found."

4. If your page isn't working in a browser without frame support, you need to add a **<NOFRAMES>** section at the end of your frameset definition (just above the final **</FRAMESET>** tag). You can include an entire page's **<BODY>** section, or just provide a message or hyperlink:

```
<noframes>
  <body bgcolor="#cccc99">
    <h1>Sailing Stories</h1>
    <p>Welcome to our library of sailing stories
    from the San Juan Islands.</p>
    <p>Your browser doesn't appear to support
    frames. Check our <a href="noframes.htm">
    Frame-Free Home Page</a>.</p>
  </body>
</noframes>
```

Note

Certain older browsers, as well as current versions of the WebTV browser, have limited support for frames. In these browsers, you might find that frames don't work as you expect. Note that the **<NOFRAMES>** section won't help in these cases, because it is used only by browsers that can't display frames at all.

Deciding when to use frames

Most web sites do without frames because of a handful of problems they cause. In your own pages, you'll probably want to use frames only where necessary. Using an ordinary table, you can create pages with a layout that looks much like a frames page—but is much easier to manage and use.

On the other hand, frames can be very useful. A frames page allows you to keep one area of the page—such as a table of contents or an advertisement area—visible at all times, even when viewers scroll through content in other frames. A frames page also allows you to bring together content from different web sites or servers into one unified page—for example, if you want to display information on a business partner's web site as if it were on your own. ▶

If you don't need these features, don't use frames. They make sites more complex and confusing, both for the designer (because there are many more files to work with) and for the viewer (because navigation and bookmarks don't work as they usually do). The additional pages can be a burden on your server and might load more slowly.

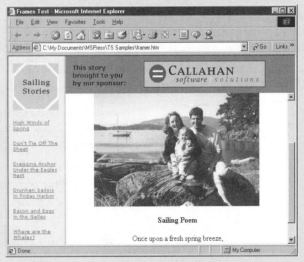

Frames are useful for displaying a table of contents or ad banner that remains in view, even when viewers scroll down the page.

The border or spacing between frames looks wrong

Source of the problem

By default, browsers display a gray border between frames with which viewers can adjust frame size. In addition, they display a margin around each frame page using the background color of that page. Depending on the content and purpose of your frames page, these margins and borders might not look right. Fortunately, using attributes of the <FRAMESET> and <FRAME> tags, you can change or remove them. ▶

However, because of differences in the implementation of frames, you might end up with changes that apply to certain browsers and not others. For example, to adjust the width of the border between frames, you use a different attribute in Netscape than you do in Internet Explorer. And if you use a design program, such as FrontPage, it probably uses an attribute that works in some, but not all, browsers.

To fix problems with frame spacing and margins, follow these steps.

The default frame borders and margins might look wrong on your page. In this frames page, the borders are too wide, and the top frame shouldn't have a border to resize.

How to fix it

1. If you don't want any border between frames, use
frameborder=0 in the **<FRAMESET>** tag. However, in order to get rid of the border in all browsers, you'll need to include additional settings. Use the following HTML (substituting your own **rows** or **cols** setting):

```
<frameset cols="120,*" frameborder=0 framespacing=0 frameborder=no border=0>
```

   Internet Explorer honors the first two attribute settings, while Netscape uses the final two. (Some versions understand both, but it won't hurt to include them all.)

2. To adjust the width of the border between frames, set both the **framespacing** and **border** attributes to the same value. If you want to change the color of the frame border from gray to

something else, most browsers also support the **bordercolor** attribute. This line of HTML, for example, creates a 5-pixel olive-colored border between frames (the default is 2 to 3 pixels):

```
<frameset cols="120,*" border=5 framespacing=5
    bordercolor="#cccc99">
```

3. If you want the pages within frames to be closer to or further from their borders (the default margin is about 12 pixels), set the **marginheight** and **marginwidth** attributes of the **<FRAME>** tag for the frame. This line of HTML, for example, causes the page to be displayed close to the frame border:

```
<frame src="adbar.htm" marginheight=2
    marginwidth=2 scrolling=no>
```

4. If a page doesn't quite fit in its frame and displays a scrollbar you don't want, you can get rid of it by adding **scrolling=no** to the **<FRAME>** tag. However, note that if the frame isn't big enough to display all its contents—if the viewer uses a larger font size, for example—there won't be any way for the viewer to move down or across the page.

5. If you still don't like the spacing or margins, look at the pages you've included in the frames. Their margins and spacing, designed for display in a larger space, might not look right inside frames—regardless of the frame settings you specify. Try adjusting the width, margins, alignment, and layout of the individual pages, and then preview them in your frames page again.

Note
If you remove the border between frames—setting **frameborder=0** (or **no**), **framespacing=0**, or **border=0**—viewers won't be able to resize your frames in the browser. You can also prevent users from changing frame size, even if you want a border between frames, using the **noresize** attribute:
```
<frame
src="navbar.htm"
    noresize>
```

Note
Netscape 4 and earlier won't position a frame page completely against its borders—even if you specify **marginheight=0** and **marginwidth=0**. Netscape still displays a 1-pixel margin.

Changing frame spacing in FrontPage

If you use FrontPage, you can set frame and frames page properties to achieve the spacing you want.

1. Right-click the frame you want to change and click Frame Properties. Set frame margins in the Width and Height boxes under Margins. ▶

2. Without leaving the Frame Properties dialog box, click Frames Page, and then click the Frames tab. Enter a value in the Frame Spacing box. If you don't want to display borders between frames, clear the Show Borders box.

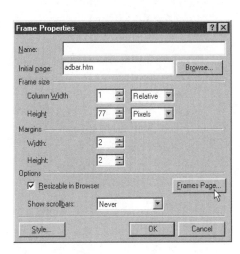

Frames are the wrong size or the layout is wrong

Source of the problem

When you create a frames page, you use a combination of <FRAMESET> and <FRAME> tags to tell browsers how to arrange the page and what page to display in each frame. Then you set attributes to determine the starting size of each frame.

Frame layout can be tricky—if you have more than two frames on your page, you might have trouble splitting frames in the right place. And frame sizing has its own problems. Remember that viewers use different sized browser windows and can change their window size—your frame settings must take this into consideration. For certain types of frames, you might want to specify a fixed width; for others, you'll want to allow them to be resized by the browser.

If your frame layout or sizing isn't working, follow these steps.

Tip

Many page design programs help you get started with frame layout. In HomeSite, for example, click the Frame Wizard button on the Frames toolbar. In FrontPage, click New on the File menu, click Page, click the Frames Pages tab, and select the page template that most closely fits your needs.

How to fix it

1. Be sure you have the right basic layout—the correct number of frames and the frame borders where you want them. ▶

2. To add another frame above or next to an existing one, add a size specification to the **rows** or **cols** attribute in the **<FRAMESET>** tag, and then insert a new **<FRAME>** tag. For three columns, for example, use this HTML:

```
<frameset cols="*,*,*">
  <frame src="left.htm">
  <frame src="center.htm">
```

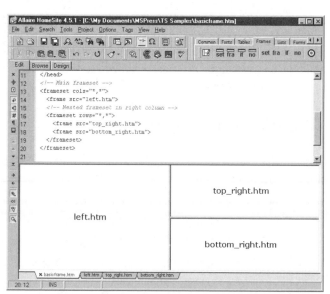

Frame layout involves experimentation and plenty of previewing. In HomeSite, you can display both the HTML and browser preview of your frames page.

```
     <frame src="right.htm">
</frameset>
```

3. To divide one row or column in two, use *nested framesets*—one **<FRAMESET>** tag inside another. For the frame you want to split, surround the existing **<FRAME>** tag with a new **<FRAMESET>** tag and add an additional **<FRAME>** tag above or below the existing one.

4. If the wrong frame is taking up a side of the frames page—the left column spans the page top to bottom, for example, when you want the top row to span left to right—rearrange tags so the frameset specifying rows comes before the one specifying columns, or vice versa.

```
<!-- Left column spans page -->       <!-- Top row spans page -->
<frameset cols="*,*">                 <frameset rows="*,*">
  <frame src="left.htm">                <frame src="top.htm">
  <frameset rows="*,*">                 <frameset cols="*,*">
    <frame src="top.htm">                 <frame src="left.htm">
    <frame src="bottom.htm">              <frame src="right.htm">
  </frameset>                           </frameset>
</frameset>                            </frameset>
```

5. Once the basic layout is right, adjust frame size using the **rows** and **cols** attributes of the **<FRAMESET>** tag. For each row or column, you can specify a number of pixels, or use percentages to specify frame sizes relative to the size of the browser window. Or, use an asterisk (*) for any row or column to let the browser distribute the remaining space equally.

Often, it makes sense to have one frame a specific size—a banner or set of links, for example—while allowing another frame to take the remaining space. For example, this HTML creates a fixed-height row at the bottom of the page and allows the remaining space to be used by the top frame.

> **Tip**
>
> If you want to prevent viewers from resizing your frames, add the **noresize** attribute to the **<FRAME>** tag. However, be aware that once you do this, adjacent frames can't be resized either. It might be better to allow viewers to resize frames in case their font or screen settings make your frame layout difficult to use.

```
<frameset rows="*,50">
  <frame src="main.htm">
  <frame src="footer.htm" noresize>
</frameset>
```

6. If pages don't fit properly in the frame size you select, you can change frame margins using the **marginheight** or **marginwidth** attributes of the **<FRAME>** tag. Also, review the HTML of the individual pages you've displayed in your frames. Adjust layout and table or image sizes in those pages, and then preview them in your frames page again.

To continue with this solution, go to the next page.

Frames are the wrong size or the layout is wrong

(continued from page 147)

Adjusting frame layout in FrontPage

If you're using FrontPage to create a frames page, you can adjust frame size by clicking the border between frames and dragging to the size you want. To change sizing options explicitly, right-click the frame you want to change, click Frame Properties, and set values in the Width and Row Height boxes under Frame Size. ▶

If you want to add a frame to your frames page, click an existing frame, click Split Frame on the Frames menu, and select Split Into Columns or Split Into Rows. Then click Set Initial Page to select the page you want the frame to display.

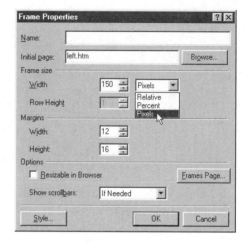

The FrontPage Frames menu items are dimmed

Source of the problem

If you have a frames page open in FrontPage, you can use items on the Frames menu to add, delete, or save frames. But when you're editing an ordinary web page—even one that you've previously designed using frames—FrontPage dims all items on the Frames menu, and you can't create frames.

If you want to add the current page to a frames page—or create a new frames page—you'll have to use a different strategy. Follow these steps.

Note
FrontPage allows you to specify compatibility settings that limit the features you can use—and if you've disabled frames support, you won't be able to use any frames features in FrontPage. Click Page Options on the Tools menu, click the Compatibility tab, select the Frames box, and click OK.

How to fix it

1. Save and close the page you're working on. In step 3, you'll display it in a frame on your frames page.

2. If you don't yet have a frames page, click New on the File menu, click Page, click the Frames Pages tab, select the frame page layout that's closest to what you're looking for, and click OK.

   If you already have a frames page, open it. (Click Open on the File menu.) To add a new frame, select an existing frame and click Split Frame on the Frames menu.

3. In the frame where you want to display the page you were working on, click Set Initial Page and select your page. ▶

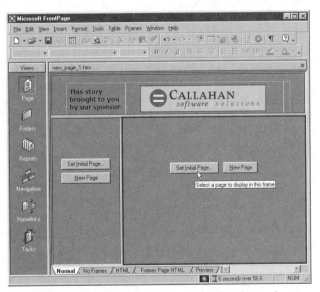

FrontPage frames features are enabled only after you've created or opened a frames page.

4. If you want to change the file displayed in an existing frame, right-click the frame, click Frame Properties, and specify your page in the Initial Page box.

Hyperlinks don't load pages into the frame I want

Source of the problem

In frames pages, you'll frequently want links in one frame to change what's displayed in another frame. You might have a navigation bar or table of contents, for example, that allows viewers to browse pages displayed in another frame. Or, you can provide special links that allow viewers to leave the frames page altogether.

But unless you specify otherwise, a hyperlink on a frames page changes what is displayed in its own frame. To get the effect you want, you need to tell the browser the *target* of each link—the frame or window that you want the link to affect. You'll need to specify proper tags and attributes in a number of places; if anything is missing, your links will either change the wrong frame or open a window you don't want.

To diagnose the problem and get your hyperlinks to work properly, follow these steps.

How to fix it

1. In the **<FRAME>** tag for each frame you want to load pages into, specify a name using the **name** attribute. You'll use this name as the target of hyperlinks that load pages into the frame. For example, this line creates a frame called main:

   ```
   <frame src="welcome.htm"
     name="main">
   ```

2. A common use of frames is to have one frame with a navigation bar or table of contents, allowing viewers to change the page that's displayed in another frame. ▶ Using the **<BASE>** tag, you can tell browsers that every link on your navigation page should load pages into a specific frame unless you specify otherwise. In the **<HEAD>** section of the navigation page—not the frames page—

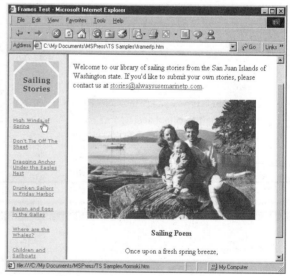

When you click a link in the navigation frame at left, you want the browser to change the page that's displayed in the main frame at the right, not display a different page in the navigation frame.

add the following line (substituting the name of a frame on your frames page):

```
<base target="main">
```

This sets the default target frame, so you don't have to set a target for each hyperlink.

3. For individual hyperlinks that you want to load into a specific frame, set the **target** attribute of the **<A>** tag. The following link, for example, opens a page in the frame called *right*:

```
<a href="winds.htm" target="right">High Winds</a>
```

4. If you link to a page that doesn't belong in your frames page—another company's home page, for example—you must use the **target** attribute to tell the browser not to load the page in a frame. To specify other pages, use either of the special target names **_top** (to open the page at the top level of the browser, outside existing frames) or **_blank** (to open a page in a new window). For example:

```
<a href="homepage.htm" target="_top">Escape the Frames</a>
```

5. If your page uses a form to submit information to a script or program—a search box in your navigation frame, for example—you can open the resulting page in a frame. Otherwise, the form page goes away when you submit the form, being replaced by the results. In the **<FORM>** tag, set the **target** attribute to the name of the frame.

```
<form action="search.asp" target="main">
```

6. You might want a link to load pages into more than one frame at a time. While you can only specify one target, you can use a simple JavaScript instruction to load a second page into another frame. For example, this HTML opens one page in the *main* frame and another in the *adbar* frame (unless that frame doesn't exist):

```
<a href="winds.htm" target="main"
   onclick="if(parent.adbar)parent.adbar.location='ad2.htm'">High Winds</a>
```

To continue with this solution, go to the next page.

Hyperlinks don't load pages into the frame I want

(continued from page 151)

Linking to frames in FrontPage

If you use FrontPage, you can change the target frame for hyperlinks on your frames page by setting hyperlink properties.

1. Be sure the frame you want to load pages into has a name. If it doesn't, right-click the frame and click Frame Properties. Type a name in the Name box, and then click OK.

2. Right-click the hyperlink you want to change and click Hyperlink Properties. (Or, to create a new hyperlink, click Hyperlink on the Insert menu.) Click the Change button at the right of the Target Frame box. In the diagram under Current Frames Page, click the frame in which you want the page to open—or, to avoid loading the link into a frame, select Whole Page or New Window under Common Targets. ▶

3. If you want all links on the current page to load pages into the same frame, select the Set As Page Default box.

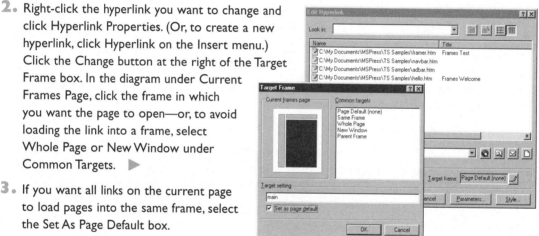

In FrontPage, you can specify the target frame for any hyperlink, or set the default target for all hyperlinks on the page.

The new page I created in FrontPage didn't get added to the frames page

Source of the problem

If you are editing a frames page in FrontPage and then use the New Page command to create a new page, your new page doesn't get added to the frames page. Instead, FrontPage creates a separate, nonframed page. For example, you might want to create a page based on a template. You click New on the File menu, click Page, and double-click the type of page you want, but your new page isn't included on the frames page.

To create a new page and include it on the frames page, follow these steps.

Note

Many FrontPage features work well with frames, but others don't. FrontPage navigation bars, shared borders, and page transitions aren't designed for use in a frames page. If you use a template or wizard to create a page—or a whole web—remember that the page might or might not be appropriate for use in frames.

How to fix it

1. Save and close the new page you're working on. ▶

2. Add a new frame in your frames page. Select an existing frame and click Split Frame on the Frames menu. Click Set Initial Page in the frame and select the page you created.

   Or, if you want to change the file displayed in an existing frame—replacing it with the new page you created—right-click the frame, click Frame Properties, and specify a page in the Initial Page box.

3. Now that your new page is included in the frames page, you can adjust frame borders, specify hyperlink targets, or make other changes on the page to get your frames page working the way you want.

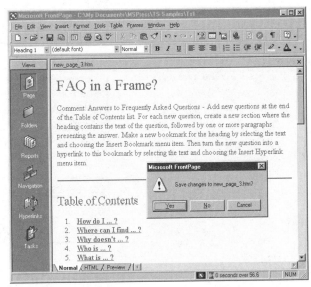

To add a new page to your frames page, you can use a template or wizard. But FrontPage doesn't add the new page to your frames page—you have to add it yourself.

Like other web design programs, FrontPage helps you concentrate on design and content rather than HTML. FrontPage is unique in that it's tightly integrated with server software—FrontPage Server Extensions—allowing you to provide interactive and graphical web features without learning additional software or programming.

But powerful features add complexity, and you are likely to run into some problems. Many FrontPage tools—its templates and wizards, for example—are designed for a specific purpose, and might not adapt easily to your needs.

To recover your footing with FrontPage, follow this flowchart. And if you're just starting out, see "Getting started with FrontPage" on page 157 and "What's in a FrontPage web?" on page 159.

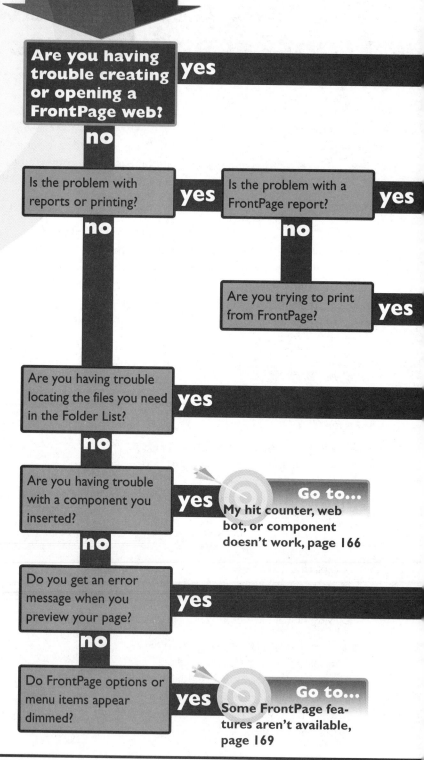

Are you having trouble creating or opening a FrontPage web?

yes

no

Is the problem with reports or printing?

yes

Is the problem with a FrontPage report?

yes

no

no

Are you trying to print from FrontPage?

yes

Are you having trouble locating the files you need in the Folder List?

yes

no

Are you having trouble with a component you inserted?

yes

Go to...
My hit counter, web bot, or component doesn't work, page 166

no

Do you get an error message when you preview your page?

yes

no

Do FrontPage options or menu items appear dimmed?

yes

Go to...
Some FrontPage features aren't available, page 169

Do you get an error message?

yes Go to...
I get an error when I try to create or open a FrontPage web, page 162

no

Go to...
A FrontPage report indicates problems or doesn't work properly, page 170

Is the problem that there isn't a template for the web you want?

yes Go to...
None of the FrontPage web templates fit my needs, page 156

no

Go to...
When I print my web, I don't get what I want, page 165

Is the problem that your web doesn't have the pages you want?

yes Go to...
FrontPage created a web that doesn't have all the pages I want, page 160

Quick fix

The Folder List and Open File dialog box display only files in the current web. To use a file in your web, import it.

1. Click Import on the File menu, and then click Add File.
2. Locate the file on your computer or network and click Open.

Quick fix

If FrontPage tells you that a page "may need to be saved or published," it means you have used a component, such as a hit counter, that must be on a web server to work properly.

1. Click Publish Web on the File menu and specify the web server address (beginning with **http://**).
2. Use your browser to preview your page on the server.

If your solution isn't here
Check these related chapters:
Or see the general troubleshooting tips on page xvii

None of the FrontPage web templates fit my needs

Source of the problem

The first step in using FrontPage is to create your FrontPage *web*—the combination of your web pages and images and the supporting files that FrontPage uses to organize your project. To help you get rolling, FrontPage offers several templates and wizards—for personal, project, customer support, and corporate webs—but it's unlikely that

any of them will be exactly what you need. ▶

Still, the web templates might give you a head start or give you ideas for your web. You can use one of them as a starting point—deleting elements you don't want and adding your own content—or you can pass them over and start fresh with your own web.

If the web templates aren't helping you get started, follow these steps.

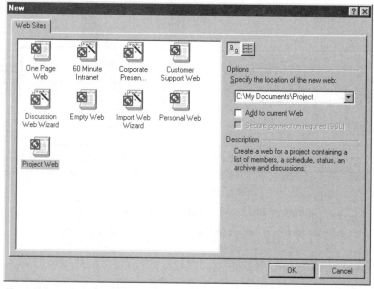

FrontPage offers several web types to choose from, but none is likely to meet your needs exactly.

How to fix it

If the type of web you want—an online store, for example—isn't among the templates, you might find a template or wizard available for download or purchase from a software vendor. (For ideas, see Appendix C.) Follow the vendor's instructions to install the template or wizard.

Try creating a sample web with a template or wizard. Even if it isn't quite right, it will help you become familiar with FrontPage features and provide ideas for your own web.

1. Point to New on the File menu and click Web. In the Web Sites section of the New dialog box, select Corporate Presence Wizard, Personal Web, or Project Web (or another template you've installed), and then specify the location of your new web in the Options section.

2. If the template-created web has some of the elements you want in your own web, keep the web as a starting point. You can always delete pages you don't want and add others.

    If you want to start fresh with your own web, close the sample web. (On the File menu, click Close.) To create a new web, point to New on the File menu and click Web, and then select One Page Web. Or, if you want to base your new FrontPage web on files that already exist—or even a complete web site—select Import Web Wizard.

Note

A FrontPage web on a server can be the server's default web—at the web root level—or it can be located in a subfolder. It's best to create sample or test webs as subfolders, because they are easy to copy or delete. In fact, you can't delete the default web on your server—if you don't want the pages and other files it contains, just delete them before adding new pages.

Getting started with FrontPage

Once you've created a web using one of the options above, you're ready to get started with your content and design. Here are some of the important steps:

1. Select a strategy for color and formatting. To set or change the web's *theme*—a set of predefined colors and styles that provide a consistent appearance—click Theme on the Format menu. ▶

    Or, if you want more control over formatting than a theme provides, set your own colors and background. (Right-click the page and click Page Properties.) Format pages as you go, or create and attach a style sheet. (See "Styles" on page 296.)

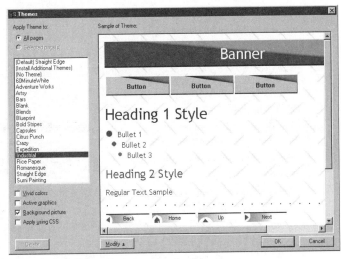

A theme provides a consistent, colorful style.

To continue with this solution, go to the next page.

None of the FrontPage web templates fit my needs

(continued from page 158)

2. Develop the basic structure of your web by creating pages and adding them to your web while in Navigation view. (Click the Navigation icon on the Views bar.) If you have other pages you want to include, drag them from the Folder List into the hierarchy. ▶

To create a new page in Navigation view, right-click an existing page and click New Page. Double-click pages to open them.

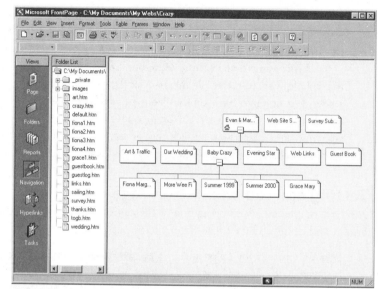

In Navigation view, you can view and modify the overall structure of your web. FrontPage uses the structure in your page banners and navigation bars.

3. Open and edit each of your pages. Insert banners and navigation bars to let FrontPage supply headings and hyperlinks based on your settings in Navigation view. Or, if you don't like FrontPage navigation bars, create hyperlinks to link pages in your own way. (See "Hyperlinks" on page 174.)

4. Create or scan pictures, logos, and other graphic images and import them. (On the File menu, click Import.) To insert an image into your page, point to Picture on the Insert menu and click From File. (See "Images" on page 188.) ▶

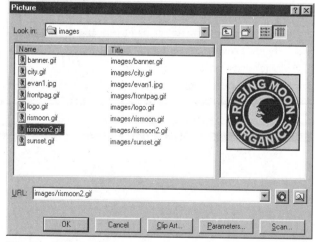

Pictures, logos, and graphical images are the key to creating effective pages.

5. Remember to try out your web at different points along the way. Click the Preview tab at the bottom of the FrontPage window, or click Preview In Browser on the File menu.

What's in a FrontPage web?

The most important elements of a FrontPage web are your HTML pages and the text and images they display—the rest is just icing on the cake. But in order to support its many features, FrontPage keeps track of much more information behind the scenes. This means that FrontPage can do plenty of powerful things that usually involve additional software, but it also means your FrontPage web takes more server space and is slower and more complex than a conventional web site.

For example, to support navigation bars and hyperlink maintenance, FrontPage stores information about how all your pages and files are linked together. When you first create the web, FrontPage adds the supporting folders and files it needs, and it maintains them whenever you work on your pages. Most of these folders and files are hidden from view, and you don't have to concern yourself with them. But if you examine your web outside of FrontPage, you'll see several folders whose names start with an underscore, such as _vti_pvt.

Most of the information FrontPage keeps track of is available to you through the six FrontPage views. You can open any of the following views by clicking the icons on the Views bar at the left side of the FrontPage window:

- **Page view**, where you view, edit, and preview your pages

- **Folders view**, where you can organize, move, rename, and delete web files

- **Reports view**, where you can view reports about your pages and links

- **Navigation view**, where you organize your pages into a hierarchy, which FrontPage uses to produce page banners and navigation bars

- **Hyperlinks view**, where you can view and check links between your pages as well as from your pages to external web sites

- **Tasks view**, where you can create a to-do list for maintaining your web

FrontPage created a web that doesn't have all the pages I want

Source of the problem

If you use a FrontPage template to create a web—a personal, project, or corporate web, for example—you'll probably find that the pages you need aren't all included. Everyone's needs are different, and a web template is just a starting point. To create additional pages, you can use page templates, import pages from other programs or webs, or create pages from scratch. Fortunately, most of the web templates provide a basic framework.

New pages that you create use the same themes, shared borders, and navigation bars as existing pages, so your web has a unified look and feel. ▶

If your new web doesn't have the pages you want, follow these steps. For other ideas on creating a web, see "Getting started with FrontPage" on page 157.

How to fix it

1. Click the Page icon on the Views bar at the left side of the FrontPage window.

2. If a new page doesn't appear, create one. Point to New on the File menu, click Page, and double-click a page template. For example, to create a Frequently Asked Questions (FAQ) page for your web, use the Frequently Asked Questions template.

   Or, to create a blank page, click the New Page button on the standard toolbar.

3. Click Save on the File menu and type a name for your new page.

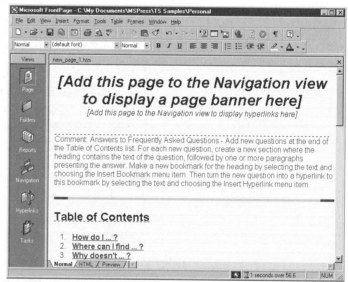

New pages in a template-created web inherit formatting, shared borders, and navigation. Once you tell FrontPage how this page fits into your web, it will automatically display a banner and links to other pages.

4. Click the Navigation icon on the Views bar. Drag the new page into its place in your web hierarchy. If it doesn't have the title you want, right-click it, click Rename, and type a name.

5. Click the Page icon on the Views bar again to view your page with its banner and navigation bars updated. ▶

6. Add text, images, and other components to your new page. If you used a template, edit existing text and follow instructions displayed in comments on the page. (Once you've finished, you can delete the comments if you like.)

7. Repeat these steps until your web has all the pages you want.

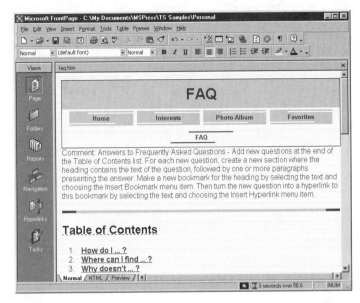

Note

If you want to include existing web pages from other webs—or if you've created web pages using Word, Excel, PowerPoint, or Access—click Import on the File menu and specify the files or folders you want to import. Then, follow steps 4 to 6 to incorporate the new pages into your web.

Note

Your new page probably already has shared borders—on a new page, these sections display a message such as "[Add this page to Navigation view to display...]." If your page doesn't have shared borders, you can add them. Click Shared Borders on the Format menu, select the borders you want, and click OK. Or, to remove shared borders (to provide your own navigation and banners, for example), clear all the boxes.

I get an error when I try to create or open a FrontPage web

Source of the problem

A web site, generally speaking, is a collection of web pages that are linked together. A *FrontPage web* is more than this; in addition to web pages, it includes several hidden folders and supporting files that FrontPage uses to make your web site work better.

When you create or open a web—whether in a file folder or on a web server—FrontPage creates or opens these files. If you're using a web server, FrontPage does this by connecting with the server via Hypertext Transfer Protocol (HTTP). If FrontPage can't connect to the server or can't create or open the files it needs, you'll see an error message. ▶

There are many reasons that a FrontPage web might not work, including problems with your network, server extensions, or permissions. To track down the problem and get your web working, follow these steps.

When you open or create a web, FrontPage tries to communicate with the server.

How to fix it

1. If you're trying to create or open a web in a folder on your computer or network (such as C:\My Documents\My Webs\TestWeb), make sure the path you've specified is valid. If the web is on a network and you get an error message, make sure you have permission to open and create files.

2. If you're trying to open a web and have specified a file folder that is not a FrontPage web, FrontPage offers to add supporting folders and files. To create a new FrontPage web in the folder, click Yes. If you specified the wrong folder, click No and try again. ▶

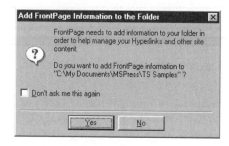

3. If you're trying to create or open a server-based web, be sure to specify **http://** at the beginning of the address, so that FrontPage knows you are referring to a web server rather than a folder on your computer. For example, type **http://Weber/Intranet** in the Folder Name box to open a web called Intranet on a server named Weber.

4. Check whether the web server you're opening is working and available. Try the root web address, such as *http://Weber or www.mydomain.com,* in your browser. If the server is available, you'll see a web page. (If there's no default page, you might see a message such as "The page cannot be found" or "Directory listing denied.") If the browser can't find the web server and displays an error, either the web server or your network connection isn't working. Try again later, contact your network administrator or Internet service provider (ISP), or see "I'm having trouble accessing the Internet" on page 44.

the Internet" on page 44.

5. In order to host a FrontPage web, the server must have FrontPage Server Extensions installed and properly configured. If you see the message "The web server at *name* does not appear to have the server extensions installed," you probably need to install server extensions or use a different server. For information on FrontPage Server Extensions, see *officeupdate.microsoft.com/frontpage/wpp/serk.* If you don't control the server, contact your network administrator or ISP.

6. To open or create a web, you need proper FrontPage permissions; otherwise, you'll get an error message saying you aren't authorized. In order to open a web, for example, you need Author permission for that web. To create a subweb, you need Administrator permission for the *parent web*—the web in which you are creating the new subweb.

If you are connecting over a Windows-based network, the server usually determines who you are based on your Windows account. Otherwise, FrontPage asks for your name and password. If you get an error telling you that you aren't authorized, ask your network administrator, your ISP, or the owner of the parent web to check your FrontPage permissions, or to create the web for you and give you Author permission. ▶

To continue with this solution, go to the next page.

I get an error when I try to create or open a FrontPage web

(continued from page 163)

7. If you specify a root web address (such as *http://server_name*) when creating a new web, you'll get an error message, because every FrontPage web server already has a root web. Instead, open the web, and then add files. Click Open Web on the File menu and type the server name.

8. If you get the message "Server Error: Cannot create folder" when creating a subweb, you might have specified a parent web location that doesn't exist. To create *http://webserver/teams/marketing*, for example, first create *http://webserver/teams*.

9. If you still get an error, your web server extensions or security settings might be incorrect or incompatible. For more ideas, see "The FrontPage security option isn't available or working" on page 274.

> **Tip**
>
> If you want to use a web template or wizard to add files to the root web—or to any other web that already exists—point to New on the File menu and click Web, click the template or wizard you want to use, and select Add To Current Web.

When I print my web, I don't get what I want

Source of the problem

FrontPage is designed for on-screen viewing, not printing. You can print your pages, HTML code, or navigation structure from FrontPage, but you might not get what you expect.

Fortunately, other programs such as Internet Explorer offer better printing features. If you're having printing problems in FrontPage, follow these steps.

How to fix it

1. You can't print from Folders, Reports, Hyperlinks, or Tasks view. In these views, the Print command is dimmed. If you want to print what you see on the screen, press **Alt+PrtScn** to copy the FrontPage window to the Windows clipboard. Then open a blank document in your word processor or graphics program, switch the page to landscape orientation, click Paste, and then click Print.

2. You can print from Page view, but you might not always get the results you want. For example, if your page contains form fields or an ActiveX control, these elements won't print properly.

   Before you print, click Print Preview on the File menu. If you don't like what you see, print your page using Internet Explorer from within FrontPage: click the Preview tab, right-click the page background, and click Print. ▶

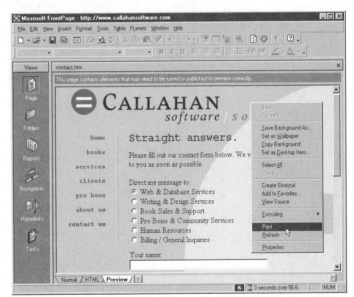

If FrontPage printing doesn't work, print from Internet Explorer.

3. You can print from HTML view, but page margins might not work properly. Also, if you select landscape orientation, ten lines of HTML are left out between each page.

   Instead, print your code using Notepad. Save and close the file, right-click the file in the Folder List, click Open With, and click Notepad. Click Page Setup on the File menu to specify printing options, and then click Print on the File menu.

My hit counter, web bot, or component doesn't work

Source of the problem

When you insert a component such as a Hit Counter, Hover Button, or Search Form on your page, FrontPage does some fancy work behind the scenes. If you look at your HTML, you'll see special information describing the component you're using and its settings. When you view the page in a browser, this code is hidden, but it tells FrontPage how you want the component to look and work. ▶

The programs and files that make each component do its thing are in hidden folders on your web or are part of the FrontPage Server Extensions. You've probably heard of some of the technologies FrontPage uses to make components work: Java applets, server-side programs, and *web bots*, the name for components in FrontPage 98 and earlier.

Because components involve complex interactions, there's a lot of room for trouble. If a component on your page doesn't work in a browser, follow these steps.

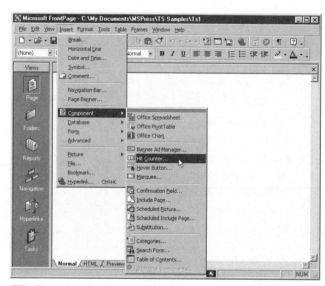

The Insert menu offers a host of components for your pages. To make them work, FrontPage uses Java applets and server extensions.

How to fix it

FrontPage allows you to insert components on any page, even one that isn't in a FrontPage web. But most components must be saved in a web to work—only the Hover Button component works outside a FrontPage web.

If you've added a component to a page that isn't in a web, you can either import the page into an existing web or create a FrontPage web in the folder that contains the page.

1. To create a web, close and save the page, click Open Web on the File menu, select the folder that contains your page, click Open, and then click Yes when FrontPage asks if you want to add

FrontPage information to the folder. Then open any pages that have components and save them again. ▶

2. Some components work in a file-based FrontPage web, while others work only on a web server with FrontPage Server Extensions. Components that require a server include Hit Counter, Search Form, Form and Database Results, and Confirmation Field.

If you are using a file-based web, FrontPage displays the following message when you preview your page: "This page contains elements that may need to be saved or published to preview correctly." To get your component working, publish your web to a server with FrontPage Server Extensions.

3. For some components, it might be important to use the matching version of the server extensions (FrontPage 2000 extensions for use with a FrontPage 2000 web). If you aren't sure which version of the server extensions you're using, contact your server administrator or ISP.

4. If you use the Scheduled Include Page or the Scheduled Picture components, you might find that your page or picture doesn't change at the time you specified. Unfortunately, these components don't work as advertised—they only change your page when the page or web gets updated. If you want scheduled changes to take place, open the page and save it again, or open the web and click Recalculate Hyperlinks on the Tools menu.

5. If you insert more than one hit counter on a single page, you might see incorrect numbering. To fix the problem, delete the extra hit counters.

6. When you upgrade a web from a previous version to FrontPage 2000, some components might break. For example, hover buttons might not work, because FrontPage stores the Java applet for the Hover Button component in a different place than it did before. To fix problems, delete components that don't work and insert them using FrontPage 2000.

7. If you use the Search Form component, you might find that search results are out of date when pages have changed. To make sure your searches return current results, open the web and click Recalculate Hyperlinks on the Tools menu.

> **Note**
> Certain components won't work in all browsers. The Marquee component, for example, uses the **\<MARQUEE\>** tag, which only Internet Explorer supports. In other browsers, such as Netscape, you'll see the marquee text, but it won't move across the screen. The Office components—Office Spreadsheet, Office PivotTable, and Office Chart—all require Internet Explorer 4 or later. In addition, they require that Microsoft Office be installed on the viewer's computer. If your web's viewers won't all have Office, don't use these components.

To continue with this solution, go to the next page.

My hit counter, web bot, or component doesn't work

(continued from page 167)

If your web server uses Microsoft Internet Information Server (IIS) with Index Server, FrontPage tries to use Index Server instead of its built-in search program. Depending on how Index Server is configured, you might get incorrect results. Also, if your web uses shared borders, the results page from Index Server might not display them. If you control your web server, it's possible to reconfigure or disable Index Server. For information, see the Microsoft Knowledge Base at *support.microsoft.com*. (Select FrontPage 2000 and search for *Index Server*.)

8. If the component displays an error or just doesn't do anything, it's possible that settings have become corrupted or that required files are missing from the web. Delete the component. (You might want to first double-click it and make note of its properties so you can re-enter them.) Insert the component again, and then preview your page.

9. If a component still isn't working or just doesn't meet your needs, you might want to consider an alternative. For example, in lieu of the Scheduled Include Page component—which doesn't work very well—you could use a simple Active Server Pages (ASP) script or server-side include (SSI) directive. Or, instead of using Banner Ad Manager—which also has serious limitations—you could purchase one of many advertising management packages from a software vendor.

Some FrontPage features aren't available

Source of the problem

FrontPage disables menus and options when they don't currently apply. If you specify custom compatibility settings for your web—telling FrontPage which browsers you want your pages to work with, for example—FrontPage disables other features that aren't compatible with your settings.

If a command or feature you want to use is dimmed, follow these steps to get back in business.

How to fix it

1. If you specify custom compatibility settings for your web, a variety of FrontPage features might become unavailable. For example, if you tell FrontPage that you won't require cascading style sheets (CSS) support, it makes sure you don't use styles in your pages.

   To enable all FrontPage features, click Page Options on the Tools menu, click the Compatibility tab, and select every check box. (Ignore the drop-down lists.) ▶

2. Editing and printing commands are dimmed unless you're editing a page. (To open a page, click Open on the File menu; to activate an open page, click the Page icon on the Views bar.) To enable Table menu commands, select a table or cell. Frames menu commands are available only in a frames page.

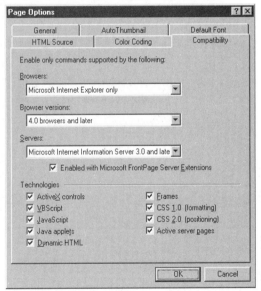

Your compatibility settings might cause FrontPage to disable features.

3. Web views (other than Page view) are disabled when you are editing a page that isn't in a FrontPage web. To open a web, click Open Web on the File menu.

4. Security features work only on a server with FrontPage Server Extensions. To change permission settings, you must open your web directly on the server. Click Open Web on the File menu and specify a web address, such as **http://server_name**. Then point to Security on the Tools menu and click Permissions.

5. To use the Check Out and Check In commands, you must first enable them. Click Web Settings on the Tools menu and select Use Document Check-In And Check-Out.

A FrontPage report indicates problems or doesn't work properly

Source of the problem

FrontPage reports, which are available by clicking the Reports icon on the Views bar at the left side of the FrontPage window, offer a great checkup for your web after you've created pages and links. (Note that reports aren't available for pages outside a FrontPage web.)

For most webs, reports correctly identify problems with components, slow pages, unlinked files, or broken hyperlinks—problems you'll want to solve before viewers discover them. You'll need to take FrontPage reports with a grain of salt, however, because they can be misleading or entirely wrong. ▶

If reports indicate problems with your web—or just aren't working as you expect—follow these steps.

How to fix it

1. The size values in the Site Summary report are inaccurate. FrontPage sums up the size of your pages and images, but leaves out supporting files, so the values tend to be 25 percent to 50 percent lower than the actual size of your web.

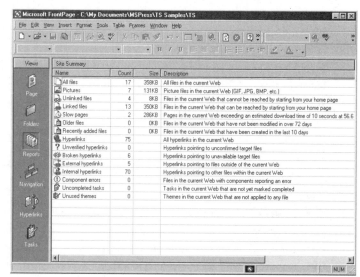

The Site Summary and other reports are helpful with web maintenance, but might not always be accurate.

If you have access to your server, or if your web is in a file folder, you can view the exact size of the folder in Windows. (Open the parent folder that contains your web's root folder, right-click the folder, and click Properties.) Or, to get a more accurate estimate, you can view hidden folders in your web. (Click Web Settings on the Tools menu, click the Advanced tab, and select Show Documents In Hidden Directories.)

2. If you're using a disk-based web that you publish to a server periodically, you might see more accurate report results if you open the web on the server. Click Close Web on the File menu. Then click Open Web and type the web address of the server (such as **http://servername**).

3. In the Unlinked Files report—which is intended to help you delete unused files so they don't take up space—you might see files that do actually belong in your web. Certain configurations with navigation bars, for example, cause FrontPage to mistakenly believe your files aren't linked. For this reason, it's important to verify whether files are unused before deleting them.

Also, if you've told FrontPage to display hidden folders—folders that store supporting files for your pages—you might see a long list of theme files, shared border files, or files that support Office-created pages. To hide these files so you can better see actual unlinked files, turn off the option. On the Tools menu, click Web Settings, click the Advanced tab, and clear Show Documents In Hidden Directories.

If a file listed in the Unlinked Files report is in fact unused—for example, an image that you removed from a page but didn't delete from the web—right-click the file and click Delete.

4. In the Broken Hyperlinks report, you'll see any links referring to files in your web that aren't there. You'll also see any *external hyperlinks*—links to files or sites outside your web—indicated as Unknown. To check external hyperlinks, click the Verify Hyperlinks button on the Reporting toolbar. Links that FrontPage can follow are marked as OK, while others are marked as Broken.

Unfortunately, the report might display links to certain types of web servers as broken, even though they work fine. Within your web as well, some valid links might show up in the report—links created by the Categories component, for example, or those from Office-created web pages to supporting files. If you suspect that links aren't really broken, preview and test the pages yourself, ignoring the list in the report.

For hyperlinks that are in fact broken, you can fix them from within the report. Right-click the link, click Edit Hyperlink on the Reporting toolbar, and specify a new file or web address. FrontPage changes the old link to the new in pages throughout your web.

Tip

When viewing the Site Summary report, you can double-click most lines to jump to the corresponding report, such as Unlinked Files or Broken Hyperlinks. But once you've done this, it might not be obvious how to get back to the summary or switch to other reports. To switch to any report, point to Reports on the View menu and click the report name, such as Site Summary.

Tip

If you make changes to your web while viewing a report, it's a good idea to refresh the report (click Refresh on the View menu). Or, to recheck all links in your web and update reports—especially if you make any changes to your web outside FrontPage—click Recalculate Hyperlinks on the Tools menu.

To continue with this solution, go to the next page.

A FrontPage report indicates problems or doesn't work properly

(continued from page 171)

5. If the Slow Pages report lists pages, you might want to try to make them smaller. (To change what constitutes *slow*, click Options on the Tools menu, click the Reports View tab, and specify settings.) To reduce a page's load time, you can try removing images from it or split it into two pages. But the main reason pages are too slow is because images are larger than necessary or are not properly optimized. For information, see "My images take too long to load" on page 194.

6. If the Component Errors report lists pages, preview the pages on your web server and test the components. If they aren't working, see "My hit counter, web bot, or component doesn't work" on page 166.

> **Tip**
>
> If you try to print a web report, you'll see that FrontPage doesn't allow it. Instead, press **Alt+PrtScn** to copy the FrontPage window into the Windows clipboard. Then open a blank document in your word processor or graphics program, and switch the page to landscape mode. (In Word 2000, click Page Setup on the File menu, click the Paper Size tab, click Landscape under Orientation, and click OK.) Click Paste and then click Print.

Hyperlinks—text or images that viewers can click to jump between pages—are the glue that holds together the web. To create a hyperlink in HTML, you use the <A> tag, specifying the web address that you want it to open. The active area for a link is usually either one or more words or an image, but can be any region or set of items on your page.

Because hyperlinks are such an important part of your pages, you'll want to make sure they look and work just right. You'll want to watch out for broken or dead-end links, and you might want to change the appearance of your hyperlinks to improve their visibility or to match better with your design.

If you're having trouble with hyperlinks, follow this flowchart. And for examples of the many types of hyperlinks you can use, see "Various types of hyperlinks" on page 179.

Is the problem with the way your hyperlinks look? **yes**

no

Are hyperlinks broken or causing "Page Not Found" errors? **yes** Go to...
The hyperlinks are broken, page 176

no

Are you having trouble making links active when viewers roll the mouse over them? **yes** Go to...
My page doesn't do anything when you move the mouse over links and images, page 184

no

Does a hyperlink open a page in the wrong frame or window, or do you want a new window? **yes**

no

Are you having trouble creating a drop-down list of hyperlinks? **yes** Go to...
I added a drop-down list for linking to other pages, but can't make it work, page 182

If your solution isn't here
Check these related chapters:
Browsers, page 42
Images, page 188
Scripting, page 280
Styles, page 296
Or see the general troubleshooting tips on page xvii

Hyperlinks

Are you trying to get rid of the underlines?

yes

Quick fix

To suppress the underlining of a link, use the style attribute of the **<A>** tag to set the **text-decoration** property:

```
<a href="link.htm" style="text-decoration: none">
```

To get rid of underlining throughout the page, add this code to the **<HEAD>** section of the file:

```
<style>
  a { text-decoration: none; }
</style>
```

no

Are you trying to change hyperlink colors or styles?

yes

Go to...

Text hyperlinks aren't the right color or style, page 180

no

Do images with links have a blue border that you don't want?

yes

Quick fix

If an image is inside an **<A>** tag, its border takes on the hyperlink color. If you don't want a border, set the **border** attribute in the **<IMG>** tag to 0:

```
<img src="pic.jpg" border=0>
```

If you want a border around your images, but don't want them to use the hyperlink color, use a style to set the **border-color** property for images and the **color** property for links within images. Place the following code in the **<HEAD>** section of the file:

```
<style>
  img {
  border-color: #000000;
  }
  a img {
  color: #000000;
  }
</style>
```

Quick fix

You control the window or frame into which a hyperlink loads a page with the **target** attribute of the **<A>** tag.

To make a link open a page in a new window, use the following HTML:

```
<a href="file.htm"
  target="_blank">
```

To load the page into a specific browser window or a frame on a frames page, set the **target** attribute to the name of the frame or window. To load a page outside frames, set **target="_top"**.

The hyperlinks are broken

Source of the problem

If the destination specified in a hyperlink isn't available—the address or file name is wrong, or the destination file has been moved or deleted—the hyperlink is said to be *broken*.

If you've ever been frustrated by dead-end hyperlinks, you know how important it is to keep yours working. When a viewer clicks a broken hyperlink, the browser tries to follow the address and the viewer gets an error message, such as "The page cannot be found."

There are a variety of reasons why a hyperlink might not work. To diagnose and solve the problem, follow these steps.

How to fix it

1. Preview your page and position the mouse pointer over the hyperlink. The mouse pointer should change to a hand with a pointing finger. If it doesn't, there might be something wrong with your HTML.

   Be sure the **<A>** tag contains only text or an image and has a closing **</A>** tag. Also, be sure that the **href** attribute is set and the address is enclosed in quotation marks. These basic text and image hyperlinks, for example, point to HTML files in the same folder as the current page:

   ```
   <a href="pr.htm">Press Releases</a>
   <a href="go.htm"><img src="gobtn.gif" width=20 height=20 alt="Go!"></a>
   ```

2. Click the hyperlink in your browser. If you see "The page cannot be found" or "HTTP Error 404," it means that your web server replied that the specified file doesn't exist. If you see "The page cannot be displayed" or "Netscape is unable to find the file or directory," it means the hyperlink points to a file on your computer or network that doesn't exist.

   Check the path and file name you've specified for the **href** attribute. Make sure it is spelled correctly—on a UNIX system, be sure to use the same capitalization—and has the correct file name extension, such as .htm or .html. Next, make sure the link address points to a file that exists. For an *absolute* link address, specify the server name and complete path. For a *relative* link address—one that doesn't specify a server or disk drive—specify the location in relation to the current page. For example, if your main page is in the folder C:\inetpub\wwwroot, both the following lines open the file C:\inetpub\wwwroot\pr\intro.htm:

   ```
   <a href="http://servername/pr/intro.htm">Press Releases</a>
   <a href="pr/intro.htm">Press Releases</a>
   ```

3. If your hyperlink doesn't include a file name, the browser tries to open the default file in the specified folder (usually named default.htm or index.html, depending on the web server). If the browser displays a folder listing—or an error message such as "You are not authorized to view this page" or "Directory listing denied"—your folder probably doesn't have a default file. The following hyperlink, for example, works only if a default page (such as default.htm) exists in the pr folder:

```
<a href="http://servername/pr/">Press Releases
</a>
```

To make the hyperlink work, add a default page to the folder. Or, change your link address to include an explicit file name at the end.

Tip
If you administer your own web server, you can specify a custom error page to appear when viewers request a page that doesn't exist (either by typing a file name or by clicking a broken link). This way, instead of the standard message, you can display a page with your company logo, a friendly message, and other links or suggestions. For information, see your web server documentation.

4. If your hyperlink is to an external web server, make sure the link address begins with **http://**, as follows:

```
<a href="http://www.risingmoon.com/">Good Food</a>
```

If the file doesn't exist at the specified location on the server, change the **href** attribute to point to an existing file (or copy or move the file to the specified location). If the server doesn't respond, it might be down, or your Internet connection might not be working. See "I'm having trouble accessing the Internet" on page 44.

Verifying and fixing hyperlinks in HomeSite

If you use HomeSite, you can check links in the current page or project and view results in the Results pane at the bottom of the window.

1. Click Verify Links on the Tools menu. (Or, if you have a HomeSite project open, you can verify links for all pages at once by right-clicking the project and clicking Verify Links.) Valid links display a green check, while broken links display a red "X" or a clock icon—indicating that the server didn't respond before the request timed out.

2. Double-click each broken link to edit the **href** attribute. (Or, make sure the file or server specified in the link exists, moving or renaming the file if necessary.)

To continue with this solution, go to the next page.

The hyperlinks are broken

(continued from page 177)

Verifying and fixing hyperlinks in FrontPage

If you use FrontPage, you can check links throughout your web anytime. Then you can update link addresses without opening each file or editing each hyperlink.

1. Point to Reports on the View menu and click Broken Hyperlinks. If there are any broken internal hyperlinks—links to nonexistent files within your web—they appear in the list.

2. If any external links display Unknown under Status, click Select All on the Edit menu, and then right-click any link in the report and click Verify.

3. Double-click each broken link to edit it. (Or, make sure the file or server specified in the link exists, moving or renaming the file if necessary.) ▶

4. After you've fixed links, click Refresh on the View menu to update the report.

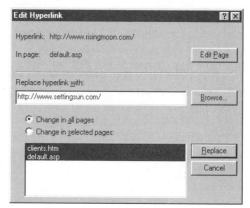

FrontPage helps you fix broken hyperlinks throughout your web.

Various types of hyperlinks

In HTML pages, you'll find all sorts of different web addresses specified in the **href** attribute. Here are examples of various types of hyperlinks you might want to try in your own pages:

- Link to page in same folder:
  ```
  <a href="other.htm">Other Page</a>
  ```

- Link to page in a subfolder:
  ```
  <a href="private/other.htm">Other Page</a>
  ```

- Link to page on another server:
  ```
  <a href="http://mspress.microsoft.com/office2000/">Microsoft Press</a>
  ```

- Link to top of page:
  ```
  <a href="#top">Top of page</a>
  ```

- Link to named position in the same page:
  ```
  <a href="#news">Read the News</a>
  ```
  To mark the position, use an **<A>** tag with the **name** attribute, but no **href**:
  ```
  <a name="news">Today's News</a>
  ```

- Link with a query string that a script can access:
  ```
  <a href="search.asp?qry=faq">See all our FAQ lists</a>
  ```

- Link that opens an e-mail message:
  ```
  <a href="mailto:anyone@microsoft.com">anyone@microsoft.com</a>
  ```
  Some browsers allow you to specify a subject for the message as follows:
  ```
  <a href="mailto:anyone@microsoft.com?subject=Website%20Feedback">
    anyone@microsoft.com</a>
  ```

- File Transfer Protocol (FTP) download:
  ```
  <a href="ftp://www.callahansoftware.com/downloads/thefile.exe">
    Download the file</a>
  ```

- Link to an image, media, or compressed Zip file:
  ```
  <a href="music/imagine.mp3">Listen to me sing</a>
  ```

- Link that opens a new browser window:
  ```
  <a href="http://www.risingmoon.com/" target="_blank">
    Our Friend's Web Site</a>
  ```

- Link that runs a JavaScript function:
  ```
  <a href="javascript:dosomething()">Do something</a>
  ```

- Link that does nothing (useful if you run a script from another event):
  ```
  <a href="javascript:void(0)"
    ondblclick="alert('Col. Mustard in the library with the wrench.')">
    Double-click for a clue</a>
  ```

Text hyperlinks aren't the right color or style

Source of the problem

If you don't specify hyperlink colors and styles for your page, the browser uses default colors—usually bright blue underlined text for hyperlinks you haven't followed yet, purple for ones you have followed, and red for ones you've just now clicked.

Designed for easy recognition rather than attractive appearance, these colors probably won't look right with your page. To get hyperlinks looking the way you want, follow these steps.

> **Note**
> Netscape allows viewers to override the color settings specified in your pages—although by default, pages use the colors you specify. If you don't see the colors you want in Netscape, check under Preferences.

How to fix it

1. The standard way to change hyperlink color is to use attributes of the **<BODY>** tag. The **link** attribute specifies the main link color, the **vlink** attribute the visited link color, and the **alink** attribute the active (clicked) link color. This **<BODY>** tag, for example, specifies a gray background and three shades of blue for hyperlinks:

```
<body bgcolor="#cccccc" link="#003399" alink="#3399ff" vlink="#0066cc">
```

2. The second way to change hyperlink color is by setting cascading style sheet (CSS) properties for the **<A>** tag. Styles are much more flexible, allowing you to specify options such as bold and italic, as well as color—or to have more than one hyperlink style in the same page. For example, adding this code to the **<HEAD>** section of your page causes hyperlinks to be dark red, bold, and never underlined:

```
<style>
  a {
    color: #993300;
    font-weight: bold;
    text-decoration: none;
  }
</style>
```

3. To specify a different color for regular, visited, and active hyperlinks, you set the color property of the **a:link**, **a:visited**, and **a:active** subclasses. You can also set a special color or style for when viewers roll the mouse over your hyperlinks, using the **a:hover** subclass. ▶

For example, adding these styles to the **<STYLE>** section above causes visited hyperlinks to be red-brown and causes hyperlinks to light up and turn italic when your viewers roll over them:

```
a:visited {
  color: #663300;
}
a:hover {
  color: #ffffcc;
  font-style: italic;
}
```

While the **a:hover** subclass is part of the CSS 2 specification, it currently works only in Internet Explorer. If the browser doesn't support it, the mouse pointer has no effect.

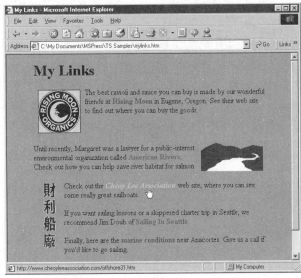

Thanks to CSS, hyperlinks don't have to be bright blue and underlined.

> **Tip**
> Even if you use styles to set hyperlink colors, you should set them in the **<BODY>** tag as well, because not all viewers will use browsers that support CSS.

I added a drop-down list for linking to other pages, but can't make it work

Source of the problem

Many web pages use a **<SELECT>** tag to provide a drop-down list of hyperlinks. This allows you to compress a lot of navigation into one small box, and is a familiar way for viewers to find the page they want. ▶

To make such a list work, you have to use a script—either in the browser or on the server. If your HTML or script code isn't exactly right, the list might not work. To get your hyperlink list working, follow these steps.

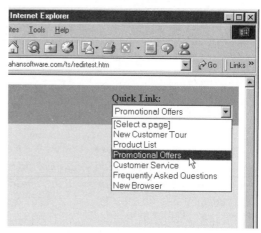

If you create hyperlinks in a drop-down list box, you need a script to redirect the browser when viewers select a link.

How to fix it

1. Place this code in the **<HEAD>** section of your page to define the **redir** function. The function redirects the browser to a new page by setting the **document.location** property to the value of the selected option in the list box:

```
<script language="JavaScript">
  <!--
  // Redirect to the URL selected in a list box.
  function redir(myList) {
    if(newURL=myList.options[myList.selectedIndex].value)
      document.location=newURL;
  }
  //-->
</script>
```

2. In the **<SELECT>** tag, use the **onchange** event to run the function—this way, the browser redirects to a new page as soon as a viewer clicks a selection in the list. In the following HTML, each **<OPTION>** tag displays descriptive text for the list, but specifies a URL in the **value** attribute. One exception is the "[Select a page]" entry at the top, which has an empty value (so it won't redirect to another page).

```
<form>
   <b>Quick Link:</b>
   <select onchange="redir(this)">
     <option value="" selected>[Select a page]
     <option value="tour.htm">New Customer Tour
     <option value="products.htm">Product List
     <option value="offers.htm">Promotional Offers
     <option value="service.htm">Customer Service
     <option value="faq.htm">Frequently Asked Questions
     <option value="http://www.microsoft.com/windows/ie/">New Browser
   </select>
</form>
```

You'll notice that the **<FORM>** tag doesn't need any action attribute or a submit button—the script runs from the **<SELECT>** tag. You should still include it, however, because Netscape requires that controls be contained inside a form.

A server script alternative

If the viewer's browser doesn't support JavaScript, the list box above won't do anything. Since not all browsers support JavaScript, be sure to provide another way to link to other pages, such as ordinary hyperlinks.

Alternatively, if your server allows scripting through Active Server Pages (ASP) or Common Gateway Interface (CGI), you can use a server script to redirect viewers—a solution nearly every browser supports. If your server supports ASP, for example, follow these steps:

1. Enter the following simple server script into a new file and save it as redir.asp, placing it in the same folder as the page that has the drop-down hyperlink menu. (You can test this script in your browser by entering **redir.asp?url=*pagename*.htm** in the address bar to open *pagename*.htm.)

```
<%@ LANGUAGE="VBScript" %>
<%
   ' Redirect to the page specified in the URL parameter.
   Response.Redirect Request("url")
%>
```

2. Use the following HTML to create the form, setting the **action** attribute to the name of the ASP script.

```
<form action="redir.asp">
   <b>Select a page:</b>
   <select name="url">
     <option value="tour.htm">New Customer Tour

         .
         .
         .

     <option value="faq.htm">Frequently Asked Questions
   </select>
   <input type=submit value="Go!">
</form>
```

My page doesn't do anything when you move the mouse over links and images

Source of the problem

It's increasingly popular nowadays, because of steadily improving browser support, to include action or interactivity on pages. Many web pages, for example, improve the visibility of hyperlinks by causing them to change or light up when viewers position the mouse pointer over them. Known as a *rollover*, this capability requires the use of JavaScript—which you can write yourself, borrow from someone else, or create using your graphics software and then paste into your page.

If your page is too static, follow these steps to create rollovers for your links.

> **Tip**
> If you use FrontPage, you'll notice that navigation bar buttons automatically have a rollover effect. Or, you can create custom rollovers by inserting a Hover Button component (point to Component on the Insert menu and click Hover Button).

How to fix it

To cause the browser to display an alternate image whenever the viewer rolls the mouse over your links, follow these steps.

1. Create a main image and an alternate (rollover) image for each link. For example, create a GIF image for your link with plain text and bullet, and a second image with glowing bold text and an arrowhead bullet. ▶

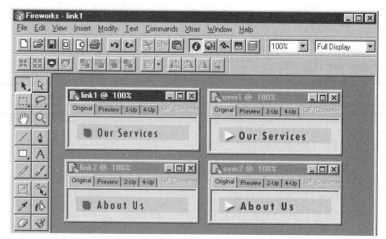

For each rollover link, create and export two similar images.

2. Inside each **<A>** tag, insert the first image for the link—the one that appears when the mouse isn't pointing—and be sure to add the **name** attribute to the **<IMG>** tag, so your code can refer to the image it swaps. In the **<A>** tag, add JavaScript that changes the image's **src** property, specifying it in the **onmouseover** and **onmouseout** attributes:

```
<a href="link.htm"
    onmouseover="img1.src='over1.gif'"
    onmouseout="img1.src='link1.gif'">
<img name="img1" src="link1.gif" border=0></a>
```

3. If you stop here, your rollovers will occur only after a slight delay, because the browser has to load your alternate image before swapping it. To avoid the delay, tell the browser to load the rollover images ahead of time by adding this code in the **<HEAD>** section of your page (for each rollover image, include another two lines and specify the image file):

```
<script language="JavaScript">
  <!--
  pre1=new Image(); pre1.src='over1.gif';
  pre2=new Image(); pre2.src='over2.gif';
  //-->
</script>
```

Displaying a status bar message

For a simple but effective rollover effect, use JavaScript to display text in the browser's status bar.

1. For each link, use JavaScript in the **onmouseover** event of the **<A>** tag to set the browser's **window.status** property.

2. Changing the message back in the **onmouseout** event is optional, but ensures that your message doesn't remain in the status bar after the viewer moves the mouse somewhere else. Here's the HTML:

```
<a href="info.htm"
    onmouseover="window.status = 'Click for more info...';return true"
    onmouseout="window.status = '';return true">Details</a>
```

Rollovers in Fireworks

Many graphics programs, such as Macromedia Fireworks and Adobe ImageReady, create the HTML and JavaScript for rollovers automatically. In Fireworks, follow these steps to create a button and incorporate it into your page. (For additional information, see "Images" on page 188.)

To continue with this solution, go to the next page.

My page doesn't do anything when you move the mouse over links and images

(continued from page 185)

1. Click New Button on the Insert menu. Create or import graphics and text for your button; then click the Over tab and click Copy Up Graphic. Modify the graphic as you want it to appear when the mouse is over it. ▶

2. Click Active Area, and then click Link Wizard. On the Link tab, specify a hyperlink address in the URL box. Close the button. (To add other similar buttons—creating a navigation bar—copy and paste the button, and then change the text and link for the new copy using the Object palette.)

3. Click Export on the File menu. Move to the folder where you store images, and specify a base name for the images. In the Style box under HTML, select Copy To Clipboard.

4. Switch to your HTML editor, such as HomeSite, click the location where you want the button(s) to appear, and click Paste.

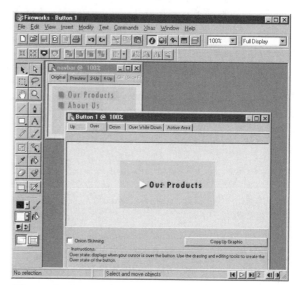

Fireworks creates the graphics, HTML, and JavaScript for rollover buttons.

Image is everything. Whether you're creating pages for your company or for yourself, photographs, maps, and graphic artwork are sure to play a part. Fortunately, graphics software offers powerful options for creating, scanning, combining, and compressing your images for use on the web.

As you create images and put them in place, there's plenty of room for trouble. Images might not look quite right or fit on the page, or they might not work at all.

To solve common problems, follow this flowchart. And for general information, see "Finding images that are legal to use" on page 192 and "Understanding web image formats" on page 197.

If your solution isn't here

Check these related chapters:

Or see the general troubleshooting tips on page xvii

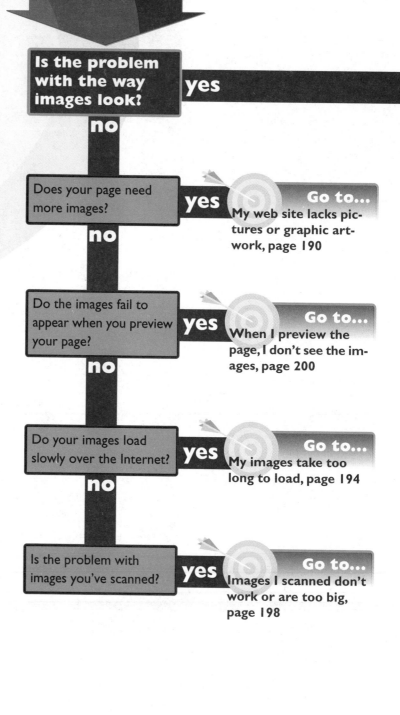

Is the problem with the way images look?

yes

no

Does your page need more images?

yes — Go to... My web site lacks pictures or graphic artwork, page 190

no

Do the images fail to appear when you preview your page?

yes — Go to... When I preview the page, I don't see the images, page 200

no

Do your images load slowly over the Internet?

yes — Go to... My images take too long to load, page 194

no

Is the problem with images you've scanned?

yes — Go to... Images I scanned don't work or are too big, page 198

Is an image distorted or compressed? **yes**

Quick fix

If the dimensions of an image are different than the **width** and **height** attributes in the **<IMG>** tag, browsers resize the image, potentially distorting it. If you change your image, make sure to update your HTML with the pixel values shown in your graphics program.

Or, if you use FrontPage or HomeSite, they can update the tag for you.

In FrontPage:

1. Right-click the picture, click Picture Properties, and click the Appearance tab.

2. Clear the Specify Size box, and then click OK.

In HomeSite:

1. Right-click the **<IMG>** tag and click Edit Tag.

2. Click Recalc Size, and then click OK.

no

Do the fonts in an image look wrong? **yes**

Go to...
The fonts in my images have jagged edges, page 203

no

Does an image display a halo around the edges? **yes**

Go to...
The image has a slight halo, page 204

no

Is an image too close to the text or other page elements? **yes**

Quick fix

Add space around an image by setting the **hspace** and **vspace** attributes of the **<IMG>** tag. For example, the following HTML positions an image at the left side of the screen, allowing text to wrap around the image but keeping at least 8 pixels between it and the text:

```
<img src="pic.jpg"
  width=80 height=120
  hspace=8 vspace=8
  align=left>
```

My web site lacks pictures or graphic artwork

Source of the problem

A picture is worth a thousand words, as they say. Perhaps the most important task in designing web pages is creating or finding images that are compelling and help get your message across. But which images will make a good impression? And where can you find them?

If you're like most web designers, you'll probably want to use a combination of images you create yourself and ready-made pictures or graphic art you find on the Internet. Putting together a graphical web page is a bit like creating a collage from magazine clippings—you collect the pieces from various sources, then cut and paste and add text to produce the desired effect. ▶

If your page doesn't have the images it needs, follow these steps.

How to fix it

1. Decide which page elements you want to create images for. For ideas, take a look at pages you like best on the Internet—and at the web sites of other organizations like yours. What combination of text, graphic art, and photographic images are you shooting for?

   For example, nearly every web site needs a logo or banner. Many also use images for navigational hyperlinks, or to make the text of a slogan stand out. If you sell a product or service, you'll probably need an image to illustrate each page. On the other hand, since images take time to download, it's best to limit yourself to those that are important to your message or design.

Like a collage, your web images can combine pictures, drawings, and text from different sources.

2. Collect the raw material for your pages from different sources, and save it in a folder on your computer. For example, if your organization or company has a logo or graphic artwork, locate online files or scan graphics from printed materials. If your pages feature products from other companies—or links or partnerships with other web sites—go to those web pages and grab their images. (To save an image from your browser, right-click the image and click Save Picture As or Save Image As.)

3. If you need additional pictures and graphics—photographs of people or merchandise, for example, or drawings or maps to illustrate your message—it's time to create or find pictures or graphic art. To create your own, take pictures with a digital camera, or use drawing software such as Adobe Illustrator. Or, look for images from clip art libraries or commercial art vendors. (See "Finding images that are legal to use" on the next page.)

4. Try to determine the approximate sizes your page needs. It may help to create a table for your page layout in your design software, or to sketch your page layout on paper. For example, if you want your logo or page banner to span the whole top of the page, you might make it 400 pixels wide by 100 pixels tall. A small logo in the corner of your page, by contrast, might be 100 by 30 pixels.

5. Choose a page background color or image, so you can be sure that images blend well with the background. (For information, see "Backgrounds" on page 14.)

6. Now you're ready to use the material you've collected to create the images for your page. In your graphics program, create a new image file with the proper size and background color. Open or import the pictures or art you want to use, and then use the features of your program to combine, resize, crop, and adjust pictures and graphics. Use the text tool to add text. ▶

Combine pictures, graphic art, and text in your graphics program, and then export a GIF or JPEG image.

To continue with this solution, go to the next page.

My web site lacks pictures or graphic artwork

(continued from page 191)

7. Save your image in the graphics program's own format—such as a Fireworks or Photoshop file—so you can make changes to it later as necessary. Then export the image as a GIF or JPEG file, saving it in a folder with your web pages (or in an images subfolder inside that folder). Use GIF for logos or graphic artwork with areas of solid color, and JPEG for photos or graphics that require smooth color transitions.

8. Place images on your page. (In HTML, use the **<IMG>** tag.) Preview your page, and then switch back to your graphics program to make adjustments.

Finding images that are legal to use

Most logos, photographs, and graphic images you see on the Internet are protected by copyright, which means you need permission to display them on your web page. For images that you can use legally on your pages, try the following sources (some offer free images, while others require purchase or royalty payment):

- Clip art and photo galleries provided with your graphics or web design software

- Stock image vendors, such as *www.corbis.com* and *www.photodisc.com*

- Map providers, such as *maps.expedia.com* and *www.mapquest.com*

- Microsoft Office clip art at *cgl.microsoft.com/clipgallerylive* (or, in FrontPage or Word, point to Picture on the Insert menu and click Clip Art)

- Search the web for *clip art*, *stock images*, *free images*, or *GIF files*

In addition, if you have partnerships with other companies or provide links to their web sites, they probably won't object to your using their logos or images.

My images take too long to load

Source of the problem

Viewers don't like to wait while a browser downloads and displays large images. While modems and Internet connections are getting faster all the time, many viewers still have slow connections, so it's important to keep download time to a minimum.

To make your page load faster, you can limit either the number of images or their size. Most important, you can use graphics software to *optimize* your images—that is, create the smallest possible GIF and JPEG files—while preserving image appearance so no one will notice the difference. Many scanning and graphics programs save high-resolution images by default. This is important if you are producing a printed brochure or magazine, but troublesome for your web pages. ▶

If your images are clogging up the Internet lines, follow these steps to make them smaller.

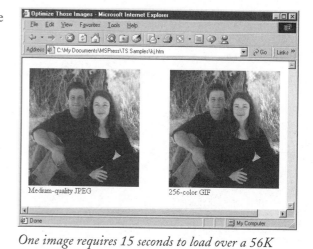

One image requires 15 seconds to load over a 56K modem, the other is optimized and takes just 3 seconds. Can you tell which is which?

How to fix it

1. Using Windows or your web design software, review the file sizes of your images. Images larger than 10 KB can take several seconds to load over some modems. If any large image file is unnecessary to your message, remove it from your page.

2. Open each image file in your graphics program. If possible, open the original scan or artwork file, such as a Photoshop or Fireworks file, since it has the best resolution to work with. (You should always keep the original, high-quality versions of your images on your computer, even though you have lower-quality copies stored in your web pages.) Make sure you're viewing the file at 100 percent magnification.

3. If the image uses more screen space than it needs, crop the image—edit out the edges—or reduce its size.

To crop an image in Photoshop 5.5, for example, select the area you want to keep, and then click Crop on the Image menu. To resize, click Image Size on the Image menu. ▶ When you enter a new value in either the width or height box, the other value changes proportionally. Make note of these new values so you can update them in your page.

4. Select optimization settings. Newer versions of graphics software, such as Photoshop 5.5 and Fireworks 3, allow you to preview an image as you try different optimization settings, so you can make your image as small as possible without sacrificing its appearance. In Photoshop, click Save For Web on the File menu. In Fireworks, click Export Preview on the File menu.

First make sure you're using the right file format. Use GIF for graphic artwork that has text or a lot of solid color. Use JPEG—which can create much smaller files due to its compression scheme—for photographs or images with subtle gradations of color. (However, if you want to let the background show through around the edges of an image—an effect called *transparency*—you must use GIF format. You can also use PNG format, but not all browsers support it. For more information, see "Many ways to let the background show through" on page 25.)

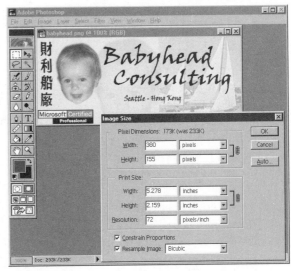

For immediate relief, reduce the dimensions of any large, colorful images on your page.

Note

While it's possible to adjust the display size of your images using **width** and **height** in the **<IMG>** tag, you're much better off resizing images in your graphics program. By reducing an image manually, you make it a smaller file; by blowing it up manually, you can better control the resolution and avoid a grainy appearance.

To continue with this solution, go to the next page.

My images take too long to load

(continued from page 195)

Next adjust the color palette and image quality. If you're using GIF, select an adaptive palette. (If you use a *web-safe* or *system* palette, your image uses a specific set of colors and can't represent gradual color changes.) Preview the image using 256 colors, and then reduce the number of colors (or in some software versions, the color depth in *bits*) as long as the color and fonts are smooth. For JPEG, start with High Quality (quality level 80 or 90) and reduce gradually as long as the image isn't too grainy, blurry, or speckled. Each lower setting will result in a smaller image file. The results can be dramatic. ▶

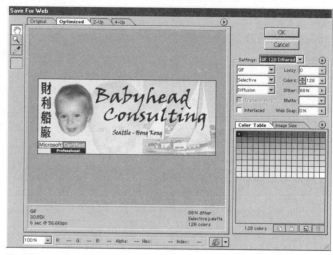

In Fireworks, Photoshop, or ImageReady, you can preview your image while adjusting quality settings.

5. Once your image is ready, export it to your web folder and preview it in your browser—but keep the previous file in case you don't like the lower-quality version. If the colors don't look right, see "Solid colors in my JPEG images look bad" on page 73 or "Colors in my GIF images are dithered or grainy" on page 74.

6. If you changed image dimensions, be sure to update your **<IMG>** tags, changing the **width** and **height** attributes to the number of pixels shown in the graphics program. Always specify these attributes; otherwise, browsers will have to adjust the layout of your page as each image downloads. The **alt** attribute is also a good idea, because it provides descriptive text that displays while the image loads:

```
<img scr="kj.jpg" width=90 height=140 alt="Photo of Kirk and Jade">
```

Tip

If you want to distract viewers while large images download, export your images as *interlaced* GIF files or *progressive* JPEG files. When the viewer opens the page, these files display in several passes as they download—first at a low quality, and then progressively better until they have downloaded completely.

Understanding web image formats

In order to allow large images to download quickly over the Internet, web image formats *compress* image information as much as possible—often ten or even a hundred times smaller than an ordinary bitmap file. Here are the three image formats and their advantages and disadvantages:

- **JPEG** can store millions of colors with a minimum of space. It is almost always the best format to use for photographic images, as it produces smoother colors and much smaller files. When you save a JPEG file, you specify the quality you want—usually on a scale of 0 to 100— and the software discards color detail according to your setting. Try quality level 70 for your web images, which is a good compromise between small file size and sharp images.

  JPEG has two notable disadvantages. First, its compression scheme causes areas of solid color to become blotchy, sharp edges to blur or discolor, and fonts to look messy. For this reason, you shouldn't use JPEG for logos or for graphic art that includes text. Also, JPEG doesn't allow you to specify transparency—so you can't let the background show around the edges of the image.

- **GIF** is best for logos and graphics, especially those that include text. It stores up to 256 different colors, referred to as the image's *palette*. To make your GIF file smaller, you can use a palette with fewer colors—a logo might require only 4 or 8 colors, for example. GIF does a great job of compressing areas of solid color—so the less detail in your image, the smaller the file.

  GIF has special capabilities. You can specify transparency, so that your image displays the page background around the edges. You can also use GIF for animation, specifying frames that play like a movie in a browser.

- **PNG** was designed as a replacement for GIF, but unfortunately, it hasn't achieved much popularity. It has all the capabilities of GIF (except animation), compresses images 5 percent to 25 percent smaller, and can store millions of colors. It also offers true transparency: not only can the background show through around the edges, but the entire image can be more or less transparent.

  Because browsers earlier than version 4 don't display PNG files, you might want to avoid them for now. In the future, however, they could become the standard.

Images I scanned don't work or are too big

Source of the problem

A scanner is a great way to create images for your page. But your scanner's software and settings might not always produce what you want.

Most scanner software lets you specify both how to perform the scan—at what resolution and color setting, for example—and how to save the file afterwards. Some scanner software also lets you crop and size your image, so you don't necessarily need to use a separate graphics program. If you select the wrong options when scanning (or use the scanner's default settings), you might end up with a very large or slow-loading image, one that's upside down or sideways, or one with unwanted space around the edges. Also, if you don't specify a file format, your image might not work in a browser.

If your scanner didn't produce the image you want, follow these steps.

How to fix it

1. If the image you scanned looks good but is too big, has space around the edges, or needs other adjustments, open and edit it in a graphics program such as Photoshop or Fireworks. Then export your image as a JPEG or GIF file to the folder with your web pages. For information, see the previous topic, "My images take too long to load."

2. If you don't have separate graphics software, or if the scan didn't work properly, scan the image again. Position your material on the scanner bed—as straight as possible—and start the scan program.

   If your scanner allows you to set a resolution for the scan, specify 72 dots per inch (dpi). Scanning programs often default to 150 or 300 dpi—which is best for images you want to print, but more detailed than necessary for the screen.

3. Once the scan is complete, select the area of the page that you want to save. ▶

Like most scanner software, the HP program allows you to specify resolution, select a page region, and then choose a destination, such as an image file.

4. Specify a destination for your scan and click Accept (or Save or Export, depending on your scanning software). If you want to make changes to the image after scanning, select your graphics program as the destination. Otherwise, select Image File.

5. Save the image in JPEG format. In HP software, for example, select JPEG Bitmap File in the Save As Type box. (Some scanning programs default to BMP bitmap format, which won't work in a web page.) ▶

The program might ask what JPEG image quality you want. To produce a smaller file that downloads faster, reduce the quality setting somewhat. However, you might also want to save a copy of your scan at the maximum quality setting. You can always reduce quality using your graphics software, but you can't go back to a higher quality from a smaller file.

6. Insert the image in your page (using the **<IMG>** tag) and then preview it in your browser.

Save your scanned image in JPEG format.

Tip

If your image is a logo or has lots of solid color, you might want to create a GIF file instead of a JPEG. However, scanner software doesn't usually produce optimized GIF files. If you want to create a GIF, send the scan directly to your graphics program and export from there.

When I preview the page, I don't see the images

Source of the problem

Web browsers can display images in GIF, JPEG, and PNG formats (although PNG isn't supported by older browsers). When the browser comes to an **<IMG>** tag in your file, it follows the file path you've specified in the **src** attribute. If the image file isn't at that location—or if there's something wrong with the **<IMG>** tag or the image itself—the browser displays an empty box with a broken image icon. ▶

To get your image working, follow these steps.

How to fix it

1. Find the **<IMG>** tag in your HTML. Make sure you've specified the **src** attribute (not **href**) and enclosed the link address in quotation marks.

   ```
   <img src="ad.gif" width=330
     height=55 alt="Advertisement">
   ```

   Make sure the **height** and **width** attributes are included, so that the page layout will be correct even if the image isn't displayed. Make sure neither **height** nor **width** is 0.

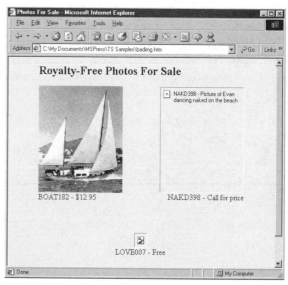

If it can't find or open your image, the browser displays a broken image icon.

2. Check the path and file name you've specified for the **src** attribute. Make sure it is spelled correctly—on a UNIX system, be sure to use the same capitalization—and has the correct file name extension (.gif, .jpg, or .png). Next, make sure the link address points to an image file that exists.

   If your image file isn't in the same folder as the page, specify the location in relation to the current page. For example, if your page is in the folder c:\inetpub\wwwroot, use the following line to display the file c:\inetpub\wwwroot\images\smile.jpg:

   ```
   <img src="images/smile.jpg" width=60 height=120 alt="Photo of Gracie">
   ```

3. If you've moved a page to a new subfolder, you'll need to move or copy the images it uses. Or, you can change the link in each **<IMG>** tag. For example, if you move your page to a new subfolder, you can either create an images folder within that subfolder (so the same **src** path will work), or else change each **<IMG>** tag as follows:

```
<img src="../images/smile.jpg" width=60
  height=120 alt="Photo of Gracie">
```

4. If your image is on an external web server, make sure the link address begins with **http://**, as follows:

```
<img src="http://www.callahansoftware.com/
  ad.gif" width=330 height=55>
```

If the file doesn't exist at the specified location on the server, change the **src** attribute to point to an existing file. If the server doesn't respond, it could be down, or your Internet connection might not be working. See "I'm having trouble accessing the Internet" on page 44.

5. If the path is correct but the image still doesn't show up, it could be corrupt or have the wrong format. Find the image on your computer or network and double-click to open it. If this doesn't work, re-create the file (open the original artwork and export the file again).

Note
Using browser options, viewers can choose not to display images—people do this to speed up Internet access—making it look as though your image links aren't working. To turn images back on (in Internet Explorer), click Internet Options, click the Advanced tab, and select Show Pictures under Multimedia.

Verifying and fixing image links in HomeSite

If you use HomeSite, you can check image links (and hyperlinks) in the current page or project and view results in the Results pane at the bottom of the window.

1. Click Verify Links on the Tools menu. (Or, if you have a HomeSite project open, you can verify links for all pages at once by right-clicking the project and clicking Verify Links.) Valid links display a green check, while broken links display a red "X" or a clock icon—indicating that the server didn't respond before the request timed out.

2. Double-click each broken image link to edit the **src** attribute. (Or, move or rename your image files, if necessary.)

To continue with this solution, go to the next page.

When I preview the page, I don't see the images

(continued from page 201)

Verifying and fixing image links in FrontPage

If you use FrontPage, you can check image links throughout your web, along with hyperlinks. If any images are missing, you can update link addresses without opening each file or editing each hyperlink.

1. Point to Reports on the View menu and click Broken Hyperlinks. If there are any broken image links—links to nonexistent image files within your web—they will appear in the list.

2. If any external links display Unknown under Status—which means that FrontPage hasn't yet verified that they work—click Select All on the Edit menu, and then right-click any link in the report and click Verify.

3. Double-click each broken link to edit it. (Or, move or rename your image files.) ▶

4. After you've fixed links, click Refresh on the View menu to update the report.

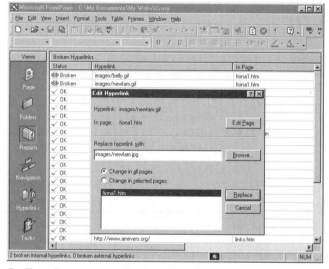

In FrontPage, use the Broken Hyperlinks report to identify image link problems.

The fonts in my images have jagged edges

Source of the problem

On a computer screen, fonts are made up of pixels, so their edges are jagged. At small sizes, this is hard to detect. But as the fonts get larger, the pixels are easier to see—and they make the text look bad.

To smooth the edges of fonts and other curved objects, graphics programs blend pixels of intermediate colors around the edges of every curve—a technique called *anti-aliasing*. ▶

Newer graphics programs anti-alias automatically, but you might have specified otherwise. Or, you might have exported a GIF file with too few colors to display fonts effectively. If your fonts have jagged edges, follow these steps.

How to fix it

1. Open your original graphics file, such as a Photoshop or Fireworks file. If you don't have the original file, you can open a GIF file, but you'll have to re-create your text.

2. Newer graphics programs allow you to edit existing text and change anti-alias options. In Photoshop 5.5, double-click the text layer in the Layers palette, and then select Crisp, Strong, or Smooth in the Anti-Alias box. In Fireworks, double-click the text object in your document and select a setting in the Anti-Alias box.

Anti-aliased type has smooth edges thanks to pixels that blend into the background.

3. In older graphics programs—or if you are editing an existing GIF file—you'll have to erase and re-create the text. Click the Eraser tool and erase the text area. Then click the Text tool, click where you want the text, and type your text, making sure to select an anti-alias option. (If your program doesn't offer anti-aliased text, it's time to upgrade.)

4. Export your image as a GIF file. Select an adaptive palette, so your GIF file can use intermediate shades of color for anti-aliasing, and make sure to specify enough colors.

The image has a slight halo

Source of the problem

In order to display color transitions in your graphics more smoothly, graphics programs use a technique called *anti-aliasing*. Simply put, they blend the colors at the edges of fonts and objects, so that some pixels actually display an intermediate color.

The problem arises when you save a transparent GIF image that has anti-aliased pixels at the edges, and then place the image on a background other than the one you specified in the graphics program. In this case, the pixels of blended color—which are intended to blend into the background—display around your image as a sort of halo. The effect is especially apparent on a dark background. ▶

If your transparent GIF image has a halo, follow these steps to get rid of it.

How to fix it

1. Open your original graphics file, such as a Photoshop or Fireworks file. (If you don't have the original file, you might need to re-create the image, because the halo and the objects are in one flat layer.)

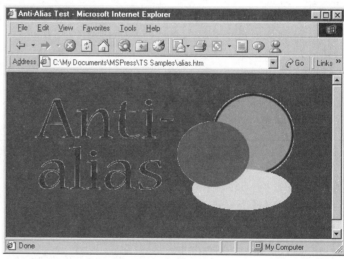

Anti-aliased pixels can produce a halo.

2. To get rid of the halo, export a new version of the GIF, telling your program to blend the edges to the background color of your page (or the approximate color, if your background is a pattern or image). In newer graphics programs, such as Photoshop 5.5 or Fireworks 3, specify a color in the Matte box (either in the Optimized palette or when exporting a GIF). ▶

   If your graphics program doesn't support a matte color, use a different strategy. Create a background layer in your image using the background color of your page—which causes text and objects to anti-alias to this color. Then, when you export the GIF file, set the background color as transparent.

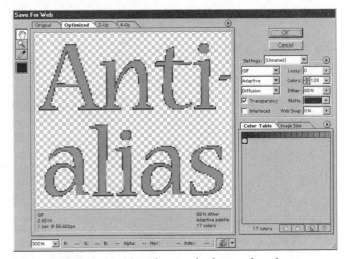

Prevent the halo by using the page background as the matte color.

Note

If you want to create a transparent file that can appear on top of any background color without a halo, create text and other objects without any anti-aliasing (use hard edges for objects and turn anti-aliasing off for text and selection tools). The edges will be jagged, but they won't have a halo.

One of the biggest challenges in web page design is controlling page layout—how your text and images should be arranged on the page. Viewers see your page using a variety of browsers, fonts, and screen sizes, all of which can affect the layout of the page. Extra space can show up where you don't expect it, and some elements of the page might end up in the wrong place.

The trouble is, HTML was designed to describe page content, not layout or presentation. You can do a pretty good job of arranging elements using ordinary tags and tables, but you'll run into a variety of issues in practice because of the limitations of HTML. For further control of layout, you can use cascading style sheets (CSS).

When you can't seem to get the layout right, follow this flowchart to find a solution. And for a general introduction to layout, see "Page layout strategies" on page 212.

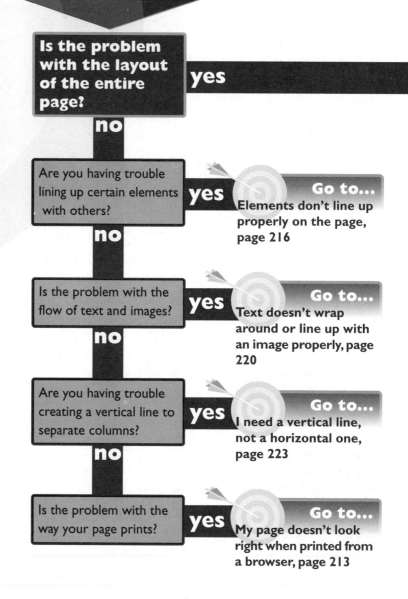

Is the problem with the layout of the entire page?

yes

no

Are you having trouble lining up certain elements with others?

yes

Go to...
Elements don't line up properly on the page, page 216

no

Is the problem with the flow of text and images?

yes

Go to...
Text doesn't wrap around or line up with an image properly, page 220

no

Are you having trouble creating a vertical line to separate columns?

yes

Go to...
I need a vertical line, not a horizontal one, page 223

no

Is the problem with the way your page prints?

yes

Go to...
My page doesn't look right when printed from a browser, page 213

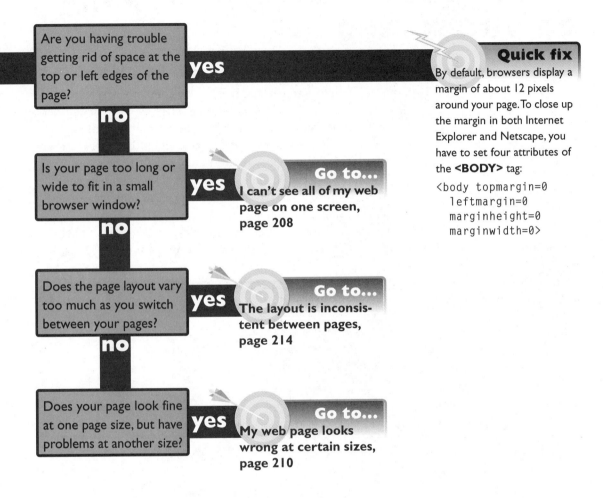

Are you having trouble getting rid of space at the top or left edges of the page? **yes**

Quick fix

By default, browsers display a margin of about 12 pixels around your page. To close up the margin in both Internet Explorer and Netscape, you have to set four attributes of the **<BODY>** tag:

```
<body topmargin=0
   leftmargin=0
   marginheight=0
   marginwidth=0>
```

no

Is your page too long or wide to fit in a small browser window? **yes**

Go to...
I can't see all of my web page on one screen, page 208

no

Does the page layout vary too much as you switch between your pages? **yes**

Go to...
The layout is inconsistent between pages, page 214

no

Does your page look fine at one page size, but have problems at another size? **yes**

Go to...
My web page looks wrong at certain sizes, page 210

If your solution isn't here

Check these related chapters:
Or see the general troubleshooting tips on page xvii

I can't see all of my web page on one screen

Source of the problem

Designers sometimes refer to the content you see on a page without scrolling as being *above the fold*—newspaper editors' terminology for what you see on the front page without opening the paper. The content that appears when your page first opens is always more likely to be seen and read. Whenever possible, you should place important content—your logo, site navigation, and primary message or page summary—above the fold.

The trouble is, people use screens of different sizes. If you use a high-resolution monitor setting, such as 1024 by 768, to design pages, you might not be aware how much of the page is lost on another screen. Viewers might have a browser window as little as 300 pixels in height, which isn't a lot of space; so many pages will have to continue below the fold. But you don't want viewers to miss the point or lose track of navigational controls, just because their window is small. ▶

If viewers often have to scroll to view your page, follow these steps.

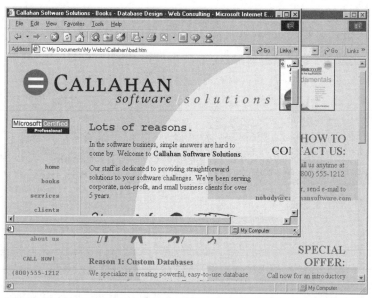

When viewed on a small monitor, the most important details and links in this page design are off to the right or "below the fold."

How to fix it

1. Preview your page in a small window to approximate what viewers might see. If your screen is set to high-resolution, you might even want to temporarily switch to a lower resolution such as 640 by 480 (using the Windows Control Panel) to get a good idea what your pages look like.

2. If you have a lot of extra space on your page, try tightening things up. For example, remove extra line breaks, wrap text around images, and reduce the **cellpadding** value in **<TABLE>** tags.

3. If critical elements of your page—your organization name and logo, the main message of the page, or major hyperlinks—aren't in view, consider moving them further up and to the left side of the page. If navigation controls or important text are beyond the right margin, reduce the width of the table that contains them.

4. If the page is long, split it up into two or more pages, taking advantage of the linked nature of web pages. As you would in a newspaper story, redesign your page to start with summary information and save all the details for later. Then, if the details aren't critical, move them to another page and provide a link to them instead. ▶

To split a page in two, copy it (or click Save As on the File menu). Replace content in the main page with a link to the details page, making sure the link is visible when the page opens. Then open the details page and remove the content that's already covered in the other.

If your pages are long, move the details to separate pages and create links between them. That way, you'll have room for the most important content and links at the top left.

5. Repeat this process for each major section of the page until it is sufficiently compact. Then turn to other pages in your web site. If you find pages containing information that's repeated elsewhere—a company profile or a list of phone numbers, for example—replace the information with a link.

My web page looks wrong at certain sizes

Source of the problem

Not long ago, web designers could depend on most viewers having a screen size of about 640 by 480 pixels. Today, there are many popular screen sizes that your pages must take into account.

If your page is too wide for viewers' screens, they'll be forced to scroll right and left to see its contents. Since most people won't do this, information or links outside the boundaries might be ignored. At the other extreme, many viewers have high-resolution screens—so your page might be too narrow or content might be too spread out.

To solve the problem, you'll want to include your page content in a large table—providing an overall grid for locating objects on the page. This lets you limit how wide the page can be, helps you to align images, and lets you set different background colors for different areas of the page. You can choose one of two basic strategies: either specify a fixed width for each section, or allow the browser to resize your content as needed to fit the page width. ▶

If your pages look wrong in a small or large window, follow these steps.

How to fix it

Your page layout table should have one column for each major section of the page. For example, you might create one column for hyperlinks, one for the main page text, and a third for images or advertisements.

1. Create a large layout table with a **<TABLE>** tag, setting the **border** attribute to 0. By default, the page is aligned at the left side of the

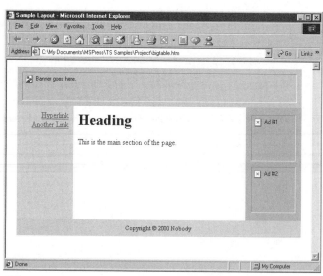

With a page layout table, you can limit the page width and arrange content into sections, making it easier to line things up.

window; if you want to split the extra space on the right and left side of the page, set the **align** attribute to **center**.

If you want columns of the table to touch one another—for example, if adjacent columns will contain images that should join edges—set the **cellpadding** and **cellspacing** attributes to 0 as well.

2. For each column (**<TD>** tag), set the **width** attribute to the pixel width of the content you expect the column to hold. If any cells need to span more than one column—a banner that goes across the whole page, for example—set the **colspan** attribute to the number of columns.

Here's a sample three-column layout table that provides cells for a page banner and footer, uses a different background color for each section, and appears in the center of the browser window. It fits in any window that's at least 600 pixels wide:

```
<table align=center border=0 cellpadding=10
  cellspacing=0>
  <tr>
    <td colspan=3 align=center
      bgcolor="#99ccff">
      <img src="banner.gif" alt="Banner goes
        here." width=590 height=60>
    </td>
  </tr>
  <tr valign=top>
    <td width=100 align=right bgcolor="#ffcc66">
      <a href="pageone.htm">Hyperlink</a><br>
      <a href="pagetwo.htm">Another Link</a><br>
    </td>
    <td width=350>
      <h1>Heading</h1>
      <p>This is the main section of the page.</p>
    </td>
    <td width=100 align=center bgcolor="#ff9933">
      <img src="ad1.htm" alt="Ad #1" width=96 height=96 vspace=6><br>
      <img src="ad2.htm" alt="Ad #2" width=96 height=96 vspace=6><br>
    </td>
  </tr>
  <tr>
    <td colspan=3 align=center bgcolor="#cccccc">
      Copyright &copy; 2000 Nobody
    </td>
  </tr>
</table>
```

To continue with this solution, go to the next page.

Note

When you specify fixed widths for all columns in a table, the browser might still change them. For example, if a cell contains an image that's too wide, the cell expands to display it. Or, if you specify a width for the whole table that's more than the sum of the cells—or omit the width setting for any one column—the browser distributes extra space inside cells.

Tip

If you want your page to fit comfortably in a certain monitor width, remember to leave room for browser controls such as scroll bars. To support a 640 by 480 screen resolution, limit page width to 623 pixels; for 800 by 600, limit it to 783 pixels. If you want a wider page, position the least important items to the far right, since some viewers won't see them.

My web page looks wrong at certain sizes

(continued from page 211)

If you want your layout to stretch when viewers change the width of the window, remove the **width** attribute from the column you want to stretch (in the preceding code, you'd delete **width=350**), and then set the **width** attribute for the **<TABLE>** tag to a relative value, such as 90% or 100%.

3. Once you get the layout table in place, move your existing content into each section of the page. Preview the page with a variety of window sizes to approximate what viewers might see, and adjust the **width** attribute in each **<TD>** tag to provide the best fit.

Page layout strategies

Successful web sites start with planning. Even if you don't know all the elements you'll need, it's a good idea to develop a basic page layout strategy. Here are some guidelines to get you started:

- First browse the Internet or company intranet to find sites that appeal to you. What main pages do they link to? What sort of graphics and color do they use? Where do they display logos, hyperlinks, and text? Does the layout change at all between pages?

- Don't reinvent the wheel. Most web sites use similar layout types because web viewers have become accustomed to them. For example, viewers expect navigation controls—hyperlinks, search boxes, and lists—to be across the top or down the left side of the page. Make sure the top of your page contains text or images that identify your organization and major message, and save details, legal notices, and miscellaneous links for a section at the bottom.

- Once you've sketched the overall layout you're shooting for, start on the physical design. Create a large table, set column widths and background colors, and insert placeholders for the major content you want. (For ideas on creating a template, see "The layout is inconsistent between pages" on page 214.)

- Decide whether you want your layout to be *flexible*—with one or more columns that adjust to the page size—or *fixed*—so columns have a set width, and extra space appears outside the main layout. (For information, see "My web page looks wrong at certain sizes" on page 210.)

- Use your layout to reinforce the message you're trying to get across. Place news, special offers, or advertisements prominently, and use borders and color to help them stand out.

- If your page is too dense, move some elements to other pages. If you're having trouble filling the space, on the other hand, create banners and images to add interest and occupy an area of the screen (such as a column at the right or a row at the bottom).

- Create one or two pages in your new layout, then review and update your template before designing other pages. It's much easier to modify the layout of one page than a whole web site.

My page doesn't look right when printed from a browser

Source of the problem

Web pages are intended for displaying on the screen. In the past, HTML standards didn't have much to say about printing—it was up to the browser to lay out and print pages. Recently, browsers have begun adding support for styles that affect printing.

If you don't see what you want when you print your page, follow these steps.

How to fix it

1. If you intend a page to be printed frequently—a form, for example—consider providing a special version of the page for printing. On that version, use black text and borders on a white background, and leave out unnecessary images. Set tables to be narrower than usual so they fit on an 8½-inch page. Print the page to test it, and then provide a link to it from the regular page.

2. If the page breaks in an undesirable place, you can use a style to specify your own page break. (Like all printing styles, this works only in recent browsers.) For the tag that you want to start on a new page, set the **page-break-before** property to **always**:

```
<table style="page-break-before:always">
```

Alternatively, set the **page-break-inside** property to **avoid** in order to prevent a break in a specific block:

```
<table style="page-break-inside:avoid">
```

3. If you use a style sheet and want to provide special styles for your page when it's printed, include them in an **@media print** section. For example, use the following **<STYLE>** block to specify a different font on the screen than in print, and to hide images when printing:

```
<style>
  @media print {
    BODY { font-family:'Times New Roman',Times; font-size:smaller }
    IMG { visibility:hidden }
  }
  @media screen {
    BODY { font-family:verdana,Helvetica,sans-serif }
  }
</style>
```

The layout is inconsistent between pages

Source of the problem

A web site is much easier to navigate and understand if the page layout doesn't change much from one page to another. When the layout changes too much, viewers can have a hard time navigating your site or reading your content. When you use a consistent and familiar model for organizing your content, viewers can find what they're looking for.

If you design each new page individually, you're likely to end up with a hodgepodge of different layouts and inconsistent styles. Instead, you should create a page template and select a strategy for creating a consistent web site. If you have pages that don't fit the model or that you have changed over time, you might need to rework them or move their content into your page template.

If your pages need a consistent layout, follow these steps.

> **Tip**
>
> If you use FrontPage, you can use shared borders to provide consistent layout and navigation across your whole web—instead of creating a layout table of your own. For more information, see "Sharing page borders across an entire web site" on page 39.

How to fix it

1. Select a general page layout, deciding where graphics, hyperlinks, and text belong on your pages. (For ideas, see "Page layout strategies" on page 212.)

2. Create a template page that you can use as a starting point for other pages. To do this, select a page that most closely approximates the page design you want, and create a copy of the page. Remove text and graphics that apply only to that page, leaving placeholders such as "Hyperlinks belong here" or "Type page summary here." ▶

A well-organized web site has the same basic layout and navigational elements on every page. A page template helps you create new pages that fit the model.

If you don't yet have a page with the right layout, start from scratch. Create a large table to provide an overall layout, adjust column widths and alignment, and set background colors. (For ideas, see "My web page looks wrong at certain sizes" on page 210.) Then add the basic text, logos, and other images that belong on every page, as well as the hyperlinks—or an image map—that link to the major pages in your web site.

Tip

If you use FrontPage, try one of the style sheets it creates. Point to New on the File menu and click Page, click the Style Sheets tab, and select a style sheet template. To apply styles to your web, save the style sheet with your web. Then click Style Sheet Links on the Format menu, click All Pages, click Add, and select your style sheet.

3. If your text formatting, borders, or margins are inconsistent, a style sheet can help. Create or open a style sheet (.css) file and specify styles that you want to apply throughout your web site. For example, if you want to indent every line of all paragraphs throughout your web site by 20 pixels, use the following style declaration in your style sheet to set the **margin-left** property (to indent only the first line, set the **indent** property instead):

```
p {
  margin-left: 20px
}
```

In your template page—and any other existing pages—delete any manual formatting or spacing that your styles will replace. Then link to the style sheet using the **<LINK>** tag:

```
<link rel=stylesheet type="text/css" href="styles.css">
```

4. Experiment with your template page, previewing to make sure it is just right. Then, if your page editor or design program allows it, save the page as a template.

In HomeSite, for example, click Save As Template on the File menu and type a name. Once you've saved the template, you can use it to create new pages. Click New on the File menu, click the Custom tab, and double-click your template.

In FrontPage, select Save As on the File menu, select FrontPage Template in the Save As Type box, and click Save. To create new pages, point to New on the File menu and click Page, and then double-click your template.

5. Using the template, create a new page for each existing page in your web site, moving text and images into the new structure. Change or add hyperlinks as necessary.

6. Preview your pages in a browser, clicking from one page to the other. If your layout still shifts from page to page, the browser is probably changing column widths to fit the changing content between pages. For example, if images are larger than the column width, the column will expand. Meanwhile, if the table is larger than the sum of the column widths, the browser distributes space inside cells.

You might need to specify the width attribute for the **<TABLE>** tag, adjust the widths of table columns, or change the size of your images to fit columns exactly. (For more information, see "I specified column widths, but they still seem to vary from the size I gave" on page 320.)

Elements don't line up properly on the page

Source of the problem

If you're accustomed to arranging items in a page layout program or a word processor, you'll probably find web page layout a bit frustrating. HTML doesn't provide reliable ways to position elements on the page.

HTML tags such as **<P>** and **<IMG>** provide attributes for specifying alignment, but their options are fairly limited. Using tables, you can create a grid for positioning elements on the page. Still, to get the layout right in a variety of browsers and screen sizes, you might need to do some experimentation.

If you're having trouble lining things up the way you want, follow these steps.

Tip

If you use FrontPage, align just about anything—a paragraph, cell, image, or other object—by selecting it and then clicking the Left Align, Center Align, or Right Align button on the toolbar.

How to fix it

1. By default, text paragraphs are aligned at the left side of the page or the left edge of the table cell that contains them. To align paragraphs of text at the center or right, set the **align** attribute of the **<P>** tag or heading tags (such as **<H1>**) to **center** or **right**:

   ```
   <p align=center>Hear Ye, Hear Ye!</p>
   ```

2. If you try to indent text using spaces or tabs within HTML, you'll quickly learn that browsers don't format text the way you enter it. When you preview your page, multiple spaces, tabs, and new lines in HTML act as if they were a single space.

   If you want a browser to arrange text just the way it appears in your HTML—using a monospace font so that a given number of characters is always the same width—use the **<PRE>** tag. (To indent text without using a monospace font, see step 3.) ▶

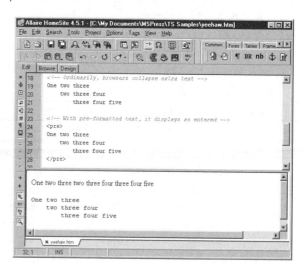

3. To line up page elements precisely in rows or columns, use a table. If you want to create space between objects or in the margin, include empty cells, specify the width attribute in the **<TD>** tag, and include a nonbreaking space ( ) to make sure browsers don't collapse the empty cell. ▶

If the contents of cells in a table aren't lining up where you want them, start by checking the alignment attributes you've set. By default, cell contents are left-aligned. To change horizontal alignment, set the **align** attribute of each **<TD>** tag to **center** or **right**. Vertically, cell contents are centered by default; if the row is longer than the cell contents, the contents shift down to the middle. If you'd like each column's content to start at the top, set the **valign** attribute of each **<TD>** tag to **top;** to align an entire row, use the **valign** attribute in the **<TR>** tag. ▶

If you use FrontPage, create a table by clicking the Insert Table button on the toolbar. Or, if you want to enclose existing text or objects in a table, select the text or object, then point to Convert on the Table menu and click Text to Table. Then, to adjust width or alignment, right-click the table and click Table Properties or Cell Properties.

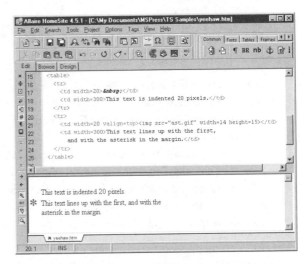

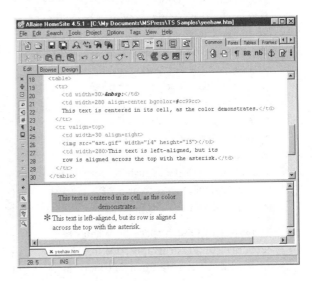

4. If the elements that don't line up are in two different tables—or if one is in a table and another is outside it—you might have trouble lining them up reliably. Make sure there's no cell spacing or cell padding for the table (set the **cellspacing** and **cellpadding** attributes of the **<TABLE>** tag to 0) and adjust column widths as necessary to line things up properly.

5. If the edges of images aren't lining up with text or with one another, check if any of them contain extra space around the edges. (Try setting the **border** attribute of the **<IMG>** tag to 2 and previewing your page to identify the edges.) If necessary, open each image in your graphics

To continue with this solution, go to the next page.

Elements don't line up properly on the page

(continued from page 217)

program, crop the image to eliminate extra space, and export it again. (Be sure to adjust the **width** and **height** attributes of the **<IMG>** tag to the new dimensions.) ▶

> If images don't flow with the text as you'd like, try setting the **align** attribute of the **<IMG>** tag to **left**, **right**, **top**, **absmiddle**, or **baseline**. (For more information, see "Text doesn't wrap around or line up with an image properly" on page 220.)

6. If the problem is with text alignment, you'll find a great deal more control with styles. For example, if your text isn't lining up with other elements as you intend, it may be because you can't control the font size or line height precisely. With CSS, you can set the **font-size** and **line-height** properties to exact point or pixel values.

> For example, if you want to line up three lines of text with another element of a certain size, such as a 100-pixel image, you could set style properties to make them exactly 35 pixels high. To set properties for a single tag, such as a **<P>** tag, use its **style** attribute. ▶

7. If there is too much space between objects or around paragraphs, use margin properties to change them. Set individual margins with **margin-left**, **margin-right**, **margin-top**, and **margin-bottom**, or set all margins at once using the **margin** property alone. ▶ facing page

8. If you want to change the positioning of a specific tag throughout the document, use a **<STYLE>** block or a separate style sheet. The following **<STYLE>** block—which you would insert in the **<HEAD>** section of your HTML to affect your whole page—causes paragraphs to be justified right and left and have less space between them (an alignment effect you can't achieve with HTML alone):

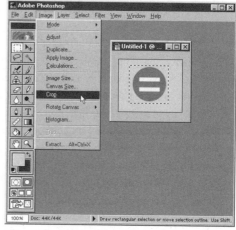

Crop extra space from around your images so they'll line up on your page.

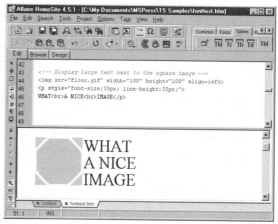

Tip

If you use FrontPage, you can set positioning of individual objects without writing HTML and CSS code. Just select the text or object you want to position, click Position on the Format menu, and specify options.

```
<style>
  P { margin-top:0;
      margin-bottom:10px;
      text-align:justify; }
</style>
```

9. If you want to adjust the position of an element, use the CSS **position** property. To adjust the placement of an object from its ordinary place on the page, set the **position** property to **relative**, and then set the **left** and **top** properties to the distance you want the object to move. (Use negative values to move up or to the left.) You'll notice that other items on the page don't adjust to fill in the space vacated by the element that moved.

The following line uses a **<SPAN>** tag to set style properties for a single word, causing it to move up 8 pixels from its normal spot:

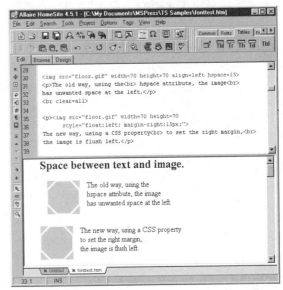

*Because the **hspace** attribute creates space on both sides of an image, you might want to set individual margin properties instead.*

```
The word <span style="position:relative; top:-8;">higher</span>
is higher than the others.
```

10. To move an element to a specific location on the page—and cause other objects on the page to appear as if it weren't there—set the **position** property to **absolute**, and set the **left** and **top** properties to the distance from the top left corner of the page that you want to locate the element. For example, this image will appear at the top of the page, exactly 200 pixels from the left edge of the page (because Netscape 4 doesn't recognize the **style** attribute for the **<IMG>** tag, it's best to use a **<DIV>** block):

```
<div style="position:absolute; top:0; left:200">
  <img src="gracie.jpg" width=100 height=150>
</div>
```

If you leave out the **top** property, the image displays 200 pixels from the left but at its normal distance from the top. What's more, you can cause absolute positions to start from another location, such as the corner of a table. Set the **position** property for the table (or other container) to **relative**, and all absolute positions within the table will refer to its top left corner.

Tip
Most viewers have browsers that support CSS, so it isn't unreasonable to use it to enhance the layout of your pages. However, it's still a good idea to use ordinary HTML—alignment attributes and tables—to provide basic layout, before refining it with styles. That way, viewers with older browsers won't be completely out of the picture, while those with newer browsers will see the page exactly as you intend.

Text doesn't wrap around or line up with an image properly

Source of the problem

Browsers give you a lot of flexibility in arranging text and images together on the page. You can align an image with the top, middle, or bottom of a line of text. You can display the image at the left or right side of the page, and the text will wrap around it. Or, you can use a table to arrange images and text.

If you don't set alignment properties correctly, your images won't end up where you want them. Or, you may find that there isn't enough space between text and images. Finally, problems might show up when viewers use a different text size or window size than you did when designing the page, because text flows differently around the images.

If your images and text are askew, follow these steps to get them into place.

Tip

If you use FrontPage, you can change image alignment and spacing without editing HTML directly. Right-click the image, click Picture Properties, click the Appearance tab, and select values in the Alignment box.

How to fix it

By default, images that you place alongside text—without any line breaks—line up with the bottom of the line of text. If they are taller than the text (which is usually the case), they'll cause the height of the line they are on to grow, so you'll see quite a bit of space between lines. And if the line is too long, the text wraps underneath the image. This probably isn't what you want. ▶

1. If your image is small enough to fit reasonably in a line of text, you might want to keep it where it is. However, if you don't like the way the image lines up vertically with the text—if it is too high or too low—

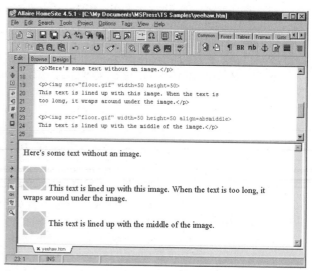

Images and text behave strangely by default. To fix the problem, change the alignment.

try changing the alignment by setting the **align** property of the **<IMG>** tag to **middle**, **top**, or **baseline**.

2. If you want the image to stand on a line by itself, so that no text flows alongside it, enclose it in **<P>** and **</P>** tags. Or, if you don't want any space above or below it, use **
** tags before and after the **<IMG>** tag.

3. If you want text to wrap around the image so that it won't change the line height, set the **align** attribute of the **<IMG>** tag to **left** or **right**. The image will display on the left or right edge of the page (or table cell), and text will align at the top of it and wrap around the image to the margin. ▶

Be sure to place the image *before* the text that you want to wrap around it; otherwise, the image will move to the next line.

4. If there isn't enough text in the paragraph next to the image, additional paragraphs or other page content will continue to flow alongside the image. If you want the next line to start below the image instead, add a **
** tag with the **clear** attribute set to **all**. (In FrontPage, click Break on the Insert menu and click Clear Both Margins.)

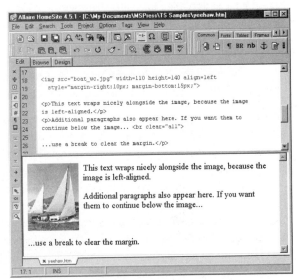

To wrap text around an image, use left or right alignment. If the text is too close, you can adjust the spacing around the image.

5. If the image is too close to the text, set the **vspace** and **hspace** attributes of the **<IMG>** tag to add space:

```
<img align=right vspace=5 hspace=8>
```

Alternatively, if you want space on one side of the image but not the other, use the **style** attribute to set the **margin-left**, **margin-right**, **margin-top**, or **margin-bottom** properties:

```
<img align=right style="margin-left:8px">
```

> To continue with this solution, go to the next page.

Text doesn't wrap around or line up with an image properly

(continued from page 221)

6. If images don't line up quite right with text or with one another, they might contain extra space around the edges. If necessary, open each image in your graphics program, crop the image to eliminate extra space, and export a new image. (Be sure to adjust the **width** and **height** attributes of the **<IMG>** tag to the new dimensions.)

7. No matter how you specify image and text alignment, it might not look right when the page width is very wide or narrow or if viewers change the text size. If you want more control of the layout of text and graphic alignment—for example, you want to keep text in a single block to the left of your image—create a table to separate images and text.

Insert a **<TABLE>** tag, setting the **border** property to 0, and then add cells (**<TD>** tags) for each image and block of text. (In FrontPage, create the table by pointing to Insert on the Table menu and clicking Table.) Move each block of text into a cell and each image into another, and then set **alignment** and **cellpadding** properties to achieve the layout you want.

> **TIP**
>
> If you can't get images to appear in the location you want—or if you want to overlap images with other page elements—you might try positioning them precisely using styles. For information, see "Elements don't line up properly on the page" on page 216.

I need a vertical line, not a horizontal one

Source of the problem

It's easy to create a horizontal line across the page—you just use the <HR> tag. But there's no corresponding tag for a vertical line.

There are two easy solutions. (Others are possible, but they involve styles that might not be supported.) The first uses the background color of a cell in the table to display the line, while the second uses an image.

If you need a vertical line on your page, follow these steps.

How to fix it

1. Add an extra cell in your table where you'd like to see the vertical line. Or, if you aren't using a table for layout, create one with three cells, placing your page content in the left and right cells. If your table has more than one row, make sure you set the **rowspan** attribute for the **<TD>** tag that will contain your line so that the line can separate all rows.

2. In the middle cell of your table, set the **bgcolor** attribute of the **<TD>** tag to specify the line color. Set the **width** attribute to the number of pixels wide you want the line to be. ▶

   For the line to work properly, you must set the **cellpadding** attribute to 0 in the **<TABLE>** tag; otherwise, the line will be wider than you bargained for. You can specify space between cells with the **cellspacing** attribute.

3. For better control over the appearance of your vertical line, use a graphics program to create a GIF image. Make the line several pixels wide and at least 100 pixels tall. Draw the line in color, set the background (canvas) color to the color of your page, add effects (such as a bevel), and then export the image as a GIF file.

   Include the line in your table using an **<IMG>** tag, adjusting the size of the line by setting the **width** and **height** attributes:

```
<img src="vline.gif" width=4 height=200>
```

With faster Internet and network connections available, we're seeing a wealth of sound and video on web pages. If you want to add multimedia to your pages, there are many tools available to produce, compress, and deliver it. And Java applets and other plug-ins can add further excitement to your pages.

Because multimedia standards are still developing, you might run into trouble here and there. There are more formats and options than ever before, and not everyone has the same browser or add-on software installed.

For general information, see "Understanding sound and video formats" on page 229 and "Recording or finding sound clips" on page 231. And if multimedia is giving you trouble, follow this flowchart to a solution.

Is the problem with the way media files are playing?

yes

no

Are you having trouble using FrontPage to incorporate sound or video?

yes → **Go to...** Sound or video isn't working in my FrontPage web, page 226

no

Does your background sound fail to play in the browser?

yes → **Go to...** My background sound doesn't play, page 234

no

Does a media player plug-in or ActiveX control fail to work on your page?

yes → **Go to...** A media player plug-in doesn't work on my page, page 236

no

Is the problem with a Java applet?

yes → **Go to...** My Java applet doesn't work, page 240

If your solution isn't here
Check these related chapters:
   Animation, page 2
   Browsers, page 42
   FrontPage, page 154
   Hyperlinks, page 174
   Styles, page 296
Or see the general troubleshooting tips on page xvii

Does a media file open in the wrong player? **yes**

Quick fix

Media players are all vying for your attention, so they often commandeer file types behind the scenes. Some even steal file types they can't play! To get file types back to the player you want, first tell the offenders to stop reclaiming file types, then tell each player which types you do want it to play.

In Windows Media Player 7:

1. Click Options on the Tools menu, and click the Formats tab.

2. Select or clear boxes for the formats you want the player to control.

In RealPlayer 8:

1. Click Preferences on the View menu, and click the Upgrade tab.

2. Click Auto-Restore Settings, and then clear options for non-RealPlayer types.

In QuickTime 4:

1. Point to Preferences on the Edit menu, and click Connection Speed.

2. Select File Type Associations in the Settings box, and then set or clear options.

3. To prevent the QuickTime plug-in from playing non-QuickTime files in a browser, select Browser Plug-in, click MIME Settings, and then double-click to clear the plus (+) symbol next to all file types other than QuickTime files.

no

Is the problem with streaming media, such as Windows Media, QuickTime, or RealAudio? **yes**

Go to...

My streaming audio or video isn't working properly, page 230

no

Do you want a sound clip to repeat? **yes**

Quick fix

To cause a sound to repeat, set the **loop** attribute of the **<EMBED>** tag to true, or of the **<BGSOUND>** tag (which works only in Internet Explorer) to –1:

```
<embed src="sound.wav" loop=true hidden=true
  autostart=true>

<bgsound loop=-1 src="sound.wav">
```

Sound or video isn't working in my FrontPage web

Source of the problem

FrontPage helps you incorporate sound and video into your pages. For example, by editing page properties, you can specify a background sound to play when your page opens. Through other menu commands, FrontPage lets you incorporate sound and video in a variety of formats. Unfortunately, you'll probably need to go beyond the easy-to-use FrontPage features for most multimedia needs—either because these features don't support the audio or video format you want to use, or because they produce pages that work only in Internet Explorer. To get the results you want, you'll need to use advanced FrontPage menu commands to insert plug-ins and ActiveX controls, and you might need to edit HTML directly.

For general information on audio and video, see "Understanding sound and video formats" on page 229. If you're having trouble getting sound and video working in FrontPage, follow these steps.

Tip

The easiest way to make any media available from your page is with a hyperlink. Click Hyperlink on the Insert menu, and select the audio or video file. Or, enter the web address of a multimedia file, such as a RealMedia (.ram) or Microsoft Media (.asx) file. If a media player is installed, it will play your audio or video when the viewer clicks the link.

How to fix it

1. To verify that audio or video is working in general, try your media file outside FrontPage. Locate the file on your computer or network and double-click it.

   If the file doesn't play, make sure your speakers are connected and turned on and the volume is adjusted. If you see a message asking what program should be used to open the file (your computer doesn't know what to do with the file type), you probably need to install or reconfigure media player software. If you see an error in the media player, there might be something wrong with the file, or it might be a newer format than your media player understands.

2. To add a background sound that plays when your page opens, click Properties on the File menu, select the General tab, and then specify a .wav or other audio file in the Location box under Background Sound. However, because FrontPage uses the **<BGSOUND>** tag in your HTML, the background sound works only in Internet Explorer.

   To play background sound in both Netscape and Internet Explorer, include the **<EMBED>** tag in your HTML. For details, see "My background sound doesn't play" on page 234.

3. To display an AVI or Microsoft NetShow video on your page, point to Picture on the Insert menu, click Video, and then enter the name of the video file. Note, however, that this causes FrontPage to use the **<IMG>** tag in your HTML. This is not the preferred method, because it works only in Internet Explorer and doesn't allow you to specify options. (FrontPage lets you change some picture properties, but some of the settings don't work in versions of Internet Explorer other than version 3.)

Instead of using this feature, include your video through a media player plug-in (see step 4 below) or ActiveX control (see step 5 on the next page).

4. FrontPage can help you include a media file that requires a plug-in to play, such as a QuickTime movie (.mov) file. Point to Advanced on the Insert menu and click Plug-In, specify the audio or video file in the Data Source box, and then specify the height and width or other settings for the plug-in. FrontPage adds an **<EMBED>** tag to your HTML. ▶

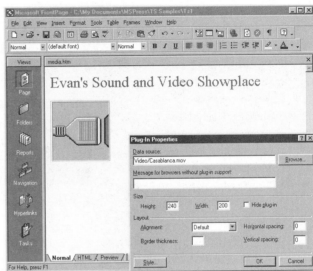

To display a QuickTime movie, use a plug-in.

Unfortunately, each plug-in has its own set of custom attributes that FrontPage doesn't know about. To set these options, you must click the HTML tab and enter them as attributes of the **<EMBED>** tag. For example, if you want to display a QuickTime movie without its controls, you would set the **controller** attribute of the **<EMBED>** tag to **false**. For more information, see "A media player plug-in doesn't work on my page" on page 236.

Note

If you select the Hide Plug-in box for your plug-in, FrontPage adds the **hidden** attribute to your **<EMBED>** tag, but doesn't give it a setting. To hide your plug-in in Netscape, edit the HTML, changing **hidden** to **hidden=true**.

To continue with this solution, go to the next page.

Sound or video isn't working in my FrontPage web

(continued from page 228)

5. If you want to display a media player ActiveX control on your page—such as the Windows Media Player or RealAudio Player—FrontPage can help. Point to Advanced on the Insert menu, click ActiveX Control, and double-click the control name. (Some controls, such as the RealPlayer G2 Control, don't automatically install themselves for use with FrontPage. Click the Customize button and select the box next to controls you want to add to the list.) Then double-click the control to set its custom properties. ▶

For example, to specify a file you want the Windows Media Player to play, double-click the player, click the

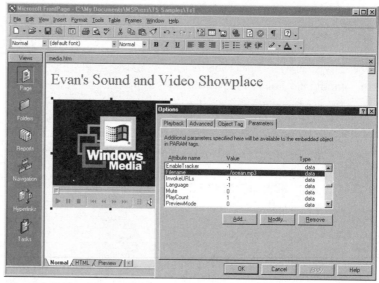

The Windows Media Player provides an ActiveX control you can insert on your page. However, it only works in Internet Explorer for Windows.

Parameters tab, double-click Filename in the Attributes box, and then enter the file name in the Data box of the Value section. These settings change the values in the **<OBJECT>** and **<PARAM>** tags that FrontPage adds to your HTML.

Because ActiveX controls work only in Internet Explorer for Windows, you might want to provide a browser plug-in or a hyperlink as an alternative to the ActiveX control. For more information, see "A media player plug-in doesn't work on my page" on page 236.

Understanding sound and video formats

Multimedia standards are continuing to develop year by year, as new technology provides better speed and quality. Compression schemes are improving greatly, as is support for *streaming*— incremental audio and video delivery that lets viewers play a file before they've downloaded the whole thing.

Sooner or later, browsers will be able to play all popular audio and video formats on the Internet. For now, it's sort of like a telephone that only lets you call people who use the same brand of phone. Unless the media file happens to be in an ordinary system format, viewers must download and install a special media player, or a plug-in player for their browser.

Here are the most popular audio and video formats and their uses:

- WAVE (.wav), µ-LAW (.au), AIFF (.aif) are the standard audio formats of Windows, UNIX, and Macintosh, respectively. They all offer a variety of *sampling rates* (quality settings), and are supported by most browsers and media players. Use one of these formats for adding short sound clips, such as a hyperlink that pronounces a difficult name. (Do you need audio? See "Recording or finding sound clips" on page 231.)

- MIDI (.mid) is a very compact format that stores a description of music rather than actual audio—an entire song takes almost no time to download. Most browsers can play MIDI through the sound card's synthesizer. Use it when you want to play a tune, but don't care how professional it sounds. Free MIDI files are widely available.

- MP3 (.mp3) audio is becoming extremely popular because of its excellent compression and music quality. It is supported by Internet Explorer 5 and most media players. To create an MP3 file, you need encoding software, such as Cool Edit 2000 (*www.syntrillium.com*) or AudioCatalyst (*www.xingtech.com*). Some servers, such as Shoutcast server, support MP3 streaming.

- For video, the primary formats are AVI (.avi) for Windows, QuickTime (.mov) for Macintosh, and MPEG (.mpg). While all three formats remain popular and are supported by most video editing software, not everyone has a player capable of displaying all of them—so it's important to provide options. QuickTime files support streaming, either from an Apple QuickTime Streaming Server or Darwin Streaming Server.

- Two competing media formats are designed especially for streaming: Microsoft Windows Media (.asf or .wma) and RealAudio or RealVideo (.ra or .rm). Both offer excellent compression for a variety of connection speeds, and can even adjust streaming speed to match the viewer's connection. To play these files, viewers need Windows Media Player or RealPlayer; to produce them, you need Windows Media Encoder, RealProducer, or video production software such as Media Cleaner Pro (*www.mediacleaner.com*).

My streaming audio or video isn't working properly

Source of the problem

What could be cooler than watching live video on your computer? It's almost like television! Streaming media is playing an increasing role on the web because it brings web pages to life. And with the right tools, you can start taking advantage of on-demand video and sound delivery from your own pages. ▶

You can create streaming media files from many sources—CD audio, WAVE files, MP3 files, AVI video, or a live video feed—using an encoding program such as Windows Media Encoder or RealProducer. You can select a variety of compression settings, or choose multiple settings so viewers with different connection speeds can have the highest possible quality.

If you've produced media files and are having trouble getting them to work with your pages, follow these steps.

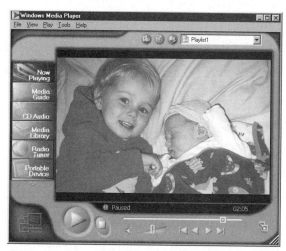

With streaming media, viewers can play your compressed audio or video without waiting for it to download..

How to fix it

1. If viewers can't play your streaming media, they might not have the appropriate media player installed. They can download Windows Media Player from *www.windowsmedia.com/download*, RealPlayer from *www.real.com*, or QuickTime Player from *www.apple.com/quicktime*.

    On your page, mention the player version and connection bandwidth required to play your media. (When you create your file using an encoding program, you might be able to select player versions that your file will support.) Also, be sure to include a link to the installation page for the required player.

    For example, the following lines of HTML provide links to a Windows media file and a RealAudio file:

Note

The easiest way to provide streaming media is through a hyperlink. But if you want live video or an audio player to display on your page—rather than in a separate media player program—you can use an ActiveX control or plug-in. For information, see "A media player plug-in doesn't work on my page" on page 236.

```
<a href="http://www.callahansoftware.com/media/ocean.asx">Play in
    Windows Media Player</a> - Requires 56k modem, <a
    href="http://www.windowsmedia.com/download/">Windows Media Player</a>

<a href="http://www.callahansoftware.com/media/ocean.ram">Play Real</a>
    Requires 56k modem, <a href="http://www.real.com/">RealPlayer G2</a>
```

Tip

Media servers, such as Windows Media Server and RealServer, can manage lots of requests to stream your files, and can change the streaming rate to match what the viewer can handle. But if you don't need advanced features, you can stream these formats from any web server. Just encode the files, create a metafile (see step 2 on this page), and stream away.

If you use an Internet service provider (ISP)—or if you have limited disk space on your web server—check how much space and bandwidth you have available. Multimedia files can be large, and multiple streams require plenty of bandwidth.

2. Some streaming formats require that you link to a *metafile*—a text file that describes the location of the media—in order to stream properly. If your link to a Windows Media file (.asf or .wma) or RealMedia file (.rm or .ra) doesn't work, or causes media files to download instead of stream, you need to link to a metafile rather than the actual media file.

Recording or finding sound clips

If you want to include custom audio on your site—whether it's a song by your garage band or an inspirational message from your company president—your best bet is to record it yourself. All you need is a decent microphone, a sound card, and recording software, such as the Windows Sound Recorder or the software provided with your sound card.

To mix audio and music or add effects, try a professional audio program, such as Cool Edit 2000 (*www.syntrillium.com*) or Sound Forge (*www.sonicfoundry.com*). When recording, try to eliminate background noise, and set the recording volume as high as possible without creating distortion.

Alternatively, you can find existing digital audio available that's free or available for purchase. Note that most sound and music you find on the Internet is protected by copyright. For audio that you can use legally on your pages, try the Microsoft Office Clip Gallery at *cgl.microsoft.com/clipgallerylive*, or search the web for *audio clips* or *wav files*.

For synthesized background music that downloads quickly, consider MIDI files. They don't actually contain recorded sound; instead, they have just a description of notes for your sound card to play. And MIDI files aren't likely to be protected by copyright. Find them in the Microsoft Office Clip Gallery or search the web for *midi files*.

To continue with this solution, go to the next page.

My streaming audio or video isn't working properly

(continued from page 231)

For example, if you have a Windows Media file called Twinkle.asf in a folder called Media on your web server, create a text file called Twinkle.asx, add the following text, and save it in the same folder:

```
<asx version="3.0">
  <entry>
    <ref href="Twinkle.asf" />
  </entry>
</asx>
```

On your page, link to the file at *http://Servername/Media/Twinkle.asx*.

You need a metafile for RealAudio and RealVideo files as well. For a RealVideo file called Star.rm, create a text file called Star.ram that contains just the following line (if you use RealServer instead of an ordinary web server, preface the link with **pnm://** instead of **http://**):

```
http://Servername/Media/Star.rm
```

3. If your web server won't play media files, it's possible it doesn't recognize the file type because MIME types aren't configured properly. (A *MIME type* is the system's code name for the file type.) One possible solution is to install either a player or a server product on the web server computer.

4. If your media file doesn't look good or stream properly for viewers, it might not be encoded correctly. Try different options in the encoding program, or consult its documentation. Of course, your streaming files won't be any better than the source audio or video you provide. For audio, try to use a high-quality microphone and eliminate background noise. You might also want to edit your audio or video, or add effects using programs such as Sound Forge (*www.sonicfoundry.com*), Adobe Premiere (*www.adobe.com*), or Media Cleaner Pro (*www.mediacleaner.com*).

Look for good (if biased) guidelines on media production at *www.microsoft.com/windows/ windowsmedia*, *www.realnetworks.com/devzone*, and *www.apple.com/quicktime/authoring*.

My background sound doesn't play

Source of the problem

Sound helps create atmosphere. Using browser extensions and plug-ins, you can play a background sound automatically when your page loads.

But perk up your ears, because the results you'll get depend on the way you link or embed media in your page. There are differences among browsers, and results can vary based on software the viewer has installed. Also, if you use FrontPage, you need to follow special steps if you want your sound to play in browsers other than Internet Explorer. (See "Sound or video isn't working in my FrontPage web" on page 226.)

For background sound, it's best to use broadly supported audio formats: WAVE (.wav), μ-LAW (.au), AIFF (.aif), or MIDI (.mid). If you use another format, your sound will play only if a media player is installed and its browser plug-in supports the HTML you've used.

For information on media players and formats, see "Understanding sound and video formats" on page 229. If you aren't sure where to find sound for your page, see "Recording or finding sound clips" on page 231. And if you're having trouble getting the background sound to play, follow these steps.

How to fix it

1. To verify that audio is working in general, try your sound outside the browser. Locate the file on your computer or network and double-click it.

   If it doesn't play, make sure your speakers are connected and turned on and the volume is adjusted. If you see a message asking what program should be used to open the file—your computer doesn't know what to do with the file type—you probably need to install or reconfigure media player software. If you see an error in the media player, there might be something wrong with the file, or it might be a newer format than your media player understands. If you have audio editing software, open and test the file. For best results, export a WAVE (.wav) file.

> **Tip**
> Chances are, you've probably run across some background audio that took time to download, and then played too long and too loudly. Before including background audio—especially a large file—consider whether it really adds anything to your page. If you do include it, consider toning it down in volume. (See step 2 on the facing page.) Or, you could include a link to your audio rather than play the sound automatically. (See step 4 on the facing page.)

2. There are several ways to play a background sound in an HTML file. To support Netscape as well as Internet Explorer, use the **<EMBED>** tag, setting the **hidden** and **autostart** attributes to **true**. Optionally, specify the volume attribute (as a percentage of the default system volume) and set the **loop** attribute to **true** or **false**:

```
<embed src="Groove.wav" hidden=true autostart=true volume=50 loop=true>
```

The **<BGSOUND>** tag is straightforward and loads audio quickly, but works only in Internet Explorer. For example, include the following tag in the **<HEAD>** section of your page to play a WAVE file when the page opens (set the **loop** attribute to **−1** if you want the file to repeat as long as the page is open):

```
<bgsound src="Groove.wav" loop=-1>
```

Finally, you can instruct the browser to open the sound file automatically using the **<META>** tag. Include the following line as the very first line of the **<HEAD>** section of your page:

```
<meta http-equiv=refresh content="0;url=Groove.wav">
```

This method doesn't actually play background sound; it causes the browser to open an external player for the file as if the viewer had clicked a hyperlink to it. (Depending on browser settings, it might also cause the browser to ask whether the viewer wants to download the file.)

3. If a background sound doesn't play, it is often because the browser can't find the audio file. (With the **<EMBED>** or **<BGSOUND>** tags, the browser won't give you any indication that it can't find the file—it is just silent.)

Check the path and audio file name you've specified in your HTML. Make sure the file name is spelled correctly and has the correct file name extension, such as .wav, .au, or .mid. (If your server is running UNIX or Linux, be sure to use the same capitalization.) Next make sure the link address points to a file that exists. For example, if you keep your audio files in a folder called Audio, use the following line to play the file Intro.wav:

Note

If audio plays outside the browser, but not using the **<EMBED>** tag, there might be a problem with browser plug-ins. See "A media player plug-in doesn't work on my page" on page 236.

```
<embed src="Audio/Intro.wav" hidden=true>
```

4. If all else fails, provide a hyperlink to the audio file—either in place of, or in addition to, the background sound—so viewers can play it in an external media player.

```
<a href="Audio/Imagine.mp3">Face the music</a> (requires MP3 player)
```

A media player plug-in doesn't work on my page

Source of the problem

One way to provide access to multimedia content on your pages is with a plug-in media player, such as Windows Media Player, RealPlayer, or QuickTime Player. Using these plug-ins (or an *ActiveX control*, which is a plug-in for Windows Internet Explorer only), you can keep viewers on your page while they watch or listen to your audio or video clips. ▶

Because browsers and media players are evolving from version to version, you might run into trouble now and then. The theory behind plug-ins is that you should be able to specify a file, and the browser will automatically select the player configured for the file. In reality, each plug-in has its own options and quirks, so you'll usually want to specify the ActiveX control or plug-in player you want viewers to use.

If you're having trouble creating media files and including them in your page, follow these steps.

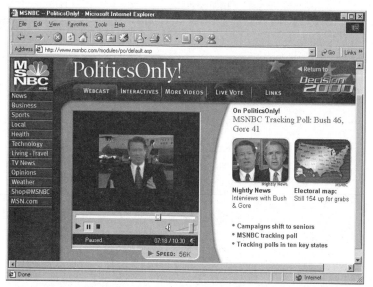

Using a plug-in or ActiveX control such as Windows Media Player, you can incorporate audio and video clips on your page—just like the big news sites.

How to fix it

1. Before you blame problems on the plug-in, verify that your media file is working in general. To play the file outside the browser, find it on your computer or network and double-click it.

   If the media file doesn't play, make sure your speakers are connected and turned on, and the volume is adjusted. If you see a message asking what program should be used to open the file (your computer doesn't know what to do with the file type), you probably need to install or reconfigure media player software. If you see an error in the media player, there might be something wrong with the file, or it might be a newer format than your media player understands.

2. If the plug-in shows up but doesn't play the clip, check the path and audio file name you've specified in the **<EMBED>** tag (or in a **<PARAM>** tag, for an ActiveX control). Make sure the file name is spelled correctly and has the correct file name extension, such as .wav, .avi, .asx, .ram, or .mov. (If your server is running UNIX or Linux, be sure to use the same capitalization.) Next make sure the file exists in the correct folder on the server. For example, the following line displays the default plug-in for AVI files and opens the Escape.avi file in the Media subfolder:

```
<embed src="Media/Escape.avi" autostart=true autoplay=true>
```

Depending on its plug-in configuration, Netscape might not know which plug-in to use for a file. If no plug-in loads, suggest a plug-in by specifying a *MIME type*—the system's code name for the file type. To specify a MIME type, use the **type** attribute of the **<EMBED>** tag. If MIDI audio doesn't play, for example, use the following to ensure that the browser knows that you want to use the plug-in for MIDI files:

```
<embed type="audio/midi" src="Takefive.mid" hidden=true autostart=true>
```

In Netscape, you can see which plug-ins and MIME types are available by typing **about:plugins** in the location bar. ▶ (Internet Explorer uses MIME types from the Windows registry.)

▶

Note

You can write JavaScript code that detects whether a plug-in is installed before trying to display it. For information, see *msdn.microsoft.com/ windowsmedia*, *www.apple.com/quicktime/ authoring*, or *www.realnetworks.com/devzone* and search for *JavaScript*.

To help diagnose problems in Netscape, get the details on installed plug-ins.

3. Depending on the plug-ins that viewers have installed—and the order in which they installed them—your page might use a different plug-in than the one you intend for the **<EMBED>** tag. For example, if a viewer has the QuickTime plug-in configured as the default player for audio, the browser uses it instead of built-in audio. This causes your audio options to be ignored, because QuickTime expects different attributes.

> **To continue with this solution, go to the next page.**

A media player plug-in doesn't work on my page

(continued from page 237)

Short of complex scripting, there is no way to support all plug-in configurations. The key is to tell users which player or plug-in to install, and then use the proper **<EMBED>** tag attributes for that plug-in. For example, the following tag uses special QuickTime attributes to play a video automatically and without any controls (note that the **autoplay** and **controller** attributes won't work with any other plug-in):

```
<embed width=280 height=200 src="sample.mov" autoplay=true controller=false
type="video/quicktime"  pluginspage="http://www.apple.com/quicktime/download/">
```

For other attributes, see the documentation for each plug-in (and samples in step 6, below).

4. Some browsers will automatically help viewers install a plug-in when one doesn't exist. To specify a web location for your plug-in, set the **pluginspage** attribute of the **<EMBED>** tag.

5. In some embedded objects, you can include a tag that's displayed only for viewers whose browsers don't support the feature. Following an **<EMBED>** tag, add an alternative message inside a **<NOEMBED>** block:

```
<embed src="mytune.mp3" type="audio/mpeg" hidden=true autostart=true>
<noembed>Your browser doesn't support plug-ins. If you have an MP3 player, <a
href="mytune.mp3">play it outside the browser</a>.</noembed>
```

6. If many of your viewers have Internet Explorer for Windows—and you want to use either the Windows Media Player or RealAudio Player on your page—you'll get the best control and results from the ActiveX controls these players provide. (If you want to control the media player using a script, you'll also have much better results with an ActiveX control.) ▶

To include an ActiveX control, use the **<OBJECT>** tag and specify settings with **<PARAM>** tags. For example, the following lines display the Windows Media Control on the page and cause it to load a streaming audio file. (The **<EMBED>** tag is optional, but allows Netscape and browsers not running under Windows to use a plug-in, if available.)

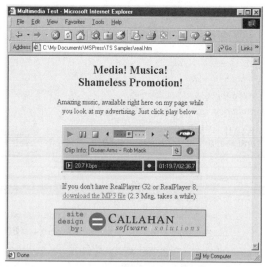

For Windows Media or RealAudio on your page, ActiveX controls are a better option if you expect viewers to have Windows and Internet Explorer.

```
<object id="MediaPlayer" width="300" height="70"
  classid="CLSID:22D6F312-B0F6-11D0-94AB-0080C74C7E95"
  codebase="http://activex.microsoft.com/activex/controls/mplayer/en/→
    nsmp2inf.cab#Version=6,4,5,715"
  standby="Loading Microsoft&reg; Windows Media&trade; Player..."
  type="application/x-oleobject">
  <param name="FileName" value="http://www.kcmu.org/listen/kcmu.asx">
  <param name="AutoStart" value="true">
  <param name="ShowDisplay" value="false">
  <param name="AnimationAtStart" value="false">
  <param name="TransparentAtStart" value="true">
  <param name="ShowStatusBar" value="true">
  <embed type="application/x-mplayer2" name="MediaPlayer"
    src="http://www.kcmu.org/listen/kcmu.asx"
    width=300 height=70 autostart=1 showdisplay=0 showcontrols=1
    showstatusbar=1 animationatstart=0 transparentatstart=1
    pluginspage="http://www.microsoft.com/isapi/redir.dll?prd=windows→
      &sbp=mediaplayer&ar=Media&sba=Plugin&">
</object>
```

Here's the code to play a RealAudio file. It uses the ActiveX control in Internet Explorer for Windows (and the plug-in anywhere else):

```
<object id="RVOCX" width="300" height="100"
  classid="clsid:CFCDAA03-8BE4-11cf-B84B-0020AFBBCCFA">
  <param name="src" value="http://www.kmcu.org/listen/live.ram">
  <param name="hidden" value="false">
  <param name="autostart" value="true">
  <embed type="audio/x-pn-realaudio-plugin"
    src="http://www.kmcu.org/listen/live.ram"
    height="100" width="300" hidden="false" autostart="true"
    pluginspage="http://www.real.com/">
</object>
```

7. If you continue to have trouble, consider a backup plan. The bottom line is, using a plug-in is always a bit risky unless you know what software your viewers will be using.

The most popular solution is to link to the audio file instead of using the plug-in, so viewers can play it in an external media player. Better yet, link to more than one version, in case they don't have the right player installed.

```
<a href="Audio/Imagine.asx">Stream with Windows Media Player</a>
<a href="Audio/Imagine.ram">Stream with RealPlayer</a>
  (best with 56k or faster connection)
<a href="Audio/Imagine.mp3">Download MP3</a> (2.3 Mb)</a>
```

My Java applet doesn't work

Source of the problem

Java is a computer language, developed by Sun Microsystems, that works on nearly all computer systems. It can be used to create entire computer applications independent of web pages, but is most commonly used to create *applets*—small, downloadable programs, stored in Java .class files, that run in just about any web browser.

Java applets are widely available and can extend your pages in a variety of ways, using visual effects, dynamic menus, databases, and interactive network applications. Look for free or low-cost applets—including plenty of toys and games—at *java.sun.com/applets* or *www.javaboutique.com* (or search the web for *java applets*).

To include a Java applet on your page, you use the <APPLET> tag. If files aren't in the right place, or if you don't provide the required parameters for your applet using <PARAM> tags, it won't work. If you're having trouble getting a Java applet to work on your page, follow these steps.

How to fix it

1. If an applet doesn't load, it is often because the browser can't find the .class file or other files it needs. Check the file name you've specified in the **code** attribute of the **<APPLET>** tag. Make sure the file name is spelled correctly and has the .class extension. (If your server is running UNIX or Linux, be sure to use the same capitalization.) Next make sure you've placed the .class file in the same folder as your page. If the applet includes a .jar file—a compressed format used to download Java files efficiently—place it in the same folder and specify the file name as the **archive** attribute.

```
<applet code=cool.class archive=cool.jar>
```

2. Check the **<APPLET>** tag to make sure you've specified all the parameters it requires and have included the end tag:

```
<applet code="chat.class" width=495 height=83>
   <param name="server" value="ares">
   <param name="user" value="evan">
   <param name="picture" value="images/evan.jpg">
</applet>
```

Many applets come with sample HTML. Rather than writing your own code, copy and paste the sample into your page and edit existing parameters.

3. To control the display of the **<APPLET>** tag, you can use most of the same attributes as in the **<IMG>** tag. For example, use the **align**, **hspace**, and **vspace** attributes to control how text flows around your applet, and apply styles using the **style** or **class** attributes.

```
<applet code="ticker.class" width=200 height=24
  align=left style="border:3px solid">
```

4. If your applet causes an error or doesn't load at all, there could be a problem with the Java Plug-in or Java Virtual Machine—or it might not be installed at all. To find out whether Java is working, test another Java applet from *java.sun.com*, or test your applet in another browser. If Java isn't working at all, you may need to upgrade or reinstall your browser.

If other Java applets work fine, there might be a bug in the applet you're trying to use. Consult the applet documentation or contact the author.

5. Because an applet might not work in everyone's browser, it's a good idea to provide an alternative display—and if necessary, an alternative page. For browsers that understand the **<APPLET>** tag but don't support Java applets, you can specify alternate text using the **alt** attribute. For browsers that don't support **<APPLET>** at all, you can include alternative HTML before the **</APPLET>** end tag:

```
<applet code=fancy.class alt="Fancy Java picture">
  <img src="no_java_pic.jpg"></applet>
```

Unfortunately, if Java isn't working, your browser might just display a blank box—even if you've specified alternative HTML.

Note

Don't confuse Java with JavaScript. While both are computer languages, Java is a complete object-oriented programming language that's used to create all sorts of computer programs.

JavaScript, by contrast, is a scripting language interpreted by Netscape and Internet Explorer. JavaScript is less powerful, but it is more accessible for web design because it deals with browser concepts you might already understand.

Note

Some applets require scripts on your page to make them work properly, while others require companion Java applications to be installed on your web server. For details, see the documentation for your Java applet.

To continue with this solution, go to the next page.

My Java applet doesn't work

(continued from page 241)

Inserting Java applets in FrontPage

1. Copy or import the .class file and other required files into your web (click Import on the File menu).

2. Point to Advanced on the Insert menu and click Java Applet. In the Applet Source box, type the path and name of the .class file (including the .class extension). ▶

Or, if sample HTML is supplied with your applet, copy it from the sample, click Paste Special on the Edit menu, and select Paste As HTML. Then, double-click the applet to edit settings.

3. Specify size and layout options. For each parameter that the applet requires (see the documentation or sample HTML for your applet), click the Add button and type a name and value. (Or, if you pasted sample code, double-click parameters to edit their values.)

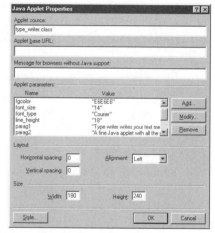

FrontPage lets you set Java applet properties and add parameters.

Web pages serve many different purposes, and there are many tools you can use to create them. Not only can you use HTML editors and designers, but also applications such as Microsoft Excel, Word, and PowerPoint. Since each program has its own strengths, you might want to create pages using more than one, and integrate them on your web site.

If web standards were perfect, moving pages between programs wouldn't be a problem. Unfortunately, Microsoft Office applications produce complex HTML, and you're likely to face a variety of issues when using them together.

If you run into problems creating pages with Microsoft Office, look for a solution in this flowchart. And for a summary of the web page capabilities in Microsoft Word, Excel, PowerPoint, and Access, see "Using HTML in Microsoft Office" on page ###.

Are you having trouble creating web pages in Microsoft Word, Excel, or Powerpoint?

yes

no

Are you having trouble incorporating pages from another program into your FrontPage web?

yes

no

Are you getting the wrong thing when you paste text or HTML into FrontPage?

yes

Go to...

A page from another program doesn't work in my FrontPage web, page 246

Quick fix

When you copy from another Office program and paste into a page in FrontPage, you might get formatting or extra HTML that you don't want.

1. Click Undo Paste on the Edit menu.

2. Click Paste Special on the Edit menu, click Normal Paragraphs, and click OK.

Or, if you copy HTML code and get extra formatting when pasting into HTML view:

1. Click Undo Text Editing on the Edit menu.

2. Click the Normal view tab, and then click in the page where you want the HTML to go.

3. Click Paste Special on the Edit menu, click Treat As HTML, and click OK.

If your solution isn't here
Check these related chapters:
Browsers, page 42
FrontPage, page 154
Hyperlinks, page 174
Publishing & servers, page 262
Styles, page 296
Or see the general troubleshooting tips on page xvii

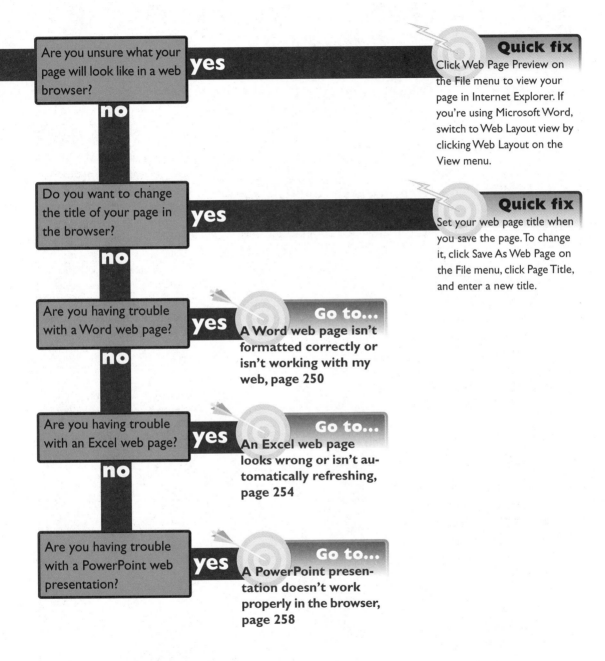

Are you unsure what your page will look like in a web browser?

yes

Quick fix

Click Web Page Preview on the File menu to view your page in Internet Explorer. If you're using Microsoft Word, switch to Web Layout view by clicking Web Layout on the View menu.

no

Do you want to change the title of your page in the browser?

yes

Quick fix

Set your web page title when you save the page. To change it, click Save As Web Page on the File menu, click Page Title, and enter a new title.

no

Are you having trouble with a Word web page?

yes

Go to...

A Word web page isn't formatted correctly or isn't working with my web, page 250

no

Are you having trouble with an Excel web page?

yes

Go to...

An Excel web page looks wrong or isn't automatically refreshing, page 254

no

Are you having trouble with a PowerPoint web presentation?

yes

Go to...

A PowerPoint presentation doesn't work properly in the browser, page 258

A page from another program doesn't work in my FrontPage web

Source of the problem

If you use FrontPage to create and manage your web, you'll probably find all the tools you need to create most pages. But for specific types of pages, other programs might do a better job. If you're creating documents that will be both printed and delivered online, for example, you might use Microsoft Word. Or, if you're writing your own scripts, you might use HomeSite, Dreamweaver, or Visual InterDev.

When you create a page in another program, you'll want to incorporate it into your FrontPage web. But some features you need are available only in the original application, while others are available only in FrontPage.

If you use other software to create a page and then have trouble using it in FrontPage, follow these steps to diagnose and solve the problem.

Note

To incorporate a Microsoft Office document into your web, you'll usually want to save it as a web page. If all your viewers are sure to have Microsoft Office, however—on your company intranet, for example—you might want to leave the file in its original format. This way, viewers using Internet Explorer can open and edit the file directly in the browser window. Those without Office, however, won't be able to view the file at all.

How to fix it

1. In the Folder List or Folders view, check to make sure your file is in the web. Also, make sure that any supporting files that the other program creates or requires are there; if they aren't, the page won't be displayed properly. For example, if you save a page from Microsoft Word, images and other supporting files get saved in a folder called *pagename*_files. ▶

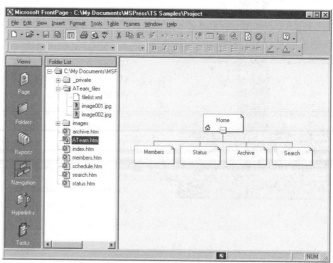

When you import into FrontPage, make sure you get all the supporting files your page needs.

If the page or its supporting files aren't there, import them into FrontPage. Click Import on the File menu, click Add File or Add Folder, and locate the file or folder on your computer or network. Or, rather than creating files elsewhere and then importing them, you might want to create or publish web files directly into your FrontPage web—that way, supporting files will always be where they belong. In Word, for example, when you use the Save As Web Page command, specify the folder that contains your FrontPage web.

If your FrontPage web is on a server and not available through a folder on the network, create a *web folder* or a *network place* to make it easier to add pages. In the Save As dialog box, click the Web Folders or My Network Places button, click the Create New Folder button on the toolbar, and type the web address of your FrontPage web server (such as **http:// servername/ webname**). ▶ (If you use Windows 2000, you might need to create a network place in Windows rather than Office. On the Windows desktop, double-click Add Network Place and then specify the web address of your FrontPage server.)

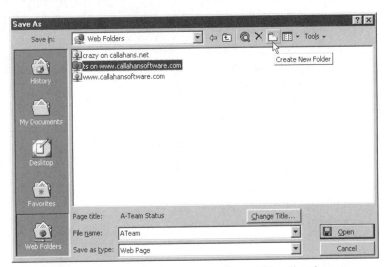

A web folder makes it easier to save pages from Office directly to your FrontPage web.

2. Once you've imported a page from another program, you can open it in the original application by double-clicking it in FrontPage. For example, you might want to update a worksheet in Microsoft Excel. Or, if your web uses a Microsoft Office theme, you'll probably want to apply the same theme to new pages—for pages created in Microsoft Word, you must apply the theme there rather than in FrontPage.

To continue with this solution, go to the next page.

A page from another program doesn't work in my FrontPage web

(continued from page 247)

3. To link the page into your navigation scheme, create links to it from other pages. If you use FrontPage navigation bars or banners, you add the new page by clicking the Navigation button, displaying the Folder List, and then dragging the page from the Folder List to its place in the navigation hierarchy. ▶

To link back to your FrontPage web, open the page in the other application and add hyperlinks to the web pages that link to the file.

4. Once you're sure that a page is the way you want it—that is, you're done making changes in the original application—you can open it in the FrontPage editor. (If you save changes in FrontPage, however, you might not be able to open it in the other application again.)

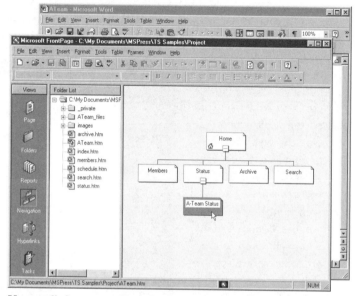

You can link to a non–FrontPage file in navigation bars—but you'll have to use the other application to add links back to your web.

For example, if you want to add shared borders, navigation bars, page transitions, or other FrontPage features, you'll need to use the FrontPage editor. Right-click the file in the Folder List, click Open With, and then double-click FrontPage.

Combining FrontPage and Office web features on the same page

If you want to use FrontPage features such as shared borders—but still want the ability to open and update page contents in the original application—use an *include page*. In FrontPage, create a blank page as a "container" for the page. Then point to Components on the Insert menu, click Include Page, and specify the page (such as a Microsoft Excel or Word web page). Link the container page to the rest of your web pages. If you update the included page in Excel or Word, be sure to open the container page and resave it, so you'll display the most recent content.

A Word web page isn't formatted correctly or isn't working with my web

Source of the problem

If you have documents created in Microsoft Word 2000, you can incorporate them into your web site by saving them as web pages. In most cases, your Word document should look just the same in a browser as it looks on the screen in Word itself. In some cases, however, the differences between an ordinary word processor document and a web page might catch you off guard. Or, when you import the page into a web, you might have some trouble integrating the page with others and providing hyperlinks between them. Finally, if you try to work with the HTML— or Extensible Markup Language (XML)—that Word creates to save document information with the page, you'll probably find it rather confusing. ▶

If you are having trouble using Word to create web pages, follow these steps.

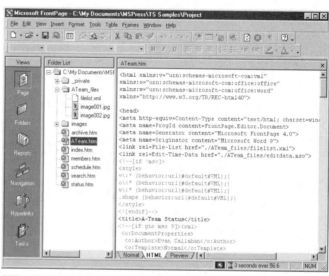

When Microsoft Word saves a web page, it places supporting files in a separate folder and stores document information in XML that only Word can interpret.

How to fix it

1. If images don't show up in your browser or if styles look very wrong (because the style sheet is missing), you may have copied or imported the Word page without its supporting files. When you save a web page, Word puts supporting files in a subfolder called *documentname*_files. Find this folder on your computer and move it to the folder containing your web files. Or, if you can't find the folder, open the original document in Word and resave it as a web page—this time to your web folder.

2. Word allows you to specify options for the browsers you want to support. If your page isn't working in certain browsers, you should select the most broadly supported options. On the Tools menu, click Options, click the General tab, and click Web Options. On the Pictures tab, clear both check boxes under File Formats. On the General tab, select the version 4.0 browsers option under Browser, and clear the Rely On CSS For Font Formatting check box. Save your page again and preview it in older browsers. ▶

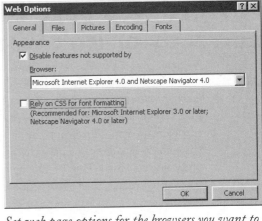

Set web page options for the browsers you want to support.

3. Unless you add them, your Word pages don't have links back to your other web pages. To allow viewers to return to your other pages, add hyperlinks (on the Insert menu, click Hyperlink).

4. Because of differences between word processed documents and web pages, some formatting might not work in the browser. In most cases, Word tells you when you save the page which elements will change, and does a reasonable job of approximating your existing formatting or layout. ▶ In some cases, you might want to replace elements that didn't work with options suggested below. (You can do this in Word or in another web design program or HTML editor.)

Elements that do not transfer to a web page include:

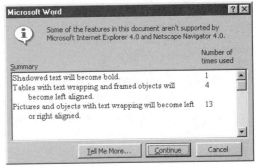

Word informs you of any formatting that it can't display in a browser.

- Printer-only fonts or fonts that don't exist on the viewer's system, special text formatting (such as animated text, vertical text, and small caps), and decorative borders and shading. If Word can't produce the layout or font effect you want, create it in a graphics program, and then import the image into your Word page.

To continue with this solution, go to the next page.

A Word web page isn't formatted correctly or isn't working with my web

(continued from page 251)

- Certain layout options, including page margins, multiple columns, and floating text boxes and pictures. To approximate a specific layout, use tables instead. Or, if you expect all viewers to have the most recent browsers, edit the HTML or the style sheet (.css) file that Word creates. (For information on cascading style sheets, see "Styles" on page 296.)

- Page features intended for printed documents, such as headers, footers, and page numbers, and most *fields*—dynamic content that Word updates automatically. In your web page, you might want to replace these elements with similar information at the top or bottom of the page. For dynamic content, such as a field that displays the current date, use a web page equivalent, such as a FrontPage component or a server script.

> **Tip**
>
> If you want to export the HTML that Word creates and incorporate it into other pages, you probably won't want the XML it contains. (The XML is there to allow you to open the page again in Word and preserve settings.) Several tools help you strip this code from a page. You can download the Office HTML Filter from *officeupdate.microsoft.com*. Or, in HomeSite, use the HTML Tidy CodeSweeper, setting the Clean Up Word 2000 Generated HTML option.

5. If you can't get a Word web page to look the way you want, consider creating an ordinary web page in FrontPage or another design program or HTML editor. Copy text and images from Word and paste them into your new page.

An Excel web page looks wrong or isn't automatically refreshing

Source of the problem

If you use Microsoft Excel to organize information and create charts, you can incorporate all this into your web site or FrontPage web by publishing Excel web pages. In some cases, you'll want to create a static web version of the information. Or, if you know that all viewers have Microsoft Office—on your company's intranet, for example—you can create dynamic spreadsheets, charts, and pivot tables that viewers can work with in their browsers.

If you don't select the right options when publishing your Excel worksheet, you might not get the page you expect. Differences between an ordinary worksheet and an Excel web page might throw you off. Finally, you might have some trouble integrating the page with others and providing hyperlinks between them. ▶

If you are having trouble using Excel to create web pages, follow these steps.

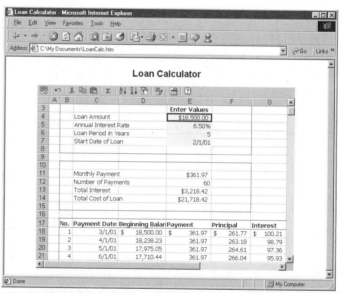

Excel creates web pages with spreadsheet information and charts. If you're sure that viewers will have Microsoft Office, you can make your pages interactive, so figures can be edited.

How to fix it

1. If images or charts don't show up in your browser, you might have copied or imported the Excel page without its supporting files. When you save a web page, Excel puts supporting files in a subfolder called *worksheetname*_files. Find this folder on your computer and move it to the folder containing your web files. Or, if you can't find the folder, open the original worksheet in Excel and resave it as a web page—this time to your web folder.

2. If you still don't see what you want, chances are you saved the wrong type of web page. Excel can save three types of static web pages (an entire worksheet, a single sheet, or a chart) and

three types of interactive web pages (a single sheet, a sheet and chart combination, or a PivotTable). Only viewers who have Microsoft Windows, Office 2000 (any version *except* Small Business), and Internet Explorer can open interactive pages, so these types of pages generally make sense only on a company or team intranet.

If you want to change the type of page, open the main worksheet again and select the sheet, chart, or range of cells you want to publish (unless you want your page to include the whole worksheet). Click Save As Web Page on the File menu, and enter a name for the page. The default is to save the entire workbook, but you can also save a particular selection. ▶

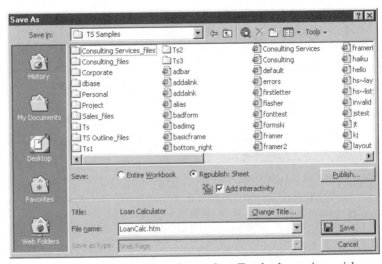

When you save or publish your web page from Excel, select options with care.

To specify additional options for publishing and interactivity, click Publish. If you don't want your page to require Office, be sure to clear the Add Interactivity check box.

3. Excel allows you to specify options for the browsers you want to support. If your page isn't working in certain browsers, you should select the most broadly supported options. On the Tools menu, click Options, click the General tab, and click Web Options. On the Pictures tab, clear both boxes under File Formats. On the General tab, clear the Rely On CSS For Font Formatting box. Save your page again and preview it in older browsers.

4. Older browsers might display columns that you've hidden in Excel. To avoid showing hidden columns, delete them before you publish the web page. (If you need the hidden data, be sure to back up the file.)

Tip

If everyone in your organization has Microsoft Office, you can include an ordinary Excel (.xls) file with your web files and link to it, rather than publish a web page. This strategy provides the easiest way for others to edit and replace the spreadsheet file (if they have appropriate permissions). Like an interactive Excel web page, however, those without Office 2000 installed won't be able to view the file at all.

To continue with this solution, go to the next page.

An Excel web page looks wrong or isn't automatically refreshing

(continued from page 255)

5. For most types of Excel web pages, it doesn't make sense to open and edit the page in another program (such as FrontPage or HomeSite), because the HTML is too complex and only Excel can understand it. If you publish a single sheet or chart, however, you might want to open the file and make changes. If you do edit the HTML and the web page no longer works, open the original file in Excel and publish it again.

6. Unless you add them, links back to your other web pages won't appear on your sheet. To help viewers return to your pages, enter some text on your sheet (for example, the word "Home"), click Hyperlink on the Insert menu, and enter the address of the page you want to link to.

7. If you can't get an Excel web page to look the way you want, consider instead creating an ordinary web page in FrontPage or another design program or HTML editor. Create a table, copy text or figures from Excel, and paste them into your new page.

Note
Depending on browsers and systems, viewers might not see the exact fonts you specified in Excel. Also, because of limitations in the Office Spreadsheet, Chart, and PivotTable components, an interactive page might not have the exact font and border formatting you specified.

A PowerPoint presentation doesn't work properly in the browser

Source of the problem

If you use PowerPoint to create a presentation, you can save it as a series of web pages and incorporate these pages into your web site or FrontPage web. When you publish a presentation, PowerPoint creates all the necessary web pages. ▶ **below**

If you don't choose the right options when publishing, viewers might not see the presentation properly in their browsers. Also, integrating the presentation with your existing pages can be tricky. In some cases, you might find that a PowerPoint web presentation just isn't the right solution for your needs.

If you're having trouble publishing a web presentation from PowerPoint, follow these steps.

How to fix it

1. By default, PowerPoint publishes a presentation for use only in Internet Explorer 4 and later. If your page displays a message such as "This presentation contains content that your browser may not be able to show properly" when you use Netscape or an older browser version, you need to publish it again using different options.

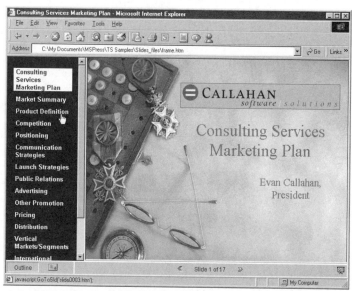

You can publish a PowerPoint presentation as a series of web pages. They work best in Internet Explorer.

Open the presentation in PowerPoint, click Save As Web Page on the File menu, click Publish, click All Browsers Listed Above under Browser Support, and click Publish. ▶

2. In Internet Explorer, presentation pages resize automatically to fit the size of the browser window; other browsers, however, might display these pages with a fixed size. If these pages are too small—or if they don't fit in the browser window on screen sizes you want to support—you can change the size of the pages.

Open the presentation in PowerPoint, click Save As Web Page on the File menu, click Publish, click All Browsers Listed Above under Browser Support, click Web Options, click the Pictures tab, and then select a screen size from the options available under Target Monitor. (To support WebTV, for example, select 544 x 376; for best results on many desktop monitors, select 1024 x 768.) Click OK, and then click Publish.

3. If you see an error in your browser such as "The Page Cannot Be Displayed" or "Page Not Found," you might have copied or imported the main presentation page without its supporting files. When you save a presentation as a web page, PowerPoint puts supporting pages and image files in a subfolder called *presentationname*_files. Find this folder on your computer and move it into the folder containing your web files. Or, if you can't find the folder, open the presentation in PowerPoint and publish it again—this time to your web folder.

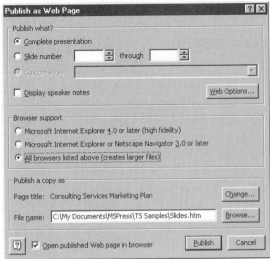

If you want your presentation to work in Netscape, specify the correct options when publishing it.

Note

Although your PowerPoint pages will show up in browsers other than Internet Explorer—assuming you use the proper publishing options—they don't work very well. Images might look wrong, sound and animation don't work, and the presentation can't be viewed full screen. Unless most everyone who views your web presentation has Internet Explorer (version 4 or later), you might not want to use PowerPoint.

To continue with this solution, go to the next page.

A PowerPoint presentation doesn't work properly in the browser

(continued from page 259)

4. Unless you add them, links back to your other web pages won't appear in your presentation. To help viewers return when they finish viewing the presentation, add a hyperlink that appears on every page. In PowerPoint, point to Master on the View menu and click Slide Master. Add text or a small image somewhere on the slide, right-click it, click Hyperlink, and enter the address of the page you want to link to. ▶

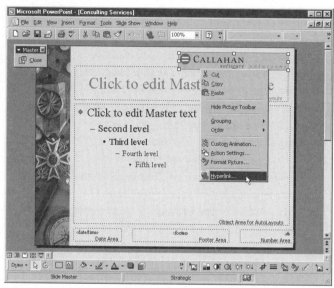

Add a hyperlink to your presentation so viewers can return to your regular pages.

Alternatively, you can make the presentation open in a separate browser window, so your page remains open and appears when the viewer closes the presentation. In the page with the hyperlink, use this HTML:

```
<a href="slides.htm" target="_blank">View slide show</a>
```

5. If you want your presentation to start in full screen mode (in Internet Explorer), you can link directly to the Fullscreen.htm file in the folder of PowerPoint supporting files. For example, use this HTML to open a presentation in full screen mode:

```
<a href="slides_files/fullscreen.htm"
   target="_blank">View slide show</a>
```

6. If your PowerPoint presentation doesn't work the way you want, consider creating ordinary pages instead—for many users, individual pages with hyperlinks are easier to navigate and understand anyway. Copy text and images from PowerPoint into web pages in FrontPage or another design program.

Tip

If everyone in your organization has Microsoft Office, you can place an ordinary PowerPoint (.ppt) file with your web files and link to it, rather than publish a web presentation. This strategy offers the most flexibility for viewing and editing, but viewers who don't have Office 2000 installed won't be able to open the presentation at all.

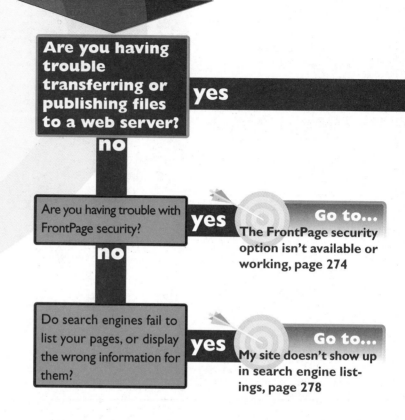

Pu

Publishing is the process of transferring your pages and other web files from your computer to a web server on the Internet or your company intranet. It is a key moment in web design, the debut of new pages. To help you transfer files, many web servers employ File Transfer Protocol (FTP), a way for authorized users to upload files. Or, in FrontPage, you'll communicate directly with the server to publish web changes.

Web servers are complex systems, and there are bound to be problems from time to time. Once you get your pages published, you'll want to make sure that they are secure, work properly, and are easy to find.

For general information, see "What are FrontPage Server Extensions?" on page 267, "Understanding web security" on page 277, and "Choosing a web server or host" on page 269. And if you're having trouble with publishing or server issues, follow this flowchart to a solution.

Are you having trouble transferring or publishing files to a web server?

yes

no

Are you having trouble with FrontPage security?

yes

Go to...
The FrontPage security option isn't available or working, page 274

no

Do search engines fail to list your pages, or display the wrong information for them?

yes

Go to...
My site doesn't show up in search engine listings, page 278

Did you move or FTP your FrontPage files to a new location or server without publishing?

yes

no

Are you having trouble publishing your FrontPage web?

yes

Go to...
When I try to publish my FrontPage web, I get an error, page 266

no

Are you having trouble transferring files in HomeSite?

yes

Go to...
I want HomeSite to transfer files, but deployment isn't working, page 270

no

Are you having other problems publishing or transferring files?

yes

Go to...
When I publish or upload my pages, I get an error, page 264

Quick fix

If you move all or part of a web manually, FrontPage doesn't have a chance to update its files, indexes, and shared borders, so the web might not work properly in a browser. Instead, you should publish the web to the new location, so FrontPage can do its thing.

1. Open the web at its previous location.

2. Click Publish Web on the File menu, specify the new web address beginning with **http://**, and then click Publish.

If the old web is no longer available, open the new web in FrontPage and click Recalculate Hyperlinks on the Tools menu. Preview your web to see if anything is missing.

If your solution isn't here
Check these related chapters:
Browsers, page 42
Databases, page 92
FrontPage, page 154
Hyperlinks, page 174
Office web features, page 244
Or see the general troubleshooting tips on page xvii

When I publish or upload my pages, I get an error

Source of the problem

Once you've created and tested a few web pages, you'll probably want to try them on the server. And when you're working on a web site with frequent updates, you'll publish pages all the time. Web design programs such as HomeSite and Dreamweaver can publish files for you automatically, transferring only files that have changed since you last published. Or, you can publish your web manually—either over the Internet using a file transfer protocol (FTP) program, or over your company network by simply copying files.

If you don't specify the right options, if your server isn't configured properly, or if you don't have the right permissions, you won't be able to transfer files or publish your web. You might see an error while you're publishing, or your pages might not work in a browser once they're published. ▶

If you're having trouble publishing your pages to a web server, follow these steps.

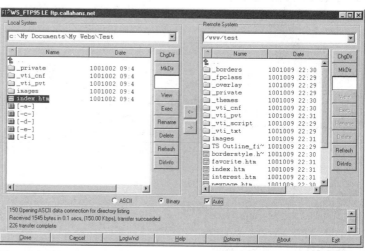

To publish files successfully, you need to use the right options in your FTP or page design program.

How to fix it

1. If you can't make a connection to the web server—whether in your FTP program or from within a design program—check the web address, user ID, and password you've entered. If you haven't used them before, contact the server administrator to make sure they are correct.

    When you use FTP, specify the server name precisely—*ftp.henry.com* might be different from *www.henry.com*, for example. Make sure you don't log in *anonymously* (that is, without providing a user ID and password), which works only for downloading files. And remember that your user ID

Tip

If you're using HomeSite, its deployment wizard can help you publish a web project efficiently. For information, see "I want HomeSite to transfer files, but deployment isn't working" on page 270.

and password are probably case sensitive, so you must use the proper capitalization.

2. If you've provided all the right information but the web server doesn't respond, the server or your Internet connection might not be working properly. Check that you can access pages on the server in a browser; if you can't, see "I'm having trouble accessing the Internet" on page 44.

3. Make sure you're uploading files to the right folder. Once you connect over FTP, the server automatically transfers you to the default folder for your FTP account. This often isn't the folder where web pages belong. They'll go in a folder called web, www, or html—and it's important that you switch to the proper folder before copying files. You might or might not see errors when uploading to the wrong folder, but the pages definitely won't show up in a browser.

If your design program uploads files using FTP, you'll generally need to specify the path for pages *relative to* your default folder. For example, if your pages are stored on a Linux server in the folder /home/miller/web but your default FTP folder is /home/miller, you should specify the destination folder as **web**, so the program will switch to that subfolder to copy files.

4. If you see a server error when uploading files, you might not have the necessary permissions to create files and folders. Or, you might be out of allotted disk space. Check your server, or contact your server administrator or Internet service provider (ISP).

5. If your newly published pages or images don't work in the browser, files might be missing. Make sure you have uploaded all supporting files, such as images or style sheets, into the folders where your pages expect them. For example, if the **src** attribute of your **<IMG>** tags refers to files such as images/picture.jpg, make sure you upload images into the **images** subfolder.

6. If pages don't work, you might have uploaded files with the wrong format or permission settings. Make sure your FTP software transfers web pages and other text-type files in *ASCII* format and images in *binary* format. (Most programs have an automatic setting that does this for you.)

If your web includes executable files, such as CGI scripts, make sure you change their permission settings so viewers can run them. (Many FTP programs let you do this; otherwise, you'll have to access the server or talk to your server administrator.)

7. If you've uploaded a default page but it doesn't appear when you request its folder (without a file name), your server might not recognize it as the default. Try a page called index.htm, index.html, default.htm, welcome.htm, or home.htm—the most commonly configured default names—or reconfigure your server to display the file you want.

8. If certain file types you've uploaded, such as streaming media, can't be retrieved from your server properly, the server might not have the right *MIME types* set up. (A MIME type is the system's code name for the file type.) Check your server documentation for how to add MIME types, and find the proper MIME type for the file from the documentation for its native program.

Note

In some cases, especially if your system and your server have different clock settings, your web server might continue providing older files because they are cached in memory. If this happens, you might have to reboot the server or wait until it retrieves the new files on its own.

When I try to publish my FrontPage web, I get an error

Source of the problem

When you've finished the first version of your web and it's ready for prime time, FrontPage can publish files to a web server on the Internet or your company intranet. Then, as you make changes to your web, you can publish again to automatically update the server, transferring only files that have changed since you last published.

If you don't specify the right options, your server isn't configured properly, or you don't have the right permissions, you'll see errors when you publish your web. ▶

If you're having trouble publishing your FrontPage web to a server, follow these steps.

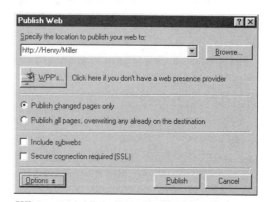

When you publish, FrontPage communicates directly with the server extensions via HTTP.

How to fix it

1. If you can't connect to the server, check the address you've provided and, if the server is on the Internet, the user ID and password as well. If you haven't used them before, contact the server administrator to make sure they are valid. (To publish a web, your user account must be designated as a web *author* in FrontPage or in the server extensions administration pages.)

   Make sure you preface the web server address with **http://**, the protocol FrontPage uses to communicate with the server extensions. For example, to create or add files to a subweb named Miller on a server named Henry, click Publish Web on the File menu and type **http:// Henry/Miller**.

   If you've provided all the right information but the web server doesn't respond, the server or your Internet connection might not be working properly. Check if you can access pages on the server in a browser—if you can't, see "I'm having trouble accessing the Internet" on page 44.

2. If you see an error such as "The server could not complete your request," your server might not have FrontPage Server Extensions installed or enabled. Server extensions are available with Microsoft Office or at *msdn.microsoft.com/workshop/languages/fp*. If your ISP doesn't support server extensions, find one that does by clicking Publish Web on the File menu and then clicking the WPP's (web presence providers) button.

If your web server doesn't have FrontPage Server Extensions, it is still possible to publish your web files, but your publishing options and FrontPage features are limited. To publish pages through an FTP account, specify an address such as **ftp://ftp.xyzee.org/web**. FrontPage copies your files, but doesn't enable any FrontPage server components. The path you specify is relative to your default FTP folder on the server, and might not be the same as the web address. In the example above, specifying **/web** in the address makes sure that FrontPage switches from the default FTP folder to the web subfolder, where this server keeps web files.

3. If FrontPage stops responding or you see an error such as "Web is busy," your web server extensions might have encountered an internal error. Cancel (or reboot) and try publishing again.

If you get the same error, you might need to fix the problem on the web server (or contact your ISP or administrator). To break the bottleneck, stop the server's HTTP service, delete the files Service.lck and Frontpage.lck in the web's _vti_pvt folder (if they are there), and then restart the HTTP service.

What are FrontPage Server Extensions?

FrontPage Server Extensions are a collection of programs that allow a web server running Windows, UNIX, or Linux to communicate with FrontPage and provide features for your FrontPage web pages. You can use FrontPage without them, but the server extensions provide several important services:

● They manage hyperlinks and synchronize changes when you publish your web.

● When you use components on your pages, the server extensions run programs on the server that make them interactive. The Form Results component, for example, saves data in a file or database, while the Search Form component allows viewers to search your web.

● They communicate with a database on the server, saving data or providing query results.

● They allow you to manage web server security using simplified procedures within FrontPage.

Microsoft Office 2000 also introduced Office Server Extensions, which extend features of Microsoft Word, Excel, PowerPoint, and Access. With Office Server Extensions, users can save files to a web more easily, comment and collaborate on Office documents and web pages in a browser, and be notified when Office documents are changed. Office Server Extensions run only on a Windows-based web server and require FrontPage Server Extensions.

To continue with this solution, go to the next page.

When I try to publish my FrontPage web, I get an error

(continued from page 267)

4. You might see messages or questions during publishing, because FrontPage performs many background tasks, such as checking hyperlinks and updating components and navigation.

If you've deleted files in your local copy of the web since you last published, FrontPage asks if you want to delete them on the server as well. If you've changed server files outside of FrontPage—or opened the web directly on the server— since last time you published, FrontPage might ask you if you want to overwrite files on the server. ▶

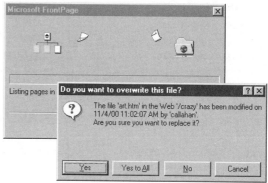

FrontPage helps you synchronize web changes and lets you resolve conflicts.

If you know that your local files are the most recent, click Yes. Beware of over-writing important server files, however. In certain cases, such as the Global.asa file that tracks database connections or text files that store form results, there might be changes to the server files that you want to preserve. (If you want the server versions of these files, open the web on the server and copy the files to your local web).

5. Other server errors might indicate an invalid configuration or an outdated version of the server extensions. Contact your server administrator or ISP, or look for information at *officeupdate.microsoft.com/frontpage/wpp/serk* or *msdn.microsoft.com/workshop/languages/fp*.

Tip

If there are files in your web that you don't want to pub-lish—or for which you want to keep a separate version on the server—you can tell FrontPage not to publish them. Right-click the file, click Properties, click the Workgroup tab, and select Exclude This File When Pub-lishing The Rest Of The Web.

Choosing a web server or host

Web servers—computers that respond to network requests for web documents—range from large UNIX servers at an Internet service provider (ISP) to personal web server software on individual workstations. If you are trying to select a web server—either for your own network or at an ISP—here are a few considerations:

● The two most popular web servers are Microsoft Internet Information Server (IIS), running on Windows NT or Windows 2000, and Apache Server, running on UNIX or Linux servers. For easier graphical administration, Active Server Pages scripting, and better integration with Microsoft Office and FrontPage, go with IIS. If you know UNIX, on the other hand, you're probably better off with Apache.

● If you use Windows and want to create a web site for your company intranet, you can install Microsoft Personal Web Server (an optional component of Windows 98 and Windows 2000) to avoid having to find web space elsewhere.

● If you want to host your web site at an ISP, both Windows-based and UNIX web servers are widely available. When you sign up, you'll have many options—some at additional cost, especially for Windows-based servers. You can choose an economical plan where your web site is on a server with many others, or you can get a dedicated server that runs only your web site.

● When selecting a hosting plan, compare SQL database support, e-commerce packages, ASP, PHP, and CGI scripting, as well as streaming media (RealServer or Windows Media) support. Consider the amount of disk space and network bandwidth you'll need.

● Hosting prices range from $15 to $500 per month (or much more for high-volume support). Don't pay for features you don't need. Most companies allow you to start small and add additional capabilities later. Free personal web hosting is also available through web sites such as *geocities.yahoo.com*.

● To find web hosting companies, talk to your ISP, look for advertisements in web publications, or search the web for *web site hosting*. If you use FrontPage, look for companies that support FrontPage server extensions at *www.microsoftwpp.com/wppsearch*.

● When you set up an Internet web site, you'll need to register a domain name. Your hosting company might do this for a fee, or you can register with any of the companies listed at *www.icann.org/registrars/accredited-list.html*.

● If you have a lot of time on your hands—and your Internet service features a *static IP address*—you can host your own Internet web site. But even if you are up to the task of administering a web server, you'll probably find that the added control and cost savings aren't worth the extra work.

I want HomeSite to transfer files, but deployment isn't working

Source of the problem

HomeSite has a powerful web publishing feature called *deployment* that can help you transfer files to a web server. Once you've set everything up properly, HomeSite creates folders, sends all your files to the right places, and gives you a report along the way. When you deploy again, it sends only the files that have changed.

Unfortunately, deployment isn't completely straightforward. You must first create a *project*—a list of files and folders that belong to your web—and set up network or FTP *deployment locations*. Then you use the Deployment Wizard to start the transfer process. If any options aren't set up right, you'll see errors and warnings.

If you're having trouble deploying your pages in HomeSite, follow these steps.

> **Note**
>
> If setting up a HomeSite project seems like overkill for your needs, you don't have to do so. But you'll need to use a separate FTP program to transfer files (or copy files over your network, if you have access to your web server).

How to fix it

1. Click the New Project button (the wand and stars) at the top of the Resource pane. Specify a name and folder for your project and click OK. ▶

   Or, if you already have a project, click the Projects tab (the globe with a plus sign, located at the bottom left corner of the window) in the Resource pane, and then select your project from the list.

2. When you create a project, HomeSite adds existing files. But, by default, when you import or create new files in a folder, HomeSite doesn't in-

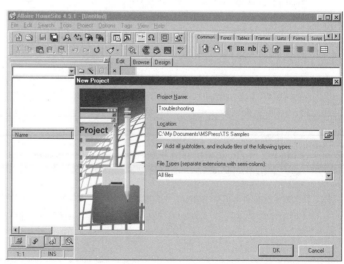

The first step is to create a HomeSite project to organize your files and folders.

clude them in your project. This can often result in necessary files not being deployed to the server.

To make HomeSite include files in a folder automatically, right-click the folder, click Properties, and select the Auto Include Files Using Filter check box. (If you want HomeSite to include only certain types of files—such as web pages or images—and exclude others, select or enter a list of file name extensions in the Filter list.)

3. Before you can deploy your project, you need to tell HomeSite where you want it to go. If you access your server through FTP, it's a two-step process—this step and step 4; to deploy over the network, skip to step 4.

To set up an FTP server, right-click Deployment Servers in the Project pane and click Add FTP Server. Specify settings, making sure to enter the path where your web pages are located in the Initial Directory box. For example, if your web files belong in the Www subfolder with respect to your default FTP folder, enter **www** in the Initial Directory box and select the Relative From Server-Assigned Directory check box. ▶

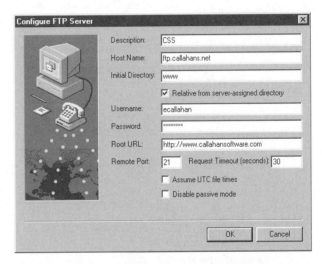

4. Right-click the main project folder, click Properties, click the Deployment tab, and click Specific Deployment Location. ▶

To deploy over your network, enter the complete network path to your web files in the Deployment Path box; for example, enter **\\servername\webfiles\salesweb**. For an FTP server, specify the path relative to the initial FTP folder you specified in step 3. If your project is a subweb, enter a path (such as **salesweb**) in the Deployment Path box; otherwise, enter just a forward slash (**/**).

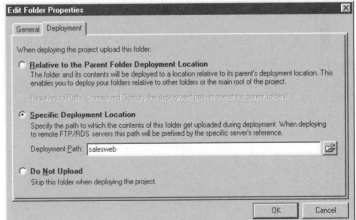

To continue with this solution, go to the next page.

I want HomeSite to transfer files, but deployment isn't working

(continued from page 271)

5. Click Deployment Wizard on the Project menu. Click Next, click Remote RDS/FTP Deployment if you are deploying via FTP (use the default option for network deployment), and click Next. When you click Finish, HomeSite starts deploying files, displaying messages in the results pane at the bottom of the window. ▶

HomeSite displays the deployment play by play. If there are errors, it's back to the drawing board.

6. If you see errors in the results pane, such as "Folder Not Found," you might have specified the wrong information or file locations. Repeat steps 3 through 5, changing values to address problems.

Tip

Setting up a project has other benefits apart from publishing. For example, you can check all the links in an entire project in one step—just right-click the project and click Verify Links.

The FrontPage security option isn't available or working

Source of the problem

Network and web server permissions are complex, so it's especially nice that FrontPage can manage most of the complexity for you. For web servers running Windows or UNIX, FrontPage can communicate with the server extensions on the web server and manage security for the folders and files in your web. From within FrontPage, you can set options to determine who can view web pages, who can change them, and who can administer the web. On a UNIX server, you can also add or remove web accounts to control access to your pages. ▶

But even though the complexity remains in the background, you could still run into problems. There are common security tasks that work only if you perform specific actions. If your server configuration is wrong, you might see errors when trying to set permissions. And, in certain cases, FrontPage can't administer security at all, so it disables the feature.

If you're having trouble using FrontPage to set permissions for your web, follow these steps.

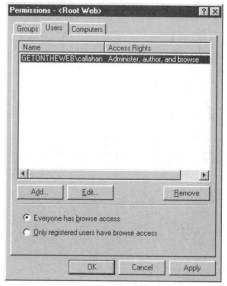

Use the FrontPage Permissions command to control access to your web.

How to fix it

1. If FrontPage can't control security for one reason or another, it disables the Security menu item on the Tools menu. This might happen because you're using a disk-based copy of your web. Make sure you have the web open on the server, and then point to Security on the Tools menu and click Permissions.

   If you have the server version open and the menu is disabled, the server doesn't support security for one of the following reasons: it is a Personal Web Server; it is a Windows NT server installed on a FAT drive instead of an NTFS drive; or security features have been disabled. Contact your server administrator or ISP, or publish the web to a server that supports FrontPage security.

2. If the Add, Edit, and Remove buttons are disabled, you're trying to set permissions on a subweb. By default, subwebs inherit the permissions of the parent web that contains them. If you want to change permissions in the subweb—leaving the main web as it is—click the Settings tab and select Use Unique Permissions For This Web. (You might want to do this to restrict access to one area of a web site.) ▶

3. If you want to limit access to your web to the accounts you've specified, click the Users tab and select Only Registered Users Have Browse Access.

Once you've done this, only users with recognized accounts will be allowed to view your pages. If your server allows *basic authentication* (text-based password transfer), Internet viewers will see a password dialog box in their browser, allowing them to log on to your pages. If Windows doesn't allow basic authentication, Internet access won't be possible (unless users can log on to the network in a secure way).

4. If you use a Windows-based server, FrontPage can't change the list of users, because Windows controls web access through its own user accounts. (On a UNIX or Linux server, you can add web user names from within FrontPage.) If you want to provide a new account with different permissions than your own—to allow password-protected access to a subweb, for example—add a new user account on the server. Once the user account is added in Windows, it will show up on the Users tab in FrontPage.

If you don't control the server, talk to your server administrator or ISP. (Many ISPs charge a fee to add a user to the system; some don't allow it at all.)

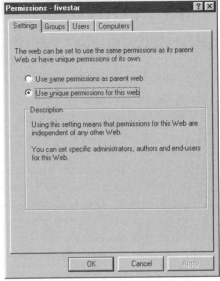

Before setting permissions on a subweb, tell FrontPage you want it to have its own settings.

> **TIP**
>
> It's best not to try to control web security outside FrontPage (using ordinary system file permissions) because your settings might confuse FrontPage. If you want to change web access for certain users, try to do it in FrontPage before changing file permissions on the server.

To continue with this solution, go to the next page.

The FrontPage security option isn't available or working

(continued from page 275)

5. If you see errors when setting permissions, or if settings don't have the intended effect, you might be able to reset them and start with a clean slate.

First, if your web is a subweb and you have access to the parent or root web, point to Security on the Tools menu, click Permissions, select Use Same Permissions As Parent Web, and click OK. Then open the parent web.

To reset permissions in the parent web, point to Security on the Tools menu, click Permissions, click the Users tab, and select Everyone Has Browse Access. Make sure your own account is listed as an administrator, but remove any IUSR_*servername* or IWAM_*servername* accounts. Next, click the Groups tab, remove all groups, and then click OK.

With everything reset, you should be ready to set permissions with better results. Set group and user permissions, changing subwebs to unique permissions if desired.

6. If you're still having problems, contact your server administrator or ISP, or see the FrontPage Server Extensions Resource Kit at *officeupdate.microsoft.com/frontpage/wpp/serk.*

Understanding web security

In order to determine who is allowed to view and change files, every file server has a list of user accounts to control access. Web servers also have security rules, but most allow *anonymous* access (without a password) to users requesting documents through a web browser. Some web sites do require users to log on just to see them, let alone make changes. For your own pages, you might want to use a combination approach, allowing anonymous access to most of the web, while restricting access to some areas. ▶

On Windows-based web servers, web server security is based on the same accounts as the network in general. If you want to allow anonymous access to your web, you grant read access for web folders to a special account called IUSR_*servername*. If you take away this access in any web or folder, the server requires viewers to be logged on and determines which files they are allowed to view or change, based on the permissions of their account in the web folders. For example, accounts with read access can browse pages, while accounts with write access can change and upload pages.

On UNIX servers, by contrast, the list of accounts for the web server is separate from the ordinary server accounts—in other words, you can allow a different set of users to access the web and the server.

If a site has access restrictions, the web browser automatically displays a login box to retrieve the user's name and password and sends it to the server. However, system and web accounts are not the only way to restrict access to web pages—in fact, they are primarily used on company intranets. Internet web sites more commonly ask viewers to sign in on a form, and then use server scripts (such as Active Server Pages) to check viewers' credentials in a database and determine whether or not to display confidential information.

When you talk about security, many people think not of access to pages, but of protecting data as it travels over the Internet. To protect data, current browsers can use Secure Sockets Layer (SSL) encryption—a scheme by which browser and server set up their own encoded private communications. When communicating via SSL, browsers use the https:// protocol. You can configure your own SSL server—many web servers support the protocol—but you'll need a registered security certificate from an agency such as VeriSign. Alternatively, many ISPs and hosting companies allow you to place pages on their secure server. You don't need to put your whole site there—just the pages with forms that submit sensitive data.

My site doesn't show up in search engine listings

Source of the problem

Once you get your pages working on a server—whether on the Internet or your company intranet—you'll want to make sure people can find them by searching. Many Internet and intranet search engines index all the text on your page, while others index only the page title or special keywords you specify. To ensure that search engines can find your page and display it properly in search results, it's important to set options in your HTML using <META> tags. Internet search sites, such as Lycos, Yahoo, and Excite, each use a different method to determine which pages they display. To get your pages listed, you'll have to follow the instructions for each, submit your page to their indexing system, and hope for the best. ▶

If your pages aren't showing up in search results or don't display the right summary information, follow these steps.

How to fix it

1. Many search engines index pages based on page title, and nearly all display the title in search results. Using the **<TITLE>** tag in the **<HEAD>** section of your page, specify a descriptive title with as many keywords as possible in a reasonable space:

```
<title>Callahan Software Solutions - Books - Database Design -
   Web Consulting</title>
```

Search engines use your page title, description, keywords, and page content to index your page and include it in search results.

2. Using **<META>** tags, specify plenty of keywords that identify your subject matter, and include a short description of the content of your page:

```
<meta name="keywords" content="consulting,
  microsoft access, database, technical writing,
  web design, computer books, seattle">
<meta name="description" content="Callahan
  Software Solutions, Seattle-Area Web and
  Database Consulting Firm">
```

Tip

The fact is, submitting to search engines is as likely to bring you more unwanted contact from salespeople as it is to bring you new business. If you really want to bring customers to your web site, consider paid advertising.

3. If your page uses lots of images instead of text, it is harder to index for searching. To help solve the problem, add text using the **alt** attribute of the **<IMG>** tag. Many search engines index this text along with ordinary text on your page:

```
<img src="images/banner.gif" width=542 height=80 border=0
  alt="Callahan Software Solutions">
```

4. To be included in Internet directories or search indexes, submit your pages using instructions they provide. For example, see *home.lycos.com/addasite.html*, *submit.looksmart.com*, *www.excite.com/info/add_url_form*, and *docs.yahoo.com/info/suggest*. Many web directories charge a fee for premium listings, but most also allow you to submit your site for free.

Setting the page title and <META> tags in FrontPage

1. In Page view, click Properties on the File menu (or right-click the page and click Page Properties on the shortcut menu), and then type your page title in the Title box.

2. Click the Custom tab.

3. For each **<META>** tag you want to add, click Add next to the User Variables box and enter a name and value for the tag. ▶

   For example, you might enter **keywords** in the Name box, and **pizza,pepperoni,food,kids,family fun,video games,delivery** in the Value box.

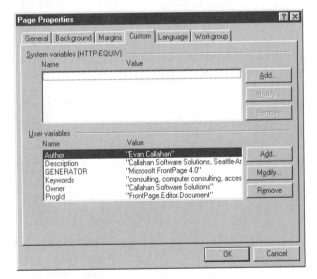

When you want to add interactivity or intelligence to your web pages, you can turn to a scripting language such as JavaScript. Using scripts, you can display different text or images at different times, create animated effects, and cause your page to change as the viewer moves the mouse. Most importantly, you can interact with your audience.

But scripting is not for the faint of heart. While there are many good tools and a wealth of documentation, the journey into the world of scripts is a tough one for any web designer. Unlike HTML, which is fairly forgiving, script languages require precise syntax to work properly.

For general information, see "Choosing client-side or server-side scripting" on page 295. And if you're having trouble with scripts, follow this flowchart to a solution.

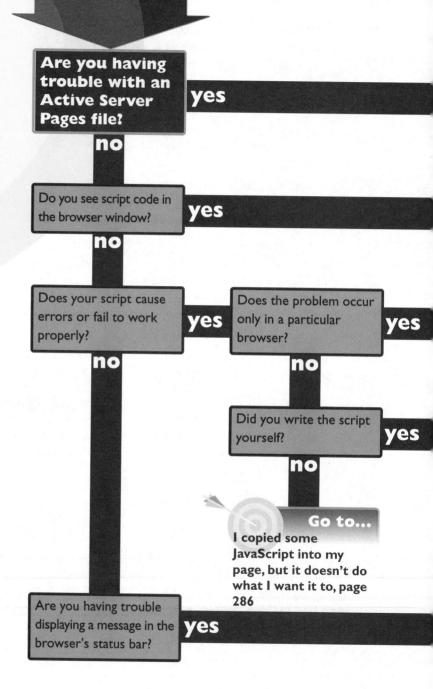

Are you having trouble with an Active Server Pages file?

yes

no

Do you see script code in the browser window?

yes

no

Does your script cause errors or fail to work properly?

yes

Does the problem occur only in a particular browser?

yes

no

no

Did you write the script yourself?

yes

no

Go to...

I copied some JavaScript into my page, but it doesn't do what I want it to, page 286

Are you having trouble displaying a message in the browser's status bar?

yes

Go to...
My Active Server Pages file doesn't work, page 292

Quick fix

1. Make sure all script code is enclosed inside **<SCRIPT>** and **</SCRIPT>** tags.

2. To prevent older browsers from displaying script, include HTML comment symbols as shown here:

```
<script language="JavaScript">
  <!--
  document.writeln('You have scripts.');
  //-->
</script>
```

Go to...
My script works in one browser but not in another, page 290

Go to...
My script doesn't work or displays an error, page 282

If your solution isn't here
Check these related chapters:
Animation, page 2
Browsers, page 42
Databases, page 92
FrontPage, page 154
Office web features, page 244
Or see the general troubleshooting tips on page xvii

Quick fix

To display a message in the status bar when a viewer moves the mouse over a link, set the **status** property of the JavaScript **window** object. This HTML uses JavaScript in the **onmouseover** property of the **<A>** tag:

```
<a href="namuch.htm"
  onmouseover=
   "window.status='Wassup.';return true">
  Check out the status bar.
</a>
```

My script doesn't work or displays an error

Source of the problem

When you're new to JavaScript, it can be a world of frustration. Even the smallest error—known as a *bug* in the language of computer programming—can stop your progress completely, and script bugs can be hard to track down. Sometimes the browser doesn't display error messages at all, even though your script doesn't perform its task.

It would be nice if your computer could tell you exactly what the problem is and how to fix it. Unfortunately, browsers aren't very helpful when they encounter errors. A message might say that the object you're trying to use "has no properties." Translation? You've used an incorrect address for the object or you haven't yet defined it in your script. There are a wide variety of reasons for this error, and just as many possible solutions to the problem. ▶

But that's the nature of scripting. If your script isn't working, here are a few simple steps you can follow to get "back with the program."

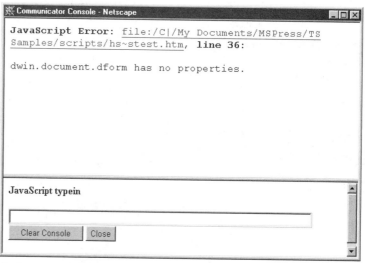

Script errors include the line number where the browser encounters the problem, and an often cryptic description of the error.

How to fix it

1. If your page has script code, it might be causing errors in the page without letting you know. Recent browser versions are designed to recover from programming errors, stopping bad scripts without reporting an error to the viewer. If your browser is configured to display script errors, however, you'll see an error message when a script is invalid or specifies an instruction that the browser can't carry out.

   If you aren't seeing error messages, your first step is to turn them on. In Netscape, type **javascript:** in the address bar to open the JavaScript Console, where errors are displayed. This window stays open to display other errors as they occur. It even allows you to type in JavaScript expressions to evaluate them immediately; for example, try entering **Date()** into the Javascript Typein box and then pressing Enter. In Internet Explorer 5, look for a warning icon at the lower left corner of the window; double-click it to display the error message. Keep an eye out for the warning icon, or if you want to see all errors in the future, select Always Display This Message When An Error Occurs. ▶

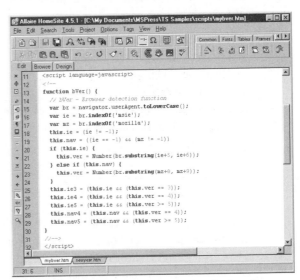

2. The error message tells you which line contains the error; in Internet Explorer, it also specifies the place in that line of script where the browser first discovers a problem. (This might not be the exact place where the error lies; the browser will cite the point at which it realizes there's a problem, even if the error occurred in an earlier line.) There also might be more than one message. Try to solve the earliest problem first—click Previous in the message window if the option is available—because later errors might be caused by the first.

Note the position of the error, then open your file and try to debug the script. Many editing programs can display line numbers in the margin to help you. If you use HomeSite, for example, select the Show Gutter and Show Line Numbers In Gutter buttons on the Editor toolbar. ▶

3. Bugs can occur for a number of reasons, but look out for these common scripting issues:

● A common type of error is a *syntax error*, where the script isn't properly formed. Check punctuation for mistakes, such as a missing bracket or quotation mark. If the error says "Expected ')'" or "Missing) after...," you have more opening parentheses than closing ones. If you include more than one statement on a line, make sure to separate them with a semicolon. (It's a good idea to always end statements with a semicolon.)

To help you with scripting, HomeSite displays line numbers and character position. It also color codes your script for easier reading.

To continue with this solution, go to the next page.

My script doesn't work or displays an error

(continued from page 283)

- Check if you've used the right operators. In particular, watch out for the difference between **=** (which assigns a value) and **==** (which compares values and returns true or false).

```
if (oneThing == another)    // comparison
   another = somethingElse; // assignment
```

- JavaScript is case sensitive. A function called **checkEmail()** is completely different from **CheckEmail()**. And built-in objects, properties, and methods, such as **Window** and **toLowerCase()**, must be capitalized precisely or they won't work.

- If the error says "Object expected" or "Object doesn't support this property or method" (or in Netscape, "[name] is not defined" or "[name] has no properties"), chances are you've either misspelled a property or method, or you've tried to use a function but haven't included it in your page.

- If you've used **document.writeln()** to insert HTML in your file, check the quotation marks you've used. You'll probably need to use quotation marks within quotation marks in order to produce the HTML you want—just make sure you use single quotation marks for JavaScript code and double quotation marks for the HTML. (You can do it the other way around, but this way tends to be least confusing.) For example, this statement uses the writeln method to produce HTML that includes a quoted string:

```
document.writeln('<p><a href="' + theLink + '">' + theText + '</a></p>');
```

  This produces HTML something like this:

```
<p><a href="somepage.htm">Some link text</a></p>
```

- Make sure your code hasn't accidentally been ignored because of comment indicators. JavaScript comments begin with **/*** and end with ***/**, or **//** makes the remainder of a line a comment. Also, make sure you have a **</SCRIPT>** end tag at the end of your script.

```
/* This function opens a window */
function aWindow() {
  it = window.open(url, 'Hello',
'width=300,height=200');
  return it;  // returns the window object
}
```

> **Tip**
>
> When scripting or tracking down errors, a language reference with code examples is a critical tool. If you don't have a book, see the Microsoft Developer Network at *msdn.microsoft.com/scripting* and *msdn.microsoft.com/workshop*, or the JavaScript documentation at *developer.netscape.com/docs*.

> **Tip**
>
> Adding comments to your script is a good way to avoid errors in the future. Make notes about what each function or block of script does.

● Make sure to follow function names with opening and closing parentheses (place function arguments inside, if there are any), both when you define them and when you use them.

4. To help find the problems in your code, you'll probably want to test whether or not your functions are executing—and what values they are coming up with. One way to do this is by inserting the **alert()** statement:

```
alert('The checkIt() function is about to return: ' + returnValue);
```

This causes the browser to pop up a message. Perhaps a better way is to send messages to a special debug information box on your page. The following HTML and JavaScript creates a small form at the top right of the screen and lets you send messages there:

```
<table align=right><tr><td>
   <form name=dform>
      <b>DEBUG:</b><br><textarea name=dtext rows=10 cols=20></textarea>
   </form>
</td></tr></table>
<script language="JavaScript">
<!--
   // Send message to debug text box.
   function debug(msg) {
      document.dform.dtext.value += (msg + "\n");
   }
//-->
</script>
```

Once you've added this at the top of your page, use the **debug** function throughout your code as follows:

```
debug( 'Here is the word: ' + word );
```

5. If you can't get your script to work, remove it before you publish your page so that viewers won't see errors.

To get the scripts you want, look into tools such as Dreamweaver that write JavaScript for you. Or, if you just want to copy a script to perform a specific task, look for sample scripts available on the web.

Using a debugger

If your scripts are long and complex, you might want to use a *debugger*—a program that lets you work through code one statement at a time, checking the value of expressions and variables at each step—and make sure things are happening the right way.

Download the Microsoft Script Debugger from *msdn.microsoft.com/scripting* or the Netscape Script Debugger from *developer.netscape.com/software*.

For a complete Internet development environment that integrates with Internet Explorer—including a debugger, HTML editor, and many other tools—try Microsoft Visual InterDev.

I copied some JavaScript into my page, but it doesn't do what I want it to

Source of the problem

If you're looking for scripting advice and sample code, the web is a friendly place. There are all sorts of sites that offer free JavaScript samples and tutorials, just waiting to make their way into your pages. For starters, try *javascript.internet.com*, *hotwired.lycos.com/webmonkey*, and *javascripts.earthweb.com*, or search the web for *JavaScript samples*. In addition, if you use programs like Fireworks, Dreamweaver, or HomeSite, they'll help you insert JavaScript into your pages. ▶

All you need to do is copy and paste the scripts you find—at least that's the theory. The trouble is, incorporating JavaScript code into your page requires an understanding of the script and how it works with your page. If you don't provide the right information to the script, or don't set up your page properly and include the elements that the script expects, it won't work. By the time you iron out all the details, you might even know enough about JavaScript to write your own.

If you've copied a script to your page and can't make it work, follow these steps.

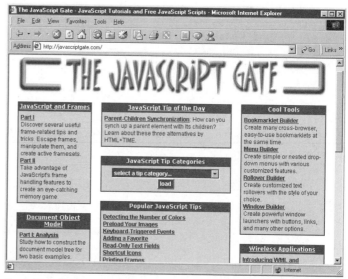

Sample scripts are widely available. What do you want your page to do today?

How to fix it

1. If your script isn't running, it might be because you haven't included it in your page properly. The script you've copied might come with instructions or sample HTML; read them carefully for clues to the problem. Look for instructions on where you should place the script, what values you need to edit, and what HTML tags the script expects on your page.

---

2. Some scripts are designed to run in the main part of your page. With this type of script, you can just paste the **<SCRIPT>** block into your HTML where you want it to display. For example, this nifty script displays the number of days left in the year:

```
<script language="JavaScript">
  <!--
  // Calculate days until New Years Day
  var now = new Date();
  var nextYear = now.getFullYear() + 1;
  var newYears = new Date(nextYear, 0, 1);
  var daysLeft = parseInt( (newYears - now) / 86400000 );
  document.writeln(daysLeft + " days until New Years " + nextYear);
  //-->
</script>
```

Make sure you enclose the code in **<SCRIPT>** and **</SCRIPT>** tags and include comment tags (**<!--** and **//-->**) as shown so that browsers that don't understand scripts won't display the script on your page. You might also need to edit the script to get the right results. In this script, for example, you might want to edit the **document.writeln** statement to add HTML formatting or change the text it displays.

3. Not all scripts are designed to run directly within your page. The script you copy is commonly written as a *function*—a reusable block of code that another script statement runs. In this case, you'll probably put the function in the **<HEAD>** section of your page to keep it from cluttering your HTML.

If you really want to keep the script out of the way, you can save it in a separate file. For example, if you copy a script that makes the viewer's browser fade in from black, you could save the script in a file called **fade.js** and include it in your page with the following **<SCRIPT>** tag (don't leave out the **</SCRIPT>** end tag, or your page won't work):

```
<script language="JavaScript" src="fade.js">
</script>
```

4. Once the function is in place, you need to make it work on your page. You can run a function in one of three ways. You can call the function in a **<SCRIPT>** block in your HTML. For example, if the fade-in function is called fadeFromBlack(), you could use the following lines to display the version on your page:

```
<script language="JavaScript">
  <!--
  // The big curtain raiser.
  fadeFromBlack();
  // -->
</script>
```

> **Note**
> JavaScript functions often include arguments—one or more names listed in the parentheses after the function name. When you use a function, you have to fill these in with the proper types of information. For example, if a script expects one text string and one number as arguments, include them in the parentheses. Make sure to enclose text strings in quotation marks:
>
> `Display('Go away!', 5);`

To continue with this solution, go to the next page.

I copied some JavaScript into my page, but it doesn't do what I want it to

(continued from page 287)

Or, you can call the function in a hyperlink. If you set the **href** attribute of an **<A>** tag to a string beginning with **javascript:**, it will run the script code rather than open another page. For example, this hyperlink calls the function named changeColor():

```
<a href="javascript:changeColor('periwinkle')">
   Click to change the color to blue.</a>
```

Finally, you can attach the function to a browser *event*—one of the predefined times, such as when the viewer clicks a button, that the browser lets you respond to viewer actions with a script. To tell the browser to run a function in response to an event, set the attribute for the event in an HTML tag. For example, if you want the changeColor() function to run when the viewer clicks a button, use the following HTML:

```
<form>
   <input type="button" onClick="changeColor('burnt sienna')"
     value="I cannot stand this color">
</form>
```

If you want a function to run when the viewer moves the mouse over an image or clicks it, use the following HTML (the **<A>** tag is there because Netscape doesn't support these events on the **<IMG>** tag):

```
<a  href="javascript:void(0)"  onMouseOver="newsFlash(66)"
   onMouseOut="noNews()"  onClick="redAlert()">
   <img src="redalert.gif" alt="Click for a special message."></a>
```

And if you want a function to run when the viewer first loads the page, set the **onload** attribute of the **<BODY>** tag:

```
<body  onLoad="specialEffect();">
```

There are many more events that can cause scripts to run—see your HTML reference. (But if you want to support Netscape 4 users, always check whether Netscape supports the event you want for a specific tag.)

5. When your script is ready to roll, preview your page in the browser. If the page doesn't work properly since you added the script—or doesn't appear at all—you might have left off the **</SCRIPT>** tag or otherwise disorganized the structure of your page. Go back to your HTML and make sure everything is in its place.

6. If the script doesn't seem to run at all, make sure you've included code to run the function (as shown in step 4). To see if the script is running at all, you can insert an **alert()** statement at the top:

```
alert('It is running.');
```

7. If you see an error such as "Object expected" or "[name] is not defined," you might have misspelled the function name. Or, the script you copied might depend on other scripts that you need to include on the page. See the instructions for your script.

8. If you're still getting an error, your script (or the code you've used to include it) has a problem or *bug*. For ideas on solving the problem, see "My script doesn't work or displays an error" on page 282.

If you can't get the script working, be sure to remove the **<SCRIPT>** block from your file to prevent viewers from seeing the error. And try copying or downloading a different script; perhaps you'll have better luck.

Note

Recent browser versions are designed to recover from programming errors without reporting an error to the viewer. Scripts on your page might be encountering errors but not mentioning them, making you believe the script isn't running at all. For information on how to display script errors, see "My script doesn't work or displays an error" on page 282.

Hiding scripts from older browsers

If you see script code on your page in an older browser, it is because the browser doesn't support scripts. To prevent viewers from seeing your scripts, surround code in the script with HTML comment marks:

```
<script language="JavaScript">
<!---
document.write('Here is a secret for those with scripting.');
//-->
</script>
```

If your script can't run, you might want to include alternative HTML as well. Following a **<SCRIPT>** block, add your code in a **<NOSCRIPT>** block. Browsers that run your script will ignore this code:

```
<noscript>
Here is a secret for those without scripting.
</noscript>
```

My script works in one browser but not in another

Source of the problem

If you use scripts—or a web design program that creates them for you—you might end up with JavaScript code that works fine in some browsers but causes errors in others. Not all viewers have the latest browser, and unless you are creating pages for a limited audience, you'll probably want to support current versions of Netscape and Internet Explorer, if not other browsers.

But as of the 4.*x* versions, Internet Explorer and Netscape have several JavaScript differences, offer varying support for cascading style sheets (CSS), and use a different *Document Object Model* (DOM)—that is, they use different names to refer to objects on the page. Fortunately, the latest versions of these browsers are converging on a standard programming model, so a great deal of script code will run unchanged between them.

If you have script code that works in some browsers but not in others, follow these steps.

Tip

In the early days of JavaScript, it was Netscape that held the upper hand, since it developed JavaScript in the first place and had the definitive implementation. Nowadays, Internet Explorer's programming model has become something of a de facto standard, at least for the time being. With the vast majority of viewers using Internet Explorer, you'll probably want to focus on programming for Internet Explorer, and then provide a reasonable fallback position—perhaps with fewer bells and whistles—for other browsers.

How to fix it

1. If you've used a design program to produce JavaScript or Dynamic HTML code, check whether the program offers options for browser compatibility—and whether the effects you're trying to use are specifically designed for a certain set of browsers. Remember that some browsers, such as WebTV and older versions of AOL, don't run JavaScript.

2. If you've written JavaScript code yourself, try to identify areas where it uses the wrong model. If your script causes an error, the message indicates a line number in your page so you can track down the problem. (For more information, see "My script doesn't work or displays an error" on page 282.)

3. Where possible, design your page so that any script or advanced feature is optional. To help support viewers whose browsers don't support scripts or embedded objects, include alternative HTML in **<NOSCRIPT>** and **<NOEMBED>** blocks.

4. If you want to move forward with your scripting in the browser where it is working, you might decide to use different features or pages for different browsers. There are many ways to detect and respond to browsers, but here are two of the easier ways.

You can check whether the browser objects you want to use are available. Suppose you want to use scripts that change styles in response to events on the page—something you can do only if the browser version has **styleSheet** objects and a **styleSheet** collection. Placed in the **<HEAD>** section of your page, this script redirects viewers with recent browser versions to a different page.

```
<script language="JavaScript">
<!--
// Redirect Netscape 5+ and IE 4+ viewers to the new site.
  if (document.styleSheets) window.location='coolsite/';
//-->
</script>
```

Alternatively, you can use a function to detect the exact browser version people are using, then use "if" statements in your code whenever you plan to use advanced features. Here's a sample function I use to detect the major browser versions. Once you've included it in a script block in the **<HEAD>** section of your page, you'll have an easy way to check the browser version whenever your script requires. (If you want to use special code for each operating system or minor version, look for a more sophisticated checker.)

```
function bVer() {
    /*  bVer - Browser detection function
        To use, create a bVer object and refer to its properties:
          bv = new bVer();
          if ( bv.ie4 || bv.ie5 || bv.nav5 ) {
              document.writeln("<p>This browser can do cool stuff.</p>");
          }
    */
    var br = navigator.userAgent.toLowerCase();
    var ie = br.indexOf('msie');
    var mz = br.indexOf('mozilla');
    this.ie = (ie != -1);
    this.nav = ((ie == -1) && (mz != -1))
    if (this.ie) {
       this.ver = Number(br.substring(ie+5, ie+6));
    } else if (this.nav) {
       this.ver = Number(br.substring(mz+8, mz+9));
    }
    this.ie3 = (this.ie && (this.ver == 3));
    this.ie4 = (this.ie && (this.ver == 4));
    this.ie5 = (this.ie && (this.ver >= 5));
    this.nav4 = (this.nav && (this.ver == 4));
    this.nav5 = (this.nav && (this.ver >= 5));
}
```

Note

A common programming issue is the difference between events in the major browsers. Netscape recognizes events for only certain objects. For example, the **click** event applies to **<A>** and **<INPUT>** tags in Netscape, but not to **<IMG>** or **<DIV>** tags as it does in Internet Explorer. In addition, Internet Explorer and Netscape have different strategies for managing events in code. For information on these and other differences, see *msdn.microsoft.com* and *developer.netscape.com*.

My Active Server Pages file doesn't work

Source of the problem

Active Server Pages (ASP) is the Microsoft framework for *server-side scripting*—page processing that happens on the web server. ASP is used to create major e-commerce web sites, but it is also easily accessible to anyone with a Windows-based web server. At the most basic level, ASP allows you to dynamically build web pages in response to requests from viewers, and to perform actions on the server based on their requests or the values they enter in forms.

When you're starting out with Active Server Pages—whether you're writing the files yourself, copying them from samples you've found, or letting a program such as Microsoft Access write them for you—there are many ways you could run into trouble. First you might not have your server or page set up properly for ASP, so the server isn't interpreting your script. Or, the script might not have the right format, so that it causes errors or isn't interpreted correctly. And once you have your script running, it might have any number of bugs or problems that are tough to track down. ▶

For ideas on when you'd want to use ASP, see "Choosing client-side or server-side scripting" on page 295. And if your Active Server Pages file isn't working, follow these steps.

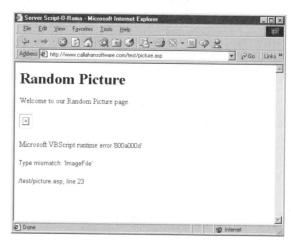

If there's something wrong with your ASP page, such as an error in your VBScript, the server displays a message on the page.

How to fix it

1. If the browser displays an error such as "Access Forbidden"—or attempts to download the ASP file—your web server isn't configured properly for ASP scripting. Make sure the server is running Microsoft Internet Information Server, Personal Web Server (with ASP installed), or ChiliASP!. Also, use the web server administration tools to make sure the web and folder allow scripting.

2. If you see ASP code on the page, your script wasn't processed by the server. Make sure the file has an .asp extension, not .htm, and make sure you've opened the file using an http:// address, not the file's location on your disk or network. Also, make sure your script code is all enclosed in an ASP script block (between **<%** and **%>**).

3. If your page is garbled, blank, or cut short, make sure the %> end tag is not missing.

4. If the browser displays a VBScript error, there's a *bug*—a formatting or programming error—in your script. There are too many possibilities to list, but here are some common ones:

Tip

Find tutorials and documentation on Active Server Pages at *msdn.microsoft.com/workshop/ server*. For tips and samples, try *www.learnasp.com*, *www.15seconds.com*, or *www.asphole.com*, or search the web for *active server pages*.

- You might have left out an = sign. For example, to tell VBScript to insert a value in your HTML, use the **<%=value%>** syntax.

```
<p>Today's Date: <%=Date%> </p>
```

- Data types are somewhat strict in VBScript—you can't combine a number and a text string, for example. If you see a "Type mismatch" error, you might need to use a conversion function, such as **CStr** or **Cint**:

```
Message = "The random number is " + CStr( Rnd )
```

- When generating HTML statements in your script or building SQL database queries, it's easy to get the quotation marks or brackets wrong, causing all sorts of errors. VBScript uses double quotation marks, but you can use single quotation marks in the HTML or SQL you create:

```
ht = "<img src='" + fname + "' height=80 width=80 alt='" + _alttxt + "'>"
Response.Write  ht
```

  If the script generates a page for the browser but the page displays incorrectly, view the HTML source to try to diagnose the problem.

- You might have used ASP server objects incorrectly. Use the **Request** object to retrieve information, such as form data, server variables, or cookies. Use the **Response** object to send HTML to the browser, redirect the browser, and set cookies. And use the **Session** object to store information that's used between pages. Here are some common examples:

```
EmailName = Request("EmailName")     ' Grab data from the form.
Response.Redirect "http://goaway"    ' Send viewer to new site.
Session("UserID") = lngUserID        ' Track this viewer between pages.
```

- If you see an error from the ODBC driver or OLE DB provider, you've written invalid database instructions. If you're having trouble connecting to the database, see "My connection string isn't connecting to the database" on page 96.

5. If your scripts are long and complex, you might want to use a *debugger*—a program that lets you step through code one statement at a time, checking the value of expressions and variables at each step. Download the Microsoft Script Debugger from *msdn.microsoft.com/scripting* or, for a complete Internet development environment, try Microsoft Visual InterDev.

> **To continue with this solution, go to the next page.**

My Active Server Pages file doesn't work

(continued from page 293)

6. If you can't get your ASP solution to work, check if the same sort of thing can be done without scripting in FrontPage. For example, if you are trying to access a database or send e-mail using a form, FrontPage can create the ASP script for you.

Using Active Server Pages in FrontPage

If you use FrontPage, you can design Active Server Pages files just as if they were ordinary web pages, switching to HTML view to add script. For example, if you want the server to insert content into your page dynamically, you can design the page in Normal view—adding tables, images and text, for example—and then switch to HTML view and add the script code that fills in your information. FrontPage displays script code in its own color to help you distinguish it. ▶

To save a new page as an .asp file, click Save As on the File menu and choose Active Server Pages in the Save As Type box. Or, to change a page in your web to an Active Server Page, rename it with the .asp extension. (FrontPage automatically changes other pages to link to the new name.)

The Preview tab doesn't run your .asp file. To preview an ASP script and see the results, click Preview In Browser on the File menu.

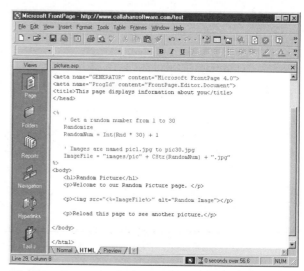

Use FrontPage to design an Active Server Page; then switch to HTML view to view VBScript code.

Note

In some cases, FrontPage can't display or design your ASP page properly in Normal view. For example, if your page builds HTML on the server using a script, FrontPage can't interpret it. Instead, you'll need to design the script in HTML view.

Choosing client-side or server-side scripting

To make web pages more dynamic, scripts can run either on the *client* computer—in the viewer's web browser—or on the web server computer. Each strategy has advantages and disadvantages, and while some tasks require one or the other, in many cases you have a choice.

For example, to display the date and time on your page, you can use the JavaScript **Date()** object in a **<SCRIPT>** block on your page; any browser that understands JavaScript can display it. However, if your web server supports server scripting, you can also insert a date and time using a server script, so the HTML sent to the browser has the date and time in it. There's no difference to the viewer, unless of course the web server is in a different time zone or has a different clock setting than that of the viewer's computer.

JavaScript is most commonly used as a *client-side* scripting language (although it can be used to control some servers as well). Server scripting comes in many flavors, including Perl and PHP for UNIX and Linux servers as well as Active Server Pages scripting for Windows-based servers.

Which should you use? In general, use client-side scripting to animate pages and to control aspects of the browser or page appearance in response to the viewer's action while they are on the page. Although you can also use it for other tasks—for example, to check and process values the viewer enters in a form or to interact with a database—most web sites use *server-side* techniques to implement these key web features. Instead of running a script in the viewer's browser, you can send form information to a program or script on the server, which in turn sends back a new page with a response to the viewer. Server scripts have the following advantages over client-side scripts:

- They don't depend as much on which browser version a viewer is using.

- They don't show up in the web page source; in fact, viewers may not be aware a script is running.

- They don't need to download with the page.

- They can more easily interact with a database and keep track of visitors as they move through a web site.

For information on server-side scripting, search the web for *Active Server Pages*, *Perl scripts*, or *PHP scripts*.

Until recently, browser support for cascading style sheets (CSS)—a powerful and flexible way to specify formatting and layout of a document—wasn't consistent enough to justify using styles extensively. Now that most popular browsers support some CSS, styles are getting much wider use.

With CSS, you can specify many styles that HTML doesn't allow. And style sheets keep formatting and layout separate from content, so you can more easily update the appearance of pages that use them.

But transitioning to styles may bring you headaches. They don't work the same in every browser, and aren't consistently supported by page design programs.

For general information on CSS, see Appendix B on page 347 and "Browser support for CSS" on page 302. And if you're having trouble getting your styles to work properly, follow this flowchart to a solution.

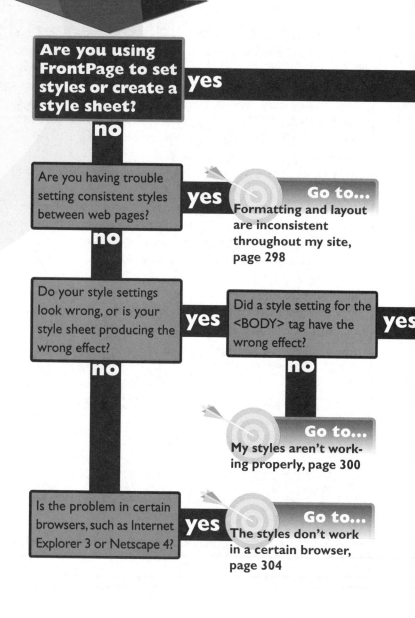

Are you using FrontPage to set styles or create a style sheet?

yes

no

Are you having trouble setting consistent styles between web pages?

yes

Go to...
Formatting and layout are inconsistent throughout my site, page 298

no

Do your style settings look wrong, or is your style sheet producing the wrong effect?

yes

Did a style setting for the <BODY> tag have the wrong effect?

yes

no

no

Go to...
My styles aren't working properly, page 300

Is the problem in certain browsers, such as Internet Explorer 3 or Netscape 4?

yes

Go to...
The styles don't work in a certain browser, page 304

Are you having trouble creating or applying styles to your entire web?

yes → **Go to...**
FrontPage doesn't let me change styles the way I want, page 306

no

Did a style setting for an image, table, or other element get applied incorrectly?

yes →

Quick fix

By default, FrontPage applies style settings such as borders and positioning to paragraphs —even if you've selected an image, table, cell, or hyperlink. To change the style of these elements, edit their properties:

1. Right-click the table or image and click Table, Cell, Hyperlink, or Picture Properties.

2. Click Style.

3. Click Format to set style properties, such as Font, Border, or Position.

Quick fix

When you specify font, color, or other styles for the **<BODY>** tag, they are applied throughout the page in different ways, depending on the browser.

If you set properties for the **<BODY>** tag, set them for individual tags as well:

```
body, td {
 font-size: 10pt;
 color: #003333;
}
h1, h2, h3 {
 color: #660000;
}
h1 {
 font-size: x-large;
}
h2 {
 font-size: large;
}
h3 {
 font-size: medium;
}
```

If your solution isn't here
Check these related chapters:
Browsers, page 42
Color, page 62
Hyperlinks, page 174
Layout, page 206
Text formatting, page 322
Or see the general troubleshooting tips on page xvii

Formatting and layout are inconsistent throughout my site

Source of the problem

When you specify style and layout of your pages using HTML—with tags such as <FONT> or attributes such as **align** and **color**—you can be sure that nearly all browsers see them as you intend. But with all this formatting spread throughout your web site, inconsistencies are sure to creep in here and there. And if you decide to change your page design or style after pages are in place, you're in for a lot of work changing all those tags and attributes. ▶

A style sheet can provide a solution to the problem if you're willing to go to the trouble of transitioning to cascading style sheets (CSS). You'll remove some existing formatting from your site, download or create a style sheet, and specify styles. The more complex your pages, the more difficult it will be to move to styles—but the more rewarding.

If the appearance of your pages is inconsistent and your formatting is difficult to modify, follow these steps.

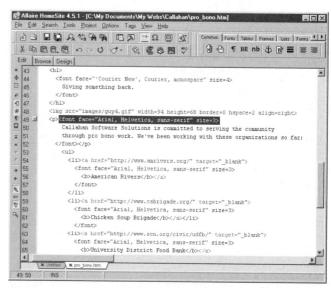

If your page is peppered with <FONT> tags, it can have inconsistencies and be difficult to modify. Using a style sheet, you can separate style and formatting from page content.

How to fix it

1. Before making the change, back up your pages in case the styles don't work the way you want.

2. Strip out all the **<FONT>** tags from your page. Optionally, take out color, background, and alignment specifications as well. (For example, you could remove the **background** and **bgcolor** attributes from the **<BODY>** tag.)

3. Make sure all your block tags, such as **<H1>**, **<P>**, and **<UL>**, have corresponding end tags. (To apply CSS consistently, browsers need to know where elements start and stop.)

4. Create a style sheet (.css) file in the folder with your web pages, or copy one into it. Find style sheet samples on the web, or use a template in FrontPage or another web design program. Or, to create a style sheet from scratch, use your HTML editor or a separate style sheet editor, such as TopStyle (available from *www.bradsoft.com*). ▶ Add style rules for HTML tags that you want to format. For example, these style rules cause headings to use green, Courier text:

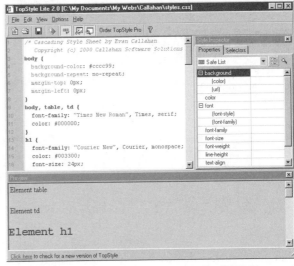

```
h1, h2, h3 {
   font-family: Courier,
      "Courier New", serif;
   color: #003300;
}
```

A style sheet contains formatting rules for HTML tags. TopStyle shows the effect of your rules in the lower pane.

5. Link to the style sheet in your pages using the **<LINK>** tag:

```
<link rel=stylesheet type="text/css"
   href="styles.css">
```

6. Preview your pages. If elements don't look right, add or modify style rules for HTML tags.

If there are areas of your page where you'd like to set special formatting, add a custom *class* to your style sheet file, specifying style rules you want to apply for page elements of that class. In the style sheet, precede class names with a period.

```
.WhiteOnBlue {
   background: #000066;
   color: #ffffff;
}
```

Apply the style to appropriate tags by setting the **class** attribute. For example, the following **<DIV>** block—in conjunction with the style rule above—creates an area of the page with white text on a blue background:

```
<div class=WhiteOnBlue>
   <!-- This is the reversed area of the page -->
</div>
```

7. Once your style sheet results in a page you like, link it to other pages as well, deleting **<FONT>** tags and other formatting information in favor of the consistent style rules.

Note Most browsers support basic style sheet properties, such as font and color styles. As long as you don't expect too many viewers using older browsers, you are probably safe using styles. But if you want your pages to look the same in every browser, don't use them. For more information, see "Browser support for CSS" on page 302.

My styles aren't working properly

Source of the problem

The cascading style sheets (CSS) language isn't complex, but it's easy to make mistakes or use styles that the browser can't interpret. As with HTML, the browser doesn't display any indication that there is something wrong; it simply ignores errors, and your page doesn't appear as you'd hoped.

You might find the problem tough to track down. Perhaps you've formatted your style sheet improperly or failed to apply styles in the right way. Maybe you've misspelled a style or property name. Or, perhaps you've used a style or combination of styles that your browser doesn't support, even though you've used valid CSS.

If your styles aren't working properly, follow these steps.

How to fix it

1. Make sure all your HTML block-level tags, such as **<H1>** or **<P>**, have corresponding end tags. The browser needs to know when to start using each style and when to stop.

2. To help rule out the browser as the problem, use a version 5 or later browser to test your styles. Then, once you get them working, try other browsers you expect viewers to use. (For ideas on solving problems with one browser, see "The styles don't work in a certain browser" on page 304.)

3. If none of the styles in a style sheet seem to be having an effect, make sure you've inserted the styles between **<STYLE>** and **</STYLE>** tags in the **<HEAD>** section of the page, or have linked the proper style sheet (.css) file using the **<LINK>** tag:

   ```
   <link rel=stylesheet type="text/css" href="styles.css">
   ```

   Also, make sure the style sheet file exists in the folder with your web pages (or in the folder indicated by whatever path you've specified in the **href** attribute).

4. Check the format of your style sheet carefully for errors, making sure each style rule uses the following format (line breaks don't matter, but always separate style selectors with a comma and rules with a semicolon):

   ```
   tag, another-tag {
     style-property: setting;
     another-property: setting;
   }
   ```

Or, for style rules included in an HTML tag with the **style** attribute:

```
<html-tag style="style-property: setting; another-property: setting">
```

5. If a style isn't applied, check that you've used the correct property name and specified a setting that the property allows. (Always keep a CSS reference table handy, such as Appendix B on page 347.)

For example, the following style rules look pretty good, but don't work:

```
body    { background: happy.gif }
p, li { font-color: #cccccc }
```

What's wrong? Web addresses, such as the GIF image file reference above, must use the **url()** identifier. And **font-color** isn't a CSS property; it's just **color**. The correct style rules are:

```
body    { background: url(happy.gif) }
p, li { color: #cccccc }
```

6. To check your style sheet for valid entries and for-matting, try the CSS valida-tion service at *jigsaw.w3.org/ css-validator*. ▶

7. Make sure HTML tags or attributes aren't overriding your style rules. For ex-ample, even if your style sheet specifies Arial font for **<P>** tags, a **<FONT>** tag could override the setting:

```
<p><font
   face="Verdana">
   Text is Verdana
</font></p>
```

8. If you've applied a custom class in a tag, make sure you include a period in the style sheet, but not in the class attribute:

```
<style>
   .blues { color: blue; font-size: 7pt }
</style>
<p class=blues>I am 7 point text, and I have the blues.</p>
```

The CSS Validation Service can point out formatting errors and other possible issues in your style sheet.

To continue with this solution, go to the next page.

My styles aren't working properly

(continued from page 301)

9. Remember that HTML elements *inherit* style settings from the block-level tags that contain them. For example, if you set the **color** property for the **<TABLE>** tag to blue, all foreground elements inside tables—headings, text, and bullets—turn blue, unless style rules for their tags specify another color.

```
table { color: blue; }   /* Everything in all my tables has the blues */
```

If you don't want a setting to apply to all contents of a block-level tag, create a class and apply it more judiciously (see step 8). Or, use a *contextual* style rule, so it applies only when you want it to. The following style rule causes **<H1>** tags to use blue text, but only within tables:

```
table h1 { color: blue; }   /* Headers in tables have the blues */
```

10. If you can't get your styles to work, try someone else's. Use a predefined style sheet from a page design program such as FrontPage, or find a sample style sheet on the web (search for *sample style sheets*) and then modify it to meet your needs.

Browser support for CSS

When designing with CSS, it can be frustrating to find out that the styles you've used aren't supported in some browsers. Although the software community has agreed on CSS standards—available on the World Wide Web consortium pages at *www.w3.org/Style/CSS*—no browser fully supports them.

When deciding how to use CSS, consider these points:

- Version 5 and later browsers, especially Internet Explorer 5.5 and later, support CSS well enough that you can use most style sheet features with confidence. Advanced features, such as printer layout and nonstandard word spacing, might not work properly.

- Internet Explorer 3 and 4, as well as Netscape 4, have fairly good support for font formatting and color. They also support some border, margin, positioning, and background styles, but with many bugs and omissions.

- Netscape 4 interprets margin and border styles so differently than do other browsers that it isn't very practical to use them. Consider a separate style sheet for Netscape 4.

- Fewer than 3 percent of viewers use a browser that doesn't understand styles at all. Even the WebTV browser interprets styles and uses them as best it can (given its limited fonts).

For a complete list of CSS property support, see charts at *www.richinstyle.com/bugs/table.html* or *www.webreview.com/wr/pub/guides/style/mastergrid.html*.

The styles don't work in a certain browser

Source of the problem

Cascading style sheets (CSS) specifications have been around for a long time, but browsers have been slow to implement them. Unless you know that your viewers all have a recent browser version, it's likely some people won't see the style settings you specify.

Worse, a browser may do a poor job of interpreting them, making your page look different from what you intended. Netscape 4 supports many style properties, for example, but its implementation can make pages look completely wrong. ▶

While there is no easy answer to this problem, there are a few good strategies you can follow. For general information, see "Browser support for CSS" on page 302. If your styles aren't working in one or more browsers, follow these steps.

How to fix it

I. Test your page in a recent browser, such as Internet Explorer 5 or later. If the styles don't work, your style sheet or HTML might have errors—perhaps because you designed the styles to compensate for problems in an older browser—or you might be using features that are too new to be supported.

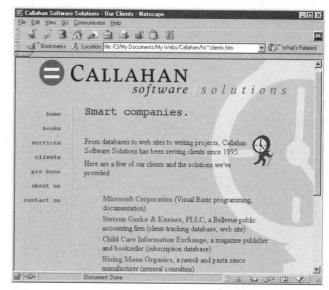

The style sheet attached to this page works perfectly in Internet Explorer. In Netscape, it's all goofed up—paragraphs have way too much space between them, and the bullets have disappeared!

Since the majority of viewers have Internet Explorer 5—and it comes closest to supporting the CSS standards—you should get your styles working there before moving forward with other browsers. (For help diagnosing problems, see "My styles aren't working properly" on page 300.)

2. For other browsers, choose one of the following strategies:

TopStyle, a popular CSS editor, has a style selector list that helps you pick style properties that work in browsers you want to support, and identify styles in your page that won't. TopStyle is available at *www.bradsoft.com*.

- If your styles work in version 5 browsers but don't look too bad in others, you might decide to not worry about the less popular browsers. (As viewers upgrade, this will become less of an issue.)

- You can use one style sheet and one set of web pages to support all browsers, limiting your style sheet to tags and properties that have the most consistent support. If you want your style sheet to work consistently across all CSS-capable browsers, stick to these style properties: **background, color, font-family, font-size, font-style, font-weight, line-height, text-align**, and **text-decoration**.

- Design separate web pages for each browser, each with its own style sheet. This way, you can get the most out of CSS and HTML in each browser while avoiding the compatibility issues. However, it's a lot more work to keep pages up to date. You'll probably want to use a server-side script to detect which browser version viewers are using in order to send the right page. (See "Choosing client-side or server-side scripting" on page 295.)

- Use one set of web pages but multiple style sheets. For example, you might create a style sheet for each major browser version, or just create a style sheet for Netscape 4 and another one for all other browsers. For older browsers, use simpler styles. In the **<HEAD>** section of your file, use JavaScript to detect the browser and link the proper style sheet:

```
<script language="JavaScript" type="text/javascript">
<!-- // Link to stylesheet - special version for Netscape 4.
   var cssfile = 'styles.css';
   if (document.layers) cssfile = 'n4styles.css';
   document.writeln(
      '<link rel=stylesheet type="text/css" href="' + cssfile + '">' );
//-->
</script>
```

This script works on the premise that only Netscape 4 has a **layers** collection. For additional ideas on scripting to support multiple browsers, see "My script works in one browser but not another" on page 290.

FrontPage doesn't let me change styles the way I want

Source of the problem

FrontPage is designed to shield the user from the complexities of cascading style sheets (CSS). As you use its formatting features, FrontPage creates styles whenever necessary—for example, when you specify font, paragraph, or border properties that can't be accomplished in ordinary HTML. Using the Styles command, you can also set your own style properties or create user-defined styles; FrontPage adds them to a <STYLE> section in your page. You can even create and attach an external style sheet, which will apply consistent styles to your pages. ▶

You can do all this without ever editing HTML or a style sheet (.css) file manually. But because this all happens behind the scenes, it's easy to lose track of what's going on. And because of limitations in the Styles command, you might not be able to set all the styles properties you want.

If you're having trouble using styles with FrontPage, follow these steps.

How to fix it

FrontPage lets you create and apply styles in three places: an external style sheet (.css) file, a <STYLE> section for a single page, or within the tag for any single element. If you want to apply consistent styles throughout your web, it's best to use an external style sheet, and then add individual style settings as required.

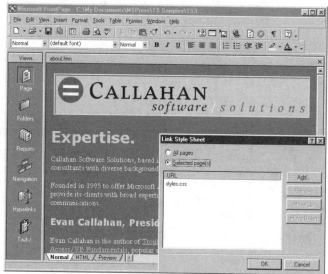

In FrontPage, you can create, edit, and apply style sheets to pages in your web. Or, you can apply styles to individual pages or elements.

I. If you've set Font formatting for individual elements and want to set it using styles instead, start by clicking Remove Formatting on the Format menu. FrontPage removes all **<FONT>** tags from your HTML, and your fonts return to the default settings.

---

2. If you have an existing style sheet, import it into your web and skip to step 5. To create an external style sheet, click New on the File menu and click Page. Click the Style Sheets tab and double-click one of the predefined style sheet templates (or Normal Style Sheet for a blank sheet).

3. In your style sheet, create all the basic style rules needed to describe your page. You'll generally want to set styles for the body, paragraph, and heading styles, and perhaps for links (the **<A>** tag) and tables as well.

For greatest control, edit the CSS rules in the style sheet directly. (For a guide, see Appendix B on page 347.) To let FrontPage create CSS style rules for you, click Style on the Format menu. To set a new style property, double-click an HTML tag name in the Styles list, then click Format in the Modify Style dialog box. For example, you might want to change the font color and background color associated with the **<BODY>** tag (which affects the whole page). In the Modify Style dialog box, click the Format button to see options. ▶

This is where it gets tricky. You can set most CSS style properties here, but the options are misleading:

Note

If your web uses a FrontPage theme, its style settings often override your own. If you want to use a style sheet to format your page, remove the theme. Click Theme on the Format menu and click No Theme in the Themes list.

You can edit a style sheet directly, or FrontPage can add and modify styles for you based on your formatting selections.

- Click Font to select a font, a font style, size, or the foreground color of any element.

- Click Paragraph to select alignment, line spacing, and margin styles for any element. (Set left and right margins under Indentation, top and bottom margins under Spacing.)

- Click Border to select borders, padding, and background colors and images. (Background styles are on the Shading tab.)

- Click Numbering to select styles for bulleted and numbered lists.

- Click Position to select alignment and absolute or relative positioning.

To continue with this solution, go to the next page.

FrontPage doesn't let me change styles the way I want

(continued from page 307)

4. Once you have styles in place for regular HTML elements, create a user-defined class for each special type of formatting you need. Precede class names with a period according to the CSS standard. For example, if you want to create a class called *tiny* for extra small text, in the Style dialog box click New, enter **.tiny** in the Name box, click Format, click Font, and enter **14px** in the Size box. ▶

5. Save the completed style sheet. To attach it to your web, open any page, click Style Sheet Links on the Format menu, click All Pages, click Add, and select the new style sheet. All your pages appear with formatting from the style sheet.

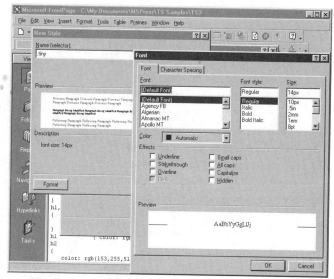

For each style or set of formatting options you want to apply in your pages, create a user-defined style (or class). Precede class names with a period, such as .tiny or .sidebar.

Applying styles, and making exceptions to the rules

Now that you have styles that are shared by all your pages, you can style individual elements. Set styles for paragraphs, and if you've created a user-defined class in the style sheet, apply it to appropriate elements. And when you want to make exceptions to the rules, specify properties that give individual page elements their own separate style settings.

1. To set the style of paragraphs or headings, click the Style box on the Formatting toolbar and select a style—such as Normal or Heading 1—or a user-defined class. To create a unique style for a single paragraph, use commands on the Format menu: Font, Paragraph, Bullets And Numbering, Borders And Shading, and Position. (Most of these commands set an in-line style using the tag's **style** attribute, except for the Font command, which adds **<FONT>** tags.)

Tip

Even if you don't create your whole style sheet with FrontPage options, you might want to use them as a tool when you can't find the style you need. For example, you can create a style in FrontPage, and then look at the HTML or style sheet to see which style properties FrontPage set.

2. To set the style of a table, cell, hyperlink, or image, don't use the options on the Format menu or toolbar. Instead, right-click the table or object and click Table, Cell, Hyperlink, or Picture Properties, and then click Style. Select a user-defined style from the Class box, or click format to set properties (as you did for the style sheet, but this time it's for just one object). ▶

For example, if you want an image to align right and have 20 pixels between it and the text, you would right-click the image, click Picture Properties, click Style, click Format, click Position, click Right,

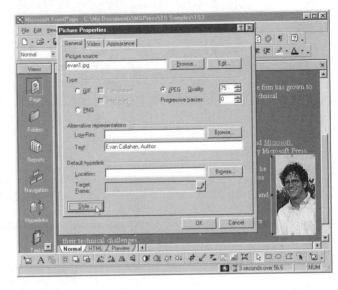

and click OK. Next, click Format again, click Paragraph, enter **20** in the Before Text box under Indentation, and click OK three times. (This procedure sets the style for just one image tag. If you want to apply this same style to other images in your web, return to the style sheet and add a class.)

3. Repeat the process for each page in your web, applying styles and adjusting the style sheet as necessary.

If you later want to make a change that applies to the whole web—increasing font size, for example—you can do it in just one place in the style sheet (in this case, by changing the **font-size** property of the **<BODY>** tag style).

4. In some cases, you might need to edit your styles directly—either in the style sheet (.css) file or in the **<STYLE>** section or style attributes of your tags—because style options are missing from FrontPage dialog boxes. ▶ For example, if you want hyperlinks not to be underlined, the Font properties box doesn't let you do this—you have to type the following rule into your style sheet manually:

```
a { text-decoration: none; }
```

Or, you might want to set new style properties that FrontPage isn't aware of, such as the **page-break-before** and **page-break-inside** properties for use with printing.

For a summary of CSS properties you can use, see Appendix B on page 347.

Tables help you arrange text and images on your page in rows and columns. Because of their flexibility and consistent support across most browsers, tables are used extensively for layout on nearly every web site.

But tables have some idiosyncrasies and differences between browsers. Originally intended only for displaying lists of data, tables have evolved into their page layout role. Whether you use a page design program or write HTML directly, it's important to understand the <TABLE>, <TR>, and <TD> tags and their attributes.

For general information, see "Fundamentals of tables" on page 313 and "Displaying table and cell borders for testing" on page 315. And to solve table problems, follow this flowchart.

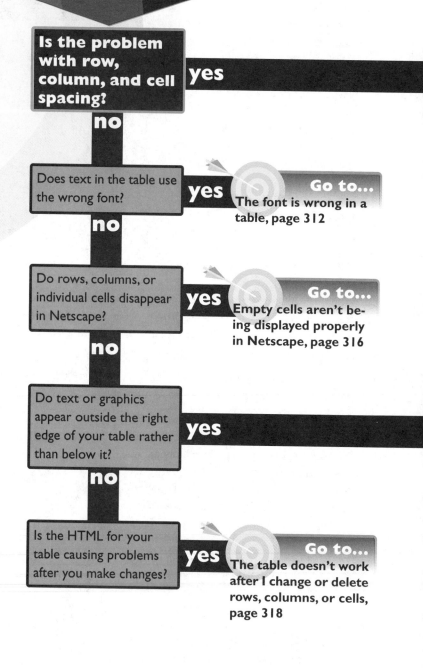

Is the problem with row, column, and cell spacing?

yes

no

Does text in the table use the wrong font?

yes

Go to...
The font is wrong in a table, page 312

no

Do rows, columns, or individual cells disappear in Netscape?

yes

Go to...
Empty cells aren't being displayed properly in Netscape, page 316

no

Do text or graphics appear outside the right edge of your table rather than below it?

yes

no

Is the HTML for your table causing problems after you make changes?

yes

Go to...
The table doesn't work after I change or delete rows, columns, or cells, page 318

Did FrontPage set cell heights and widths incorrectly?

yes

no

Are columns in your table the wrong width, especially when you resize the browser window?

yes

Go to...
I specified column widths, but they still seem to vary from the size I gave, page 320

no

Is there extra space around or at the bottom of some cells?

yes

Go to...
I can't get rid of the extra space in or between cells, page 314

Quick fix

When you drag rows or columns in a table, FrontPage sets the width of all cells in your table, estimating the width you've indicated.

To specify a row or column size precisely, select the column or row, right-click the cells, click Cell Properties, and specify percentage or pixel values in the Height and Width boxes.

Or, to remove all the height and width attributes from a table so it resizes automatically in the browser, click the table, and then click AutoFit on the Table menu.

Quick fix

If a table is left-aligned, other elements wrap around it on the right, just as with an image. If you want these elements to appear below the table, add a line break after the end of the table, setting the **clear** attribute to **all**:

```
<br clear="all">
```

Or, in FrontPage:

1. Click Break on the Insert menu.

2. Select Clear Both Margins.

If your solution isn't here
Check these related chapters:

Browsers, page 42
FrontPage, page 154
Images, page 188
Layout, page 206
Styles, page 296
Or see the general troubleshooting tips on page xvii

The font is wrong in a table

Source of the problem

When you set the typeface or text size, using either the <FONT> tag or a style, you expect your setting to affect all the text within the area you styled. But it doesn't always work that way. Depending on the viewer's browser, text inside tables might not use the font or text size that you specify outside the table. Netscape 4, in particular, treats font styles in a different way than you might expect. ▶

If you're seeing the wrong font in a table, follow these steps.

How to fix it

1. For browsers that support styles—nearly all browsers now support the minimum CSS font styles—you can set the page or table font using a style. However, don't assume that the setting for the **<BODY>** tag will be inherited by tables or paragraphs, as it should; in Netscape 4, it isn't. Instead, set the font style rule for the **<P>** and **<TD>** tag as well as the **<BODY>** tag.

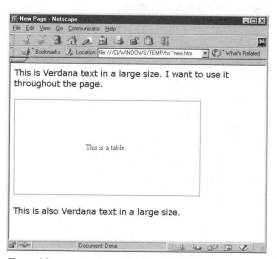

Even if you set a font for the whole page, your table might use the default font.

For example, place this **<STYLE>** block in the **<HEAD>** section of your page to set both the typeface and text size for the whole page (avoiding the clutter of **<FONT>** tags throughout your HTML):

```
<style>
body, p, td {
    font-family: Verdana, Helvetica, sans-serif;
    font-size: 12pt;
}
</style>
```

2. If you want to support older browsers, don't depend on a style to set fonts—use the **<FONT>** tag instead. To set fonts reliably in tables, however, you must include the **<FONT>** tag in every single cell (within every **<TD>** block):

Note

If you use FrontPage, it takes care of this font issue by performing step 2 for you. In fact, if you view HTML for a page in which you've changed the font, you'll see that FrontPage adds a **<FONT>** tag not just to cells, but to every single paragraph in your page.

```
<table>
  <tr>
    <td><font face=verdana size=+1>This is Verdana.</font></td>
    <td><font face=verdana size=+1>This is also Verdana.</font></td>
  </tr>
</table>
```

Fundamentals of tables

Create tables using the **<TABLE>**, **<TR>**, and **<TD>** tags (and, if desired, the **<TH>** tag for column headings). Always remember to include the end tag for each block in a table.

Tables serve three primary functions. First, they can display a list of information—their original *raison d'être*. Second, they can provide the overall layout for your page, dividing it into rows and columns. And finally, they can act as a container for positioning or grouping text or images, such as the **<INPUT>** fields on a form.

The primary table and cell options are:

- **Table dimensions and alignment.** If you want to set the overall size of a table, use the **width** and **height** attributes of the **<TABLE>** tag. And for centering the table or aligning it with the left or right margin, the **align** attribute of the **<TABLE>** tag works the same way it does for the **<IMG>** tag.

  ```
  <table width=300 align=center>
  ```

- **Cell padding, spacing, and borders.** To display a border around the table and between cells, set the **border** attribute. To control the space between cell contents, experiment with the **cellpadding** and **cellspacing** attributes. Padding is the space between the cell's contents and its border, while spacing is between the cell borders. For a layout table with no borders and cells whose edges touch, set all three attributes to 0:

  ```
  <table cellpadding=0 cellspacing=0 border=0>
  ```

- **Column width and row height.** By setting the width and height attributes of the **<TD>** tag, you can specify column and row sizes. If you don't, the browser draws the table just large enough to fit the contents of the cells. Specify either a number of pixels or a percentage of available space.

  ```
  <td width=30%>Narrow column</td>     <td height=30%>Narrow row</td>
  <td width=70%>Wide column</td>       <td height=70%>Wide row</td>
  ```

- **Cell alignment.** To control how the contents of each cell line up, set each **<TD>** tag's **align** attribute (to left, center, or right) or **valign** attribute (to top, middle, bottom, or baseline).

  ```
  <td align=right valign=top>E-mail name:</td>
  ```

- **Spanning columns or rows.** To make a cell span more than one column or row—for example, if you want an image to appear across an entire row—use the **colspan** or **rowspan** attribute.

  ```
  <td colspan=2><image src=banner.gif width=400 height=80></td>
  ```

I can't get rid of the extra space in or between cells

Source of the problem

When you use a table to position images or to create lines or borders on your page, you'll probably want your cells to be exactly the height you specify. But by default, browsers add a few pixels of extra space around cell contents. And even if you specify that you don't want this space, your cells might end up with the extra space because of strange browser behavior. ▶

If you want to get rid of space between cells, follow these steps.

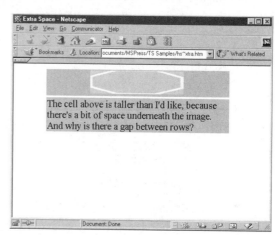

It's sometimes tricky to figure out why there's extra space around the cell contents.

How to fix it

1. In general, space around and between cells is controlled using the **cellpadding** and **cellspacing** attributes. To collapse all space so that cell contents are adjacent, set both attributes to 0.

Although tables don't usually display a border by default, Netscape displays blank space where the border would be, even when a border isn't specified. To make sure there's no extra space, you should also set the **border** attribute to 0:

```
<table cellpadding=0 cellspacing=0 border=0>
```

2. If you do use the **cellspacing** attribute to create space between cells—and your table has a background color—you'll find that in Netscape, this space uses the wrong color. To fix the problem, use **cellpadding** instead.

3. If a row of a table is taller than you intend, the browser might be adding a bit of space at the bottom, just under the image. To fix the problem, move the cell's end tag (**</TD>**) to the same line as the cell contents, with no space before the end tag:

Note

Often, extra space inside cells results from the way browsers choose column widths based on your settings. By displaying cell borders (see the facing page), you can determine whether columns are too wide. If they are, see "I specified column widths, but they still seem to vary from the size I gave" on page 320.

```
<td height=30>
  <img src=textbar.gif width=100 height=30></td>
```

4. If a cell in your table contains a form, browsers always display some extra space after the **</FORM>** tag. If you're trying to fit the form field into a small space or don't want blank space underneath, move the **<FORM>** block outside the cell (and leave no space before the **</TD>** tag, as in step 3):

```
<form>
  <td align=baseline>Search:
  <input type=text name=srchtext size=5>
  <input type=image src=go.gif width=16 height=16></td>
</form>
```

Displaying table and cell borders for testing

When troubleshooting problems with a table, it's a good idea to turn on table borders for all tables temporarily. This will help you see cell width and layout when you preview the page.

If your browser supports table border styles (as does Internet Explorer 5), use the following style block at the beginning of your page to create borders in all tables. It creates a solid gray border around the perimeter of the table and a gray dashed line around each cell. (If gray doesn't show up with your colors, change to **blue**, **yellow**, or **red**.)

```
<!-- Remove after tables are working -->
<style>
  table { border:2 solid gray }
  td, th { border:1 dashed gray }
</style>
```

If this doesn't work in your browser, set the **border** attribute to 1 for tables that don't already have a border. After you've solved table problems, you can hide the borders again.

```
<!--Return border to 0 after tables are working
-->
<table cellpadding=0 cellspacing=0 border=1>
```

Empty cells aren't being displayed properly in Netscape

Source of the problem

If you're using a table for page layout, you will likely create some cells that don't have anything in them. Perhaps you are trying to create some blank space to spread things out or provide a generous margin. Or, you might want to use table background colors to create lines or borders on your page. ▶

For most browsers, there's no special trick to creating empty cells that take up space. But in many versions of Netscape, your empty cells won't show up; even if you set a width or height for an empty cell, Netscape collapses the cell as much as possible. Even if it can't collapse an empty cell, Netscape doesn't fill the space with the background color. (In recent versions, Netscape doesn't collapse empty cells, but it still doesn't display background color.) ▶

The answer, it turns out, is to put something in the cell so that it isn't empty, using an invisible placeholder. If your cells are collapsing in Netscape and you want to set their size with confidence, follow these steps.

How to fix it

1. Set the **width** and **height** attributes for every **<TD>** tag in the table. If you want the empty cell to display a different color than that of the background, set the **bgcolor** attribute as well.

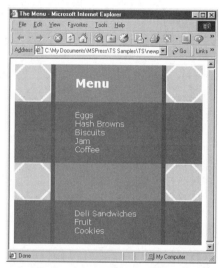

Empty cells create colored boxes and lines.

Netscape doesn't display the background color of empty cells. Some versions collapse cells so they don't show up at all.

2. To keep empty cells from collapsing, fill them with one of the following:

- A nonbreaking space ( ), line break (**
** tag), or any single character with the font color set to the background color. This example uses a nonbreaking space:

```
<td width=100 height=50 bgcolor=#339966> </td>
```

This is the simplest solution, but has a serious limitation: you can't use it for very short cells because the space or line break won't fit in the allotted space. (For a very narrow cell used to display a vertical line, use a line break.) Also, the size of a cell held open this way might change as the browser window is resized.

Note

If you use FrontPage to create tables (in Normal view, rather than by entering HTML), it automatically includes a nonbreaking space in each empty cell to address this problem.

- A **<SPACER>** tag—the only way in Netscape to add space on the page. Set the **width** and **height** attributes of the **<SPACER>** tag to the same values as those of the **<TD>** tag:

```
<td width=5 height=200 bgcolor=#339966>
   <spacer type=block width=5 height=200></td>
```

Other browsers ignore this tag, but they don't collapse cells anyway.

- A one-pixel transparent GIF image. A popular cross-browser solution for adding extra space, a transparent *shim* is perhaps the best solution of all. If you don't have a shim, open your graphics program (such as Photoshop or Fireworks), create a 1-pixel by 1-pixel image, and export it as a transparent GIF (with the minimum number of colors).

    To hold open the cell, insert the shim using the **<IMG>** tag. Set the **width** and **height** attributes to the cell size you're looking for; the browser expands the shim to any size you want.

```
<td width=5 height=200 bgcolor=#339966>
   <img src="shim.gif" width=5 height=200></td>
```

An image can't collapse, so the cell will always be at least the specified size.

The table doesn't work after I change or delete rows, columns, or cells

Source of the problem

When you use large tables for page layout, your HTML can become complex. If you make changes to a table and accidentally end up with missing **<TR>** and **<TD>** blocks or end tags, your table won't display correctly (or at all).

The problem is compounded if you use *nested tables*—tables within tables—for layout or positioning of elements on your page. ▶

It can be tough to get your tables looking right again. The key is to format your table and your HTML code so that you can find the problem. Then you can add missing tags or rearrange elements to get it back into proper form.

If your table doesn't look right and you suspect you've mixed up tags, follow these steps.

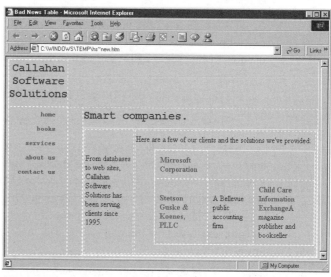

When table tags are missing or in the wrong order, you'll often see blank areas at the right side of your table. Messy HTML makes the problem hard to diagnose.

How to fix it

1. Format your HTML so that every table tag is on its own line, and indent the table tags in the following form (to help you see whether any tags are missing):

```
<table>
  <tr>
    <td>
    </td>
  </tr>
</table>
```

If you don't want to format your HTML by hand, you can use a formatting tool. For example, if you use

> **Tip**
> When troubleshooting table problems, it's a good idea to turn on table borders. For more information, see "Displaying table and cell borders for testing" on page 315.

HomeSite, the CodeSweeper feature can format code for you. Save your page, and then click the CodeSweeper button on the HomeSite toolbar.

The HTML Tidy formatter (in HomeSite or available at *www.w3.org*) not only formats the code, but also adds missing end tags—a great shortcut to fix your table. However, if your table tags are badly mixed up, the results might not be what you intend. Save your page before running HTML Tidy so you can go back to the original if necessary. To run HTML Tidy in HomeSite, point to CodeSweeper on the Tools menu and click Allaire Default HTML Tidy Settings.

Tip

Another way to find structural problems with your table—without actually changing HTML or table formatting—is to use a validation tool. In HomeSite, click Validate Document on the Tools menu. For more information, see "An HTML validation tool reports errors in my code" on page 86.

2. Look through your HTML carefully once it is indented. If the final end tags (**</TD>**, **</TR>**, and **</TABLE>**) aren't indented at the same level as the opening tags, something is missing. Starting in the middle of your HTML, look at each table to make sure it has the right structure. Add matching end tags where necessary, and then reformat again.

3. If you see extra blank cells when you preview your page, count the number of cells (**<TD>** blocks) in each row. If they aren't the same, you need to add or delete cells. Or, you can specify that a cell should take up the space of more than one ordinary cell by setting the **colspan** or **rowspan** attributes for the **<TD>** or **<TH>** tag.

Also, if rows have too many cells—or table contents extend too far to the right—look for missing **<TR>** tags. Since these tags tell the browser when to start a new row, cells keep squeezing in side by side until you indicate a new row.

4. If you can't get the table right, it might make sense to create a new one with the proper structure and move elements one by one into the new table. A page design program, such as FrontPage, can make this process easier: insert a new table with the right number of rows and columns, and then move elements into the new cells. ▶

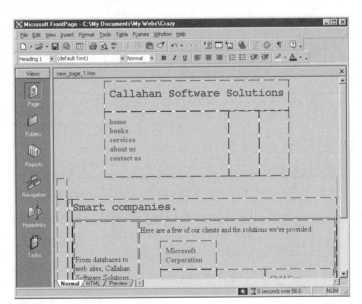

When table tags are missing or in the wrong order, you'll often see blank areas at the right side of your table.

I specified column widths, but they still seem to vary from the size I gave

Source of the problem

When you set the width or height of the cells in a table—either to an exact pixel width or a percentage of available space—you naturally expect them to display at the size you've provided. In reality, when viewers resize their browser windows or default fonts, the widths of your columns might change. If your graphics and text are designed to fit in a specific space, you won't like the result. ▶

This browser behavior isn't a bad thing, as long as you know what to expect. Here's how it works. When the browser window is too small for your table—or when your content is too large for the space available—cells with extra space collapse to fit, if possible. And when the overall table width is greater than the sum of its columns and spacing, browsers include the extra space in the table.

If you want more control over the size of your columns, follow these steps.

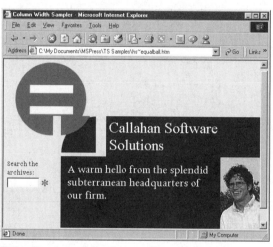

When images or text layout depend on your columns being a certain width, it's critical to set widths deliberately and test in various browsers.

How to fix it

1. Test your table in major browser versions to figure out what it does. Resize the window to full screen, then to very small, noting which columns are changing and what needs to be fixed.

2. Make sure that every **<TD>** tag has its **width** attribute set to a pixel value—unless you want to allow browsers to add space to the column.

```
<td width=100 align=center>
</td>
```

However, if you want one specific column to stretch to fit available space, set its **width** attribute to **100%** (but watch out for other columns collapsing).

Tip

When troubleshooting table problems, it's a good idea to turn on table borders. For more information, see "Displaying table and cell borders for testing" on page 315.

3. To nail down the overall width of your table—so that columns don't resize at all, as long as the contents fit—set the **width** attribute for the **<TABLE>** tag to a pixel value. Make sure you allow enough space for the contents, but not more than the sum of the columns (plus cell spacing and padding, if any). For example, this table's column widths add up to 610, so these settings ensure that the columns won't change size under normal circumstances:

```
<table width=610 cellpadding=0 cellspacing=0 border=0>
  <tr>
    <td width=100><!--Insert something 100 pixels or smaller--></td>
    <td width=400><!--Insert text here--></td>
    <td width=110><!--Insert something 110 pixels or smaller--></td>
  </tr>
</table>
```

Alternatively, if you want your table to use the column widths from the **<TD>** tags most of the time, but want to allow text columns to become narrower when the window is small, don't set the **width** attribute for the **<TABLE>** tag.

Finally, if you want the table always to stretch to fit the available space, set its **width** attribute to a percentage value, such as **100%**.

4. If columns become too wide when you make the window larger—space creeps in around your graphics, for example—reduce the value of the **width** attribute in the **<TABLE>** tag.

5. If columns become too narrow when you make the window small—other columns expand into their space and wreak havoc on your layout—you might want to prevent cells from shrinking. If the column contains one line of text or a series of images, one strategy is to enclose them within **<NOBR>** and **</NOBR>** tags to tell browsers not to break to a new line. For example, this HTML prevents the image from splitting from the text—the cell will always be wide enough for both words.

```
<td>
  <nobr>Sweet Lorraine <img src="arrow.gif" height=16 width=30></nobr>
</td>
```

To guarantee that a column won't shrink, include an image that's the minimum width you want for the column. For example, you might use a *shim*—a 1-pixel transparent GIF image—to hold the space open. If you don't have a shim, open your graphics program (such as Photoshop or Fireworks), create a 1-pixel by 1-pixel image, and export it as a transparent GIF (with the minimum number of colors). To set the minimum cell width, insert the shim using the **<IMG>** tag, setting the **height** attribute to 1 and the **width** attribute to the cell width you want.

```
<td width=5 height=200 bgcolor=#339966>
  This is my message and I don't want it to shrink.
  <img src="shim.gif" width=350 height=1></td>
```

A cell can't shrink to a size smaller than that of the image, so the column will always be at least the specified width.

Because of technical issues and differences between browsers, web pages have not traditionally been flexible in the area of typography and text formatting. With new browsers, however, text formatting options are becoming more accessible.

Still, it can be tough to format text the way you want. HTML doesn't allow the precise formatting found in a word processor, and support for cascading style sheets (CSS) varies between browsers.

If you want to insert symbols on your page, see "Common special character codes" on page 329. And to solve text formatting problems, follow this flowchart.

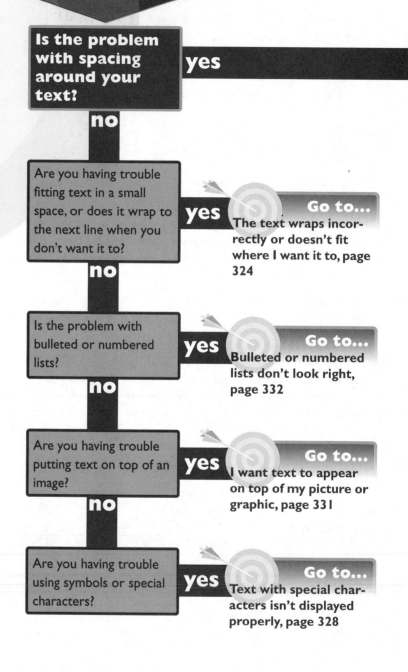

Is the problem with spacing around your text?

yes

no

Are you having trouble fitting text in a small space, or does it wrap to the next line when you don't want it to?

yes — Go to... The text wraps incorrectly or doesn't fit where I want it to, page 324

no

Is the problem with bulleted or numbered lists?

yes — Go to... Bulleted or numbered lists don't look right, page 332

no

Are you having trouble putting text on top of an image?

yes — Go to... I want text to appear on top of my picture or graphic, page 331

no

Are you having trouble using symbols or special characters?

yes — Go to... Text with special characters isn't displayed properly, page 328

Text formatting

Are you trying to reduce the space between paragraphs?

yes

Go to...
There's too much space between paragraphs, page 327

no

Are.you trying to indent text from the left margin?

yes

Quick fix

Use the **style** attribute of either the **<P>** or the **<DIV>** tags to set the **text-indent** or **margin-left** property (**text-indent** affects the first line, **margin-left** the entire paragraph):

```
<p style="text-indent:20px;">
  A foolish consistency is the
  hobgoblin of little minds.</p>
```

In FrontPage:

1. Click Paragraph on the Format menu.

2. Enter values in the boxes under Indentation, and then click OK.

no

Are you trying to justify text in a paragraph or cell, aligning both the left and right sides?

yes

Quick fix

Use the **style** attribute of either the **<P>** or the **<DIV>** tags to set the **text-align** property:

```
<p style="text-align:justify;">
  Trust thyself: every heart
  vibrates to that iron string.</p>
```

(You can also set the property for other tags, such as **<TD>**, but your setting won't apply in Netscape 4.)

In FrontPage:

1. Click Paragraph on the Format menu.

2. Select Justify in the Alignment box, and then click OK.

If your solution isn't here

Check these related chapters:

Or see the general troubleshooting tips on page xvii

The text wraps incorrectly or doesn't fit where I want it to

Source of the problem

When designing a page with text, it's tempting to adjust the type and line breaks just how you want them, assuming that the page will always look this way. But a viewer's browser might display text differently, because your font isn't available or the viewer changed the font or window size. This could make the text grow beyond the space you've provided, so it's generally a good idea to provide plenty of room for text to expand.

There are times, however, when leaving extra room isn't the answer. You could have many reasons for wanting text to fit in a specific space: to line up with an image, fit inside a narrow row or column, or to preserve its line breaks. ▶

Fortunately, there are plenty of ways to control the space that text occupies on your page. When text doesn't fit where you want it to, follow these steps.

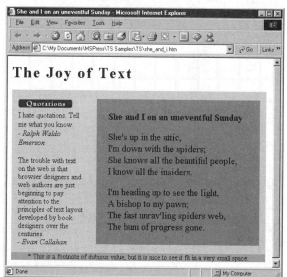

When you want text to fit into specific spaces, there are many strategies to choose from.

How to fix it

1. When you use the default font size, text might not fit where you want it to. The simplest way to change text size—and the only way that works in older browsers—is to use the **<FONT>** tag:

```
<font size=2>I hate quotations.</font>
```

2. When you set font size using the **<FONT>** tag, you might have trouble getting the size you want—browsers might interpret size settings differently, or viewers might change

> **Note**
> Even if you set precise font sizes using a style, Netscape allows viewers to expand or reduce font size. Internet Explorer, too, includes an accessibility option to override fonts specified in your page.

font size. If you want to adjust the size of text precisely, use a style. To set the font size to a specific number of points or pixels, use the **font-size** property. To adjust the space between lines of text—or to make a single line take less space vertically—use the **line-height** property. For example, the following HTML creates a paragraph with text exactly 14 pixels high and with a minimum of extra space above and below:

```
<p style="font-size:14px; line-height:16px">
* This is a footnote of dubious value, but it is nice to see it
    fit in a very small space.</p>
```

3. If text wraps to a new line when you don't want it to, you can add a line break, forcing it to break earlier. To add a line break, use the **
** tag. (If you use FrontPage, insert a line break on your page by pressing Shift+Enter.)

```
She's up in the attic,<br>
I'm down with the spiders,<br>
```

On the other hand, you might want to prevent text from breaking. If you want browsers to keep a line intact even when the text would normally break to a new line, enclose it inside **<NOBR>** and **</NOBR>** tags:

```
<nobr>Ode to the text displayed on one line</nobr>
```

4. If your text doesn't fit in a cell in a table, you might need to make the column wider by setting the **width** attribute of the **<TD>** tag:

```
<td width=300>She and I on an uneventful Sunday</td>
```

Or, if you want the table to stretch to fit your text when viewers change font size, omit the **width** attribute from the **<TABLE>** and **<TD>** tags. (If you use FrontPage, you can remove width settings by clicking the table and then clicking AutoFit on the Table menu.)

5. Recent browsers, such as Internet Explorer 5 and later, allow you to specify the exact size of a paragraph box and to clip or scroll using the CSS **width**, **height**, and **overflow** properties. For example, this paragraph is guaranteed to be exactly 120 x 80 pixels, and displays a scrollbar at the right if there isn't room for the text:

```
<p style="width:120; height:80; overflow:auto; border:1 solid;">
   I do not like to be restricted to a very small space, but I
   do not mind being tight with others.</p>
```

To continue with this solution, go to the next page.

The text wraps incorrectly or doesn't fit where I want it to

(continued from page 325)

6. Another way to guarantee that text is a specific size—and will always look the same—is to create an image to display the text. In your graphics program, such as Photoshop or Fireworks, create a new image that's the exact size you want the text to take up on your page. (Set the canvas color to the background color of your page.) Use the text tool to add, size, and style your text. ▶

   Then export the image as a GIF file and insert it in your page using the **<IMG>** tag:

```
<img src="quotes.gif" width=115
height=17 border=0
alt="Quotations">
```

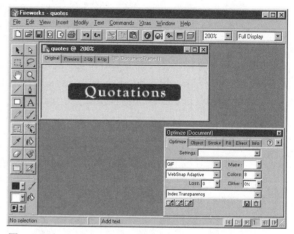

To guarantee that text is exactly the same size and appearance in every browser, create an image.

Note

While text in images often looks better than ordinary web text, it has its disadvantages. Images take more time to download, text inside images isn't indexed, and viewers can't use a browser to copy or search the text. When you do use images for text, always set the **alt** attribute of the **<IMG>** tag, so that viewers who don't display images can read the text, and search engines can index it.

There's too much space between paragraphs

Source of the problem

To move to a new line in HTML, you can insert a line break using the <BR> tag, which moves immediately to the next line without inserting any space. Or, you can start a new paragraph using the <P> tag, which inserts a blank line between paragraphs.

If you want to change the space between paragraphs, before and after headers, or between other elements, you have to turn to cascading style sheet (CSS) styles. By setting CSS properties for the <P> tag, you can control spacing.

If you want to change the space between paragraphs, follow these steps.

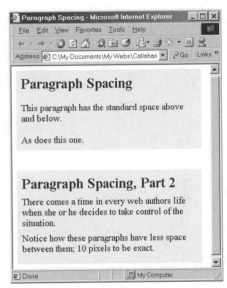

By default, there's a double space between paragraphs. You can adjust the spacing with styles or a table.

How to fix it

1. Set the CSS **margin-top** and **margin-bottom** properties for the **<P>** tag (and for other tags as desired). The following **<STYLE>** block, if placed in the **<HEAD>** section of your page, creates a margin of 10 pixels between all paragraphs and headings:

```
<style>
  p { margin-top:10; margin-bottom:10 }
  h1, h2, h3 { margin-bottom:10 }
</style>
```

If you use FrontPage, you can set these properties more easily. Select the paragraphs you want to change, click Paragraph on the Format menu, and type values in the Before and After boxes under Spacing.

Note

You might expect 10-pixel margins bottom and top to add up to a 20-pixel margin. But the actual vertical space between two elements is the greater of the two margins— not their sum.

2. The solution in step 1 doesn't work in browsers that don't support CSS, and it creates extra space between headings and paragraphs in Netscape 4. If you want paragraphs to appear closer together in all browsers, create a table and place each paragraph in a separate cell. Then, to adjust the space between paragraphs, change the value of the **cellpadding** attribute in the **<TABLE>** tag.

Text with special characters isn't displayed properly

Source of the problem

When you use *special characters*—characters or symbols that aren't in the standard set of computer characters—they might not always display properly in a browser. Special characters you might want to use include the copyright and trademark symbols (©, ®, and ™), currency and math symbols (such as ¢, ÷, and ½), and accented letters (such as é and ô). In particular, special characters are likely to cause trouble for viewers who use a different operating system or language setting than you do.

Additionally, four symbols have special meaning in HTML because they are used to specify tags and attributes. They are the ampersand (&), less-than and greater-than symbols (< and >), and quotation marks ("). If you try to use these special characters within paragraphs of text in your HTML—or inside the values you specify for attributes—your page won't work.

If special characters are causing you trouble, follow these steps.

How to fix it

1. Scan the text on your page—including your page title, headings, and the values of attributes—for the HTML reserved characters (&, <, >, and "). Replace them with their HTML equivalent names: **&**, **<**, **>**, and **"**. For example, if you want the title of your page to be >> *Review: "Troilus & Cressida"* <<, use the following HTML:

```
<title>&gt;&gt; Review: &quot;Troilus &amp; Cressida&quot; &lt;&lt;</title>
```

2. If you want to insert symbols or special characters so that they appear on your page in any browser or system, use their character codes. For example, to insert a copyright symbol, use **©**:

```
<p>Copyright &copy;2001 Evan Callahan</p>
```

   Named references such as © have been added to the HTML specification over time. For better browser support, you can also use ISO-standard code numbers to refer to characters. For example, in version 5 browsers, you can produce the trademark symbol (™) with ™ but only ™ does the trick in Netscape 4. For a list of character code names and numbers, see "Common special character codes" on the facing page.

> **Note**
>
> If a viewer's browser doesn't know about the special character you've used, it displays the HTML code value (such as ™) on the page. With a numbered character code, it's not quite as bad: browsers display a question mark or a small box.

Common special character codes

Use the following character codes in HTML to produce the character shown at right. Use named references for the first 30 in this list; beyond that, use the numbered reference to support older browsers. For a complete list of character codes, see *www.w3.org*.

Number	Name	Character		Number	Name	Character
"	"	"		½	½	½
&	&	&		¾	¾	¾
<	<	<		¿	¿	¿
>	>	>		À	À	À
				Á	Á	Á
¡	¡	¡		Â	Â	Â
¢	¢	¢		Ã	Ã	Ã
£	£	£		Ä	Ä	Ä
¤	¤	¤		Å	Å	Å
¥	¥	¥		Æ	Æ	Æ
¦	¦	¦		Ç	Ç	Ç
§	§	§		È	È	È
¨	¨	¨		É	É	É
©	©	©		Ê	&Eirc;	Ê
ª	ª	ª		Ë	Ë	Ë
«	«	«		Ì	Ì	Ì
¬	¬	¬		Í	Í	Í
®	®	®		Î	Î	Î
¯	¯	¯		Ï	Ï	Ï
°	°	°		Ð	Ð	Ð
±	±	±		Ñ	Ñ	Ñ
²	²	²		Ò	Ò	Ò
³	³	³		Ó	Ó	Ó
´	´	´		Ô	Ô	Ô
µ	µ	µ		Õ	Õ	Õ
¶	¶	¶		Ö	Ö	Ö
·	·	·		×	×	×
¸	¸	¸		Ø	Ø	Ø
¹	¹	¹		Ù	&Ugrave	Ù
º	º	º		Ú	Ú	Ú
»	»	»		Û	Û	Û
¼	¼	¼		Ü	Ü	Ü

> **To continue with this solution, go to the next page.**

Text with special characters isn't displayed properly

(continued from page 329)

Number	Name	Character
Ý	Ý	Ý
Þ	Þ	Þ
ß	ß	ß
à	à	à
á	á	á
â	â	â
ã	ã	ã
ä	&auml	ä
å	å	å
æ	æ	æ
ç	ç	ç
è	è	è
é	é	é
ê	ê	ê
ë	ë	ë
ì	ì	ì
í	í	í
î	î	î
ï	ï	ï
ð	ð	ð
ñ	ñ	ñ
ò	ò	ò
ó	ó	ó
ô	ô	ô
õ	õ	õ
ö	ö	ö
÷	÷	÷
ø	ø	ø
ù	ù	ù
ú	ú	ú
û	û	û
ü	ü	ü
ý	ý	ý
þ	þ	þ

Number	Name	Character
ÿ	ÿ	ÿ
Œ	Œ	Œ
œ	œ	œ
Š	Š	Š
š	š	š
Ÿ	Ÿ	Ÿ
ˆ	ˆ	ˆ
˜	˜	˜
–	–	–
—	—	—
‘	‘	'
’	’	'
‚	‚	‚
“	“	"
”	”	"
„	„	„
†	†	†
‡	‡	‡
‰	‰	‰
‹	‹	‹
›	›	›
€	€	€
…	…	…
™	™	™
←	←	←
↑	↑	↑
→	→	→
↓	↓	↓
↔	↔	↔
♠	♠	♠
♣	♣	♣
♥	♥	♥
♦	♦	♦

I want text to appear on top of my picture or graphic

Source of the problem

HTML tags generally place elements on the page sequentially, with no element overlapping another. Sometimes you'd like text to appear on top of an image. To do this, you can either put the image in the background so text appears on top, or add the text to the image itself. ▶

If you're having trouble getting text on your image, follow these steps.

How to fix it

Sometimes things just don't look right.

1. Browsers can display a picture as the background of the whole page, or as the background of a table or a single cell. To display an image behind text in a cell, set the **background** attribute for the **<TD>** tag:

```
<td background="powerguy.gif" width=200 height=100 align=center>
   Never underestimate the power of a picture.</td>
```

   To make the entire image appear, set the cell's **width** and **height** attributes to the dimensions of the image. If the image is smaller than the cell, it's tiled to fill the cell.

2. If you need greater control over the placement or appearance of text over your image, you might prefer to add the text to the image itself. Open the image in your graphics program, such as Photoshop or Fireworks. Use the text tool to add, size, and style your text.

   Then export the image as a GIF file and insert it in your page using the **<IMG>** tag (set the **alt** attribute to the text you've added, in case viewers choose not to display images):

Tip

If you use FrontPage, you can add text to an image without using separate graphics software. Click the picture, click the Text button on the Picture toolbar, and then type your text. Drag the text box to move or resize it, and use the Formatting toolbar to change the font. FrontPage automatically creates a graphic combining your image and the text and displays it on your page.

```
<td align=center>
   <img src="powerguy.gif" width=200 height=120 border=0
   alt="Never underestimate the power of a picture."></td>
```

Bulleted or numbered lists don't look right

Source of the problem

HTML provides several tags for creating lists, but only three are widely used: `<UL>` (for unordered lists, also called bulleted lists); `<OL>` (for ordered lists, also called numbered lists); and `<LI>` (for individual list items). The attributes of these tags provide some control over the list—the type of numbers or bullets, for example—but they don't allow you to alter the appearance or layout of the list very much. ▶

But there are a variety of ways to customize your lists. In browsers that support cascading style sheets (CSS), you can set styles to format your lists. However, since list appearance involves more than one tag and many browser differences, it's easy to run into trouble. And if you don't want to depend on browsers supporting CSS, you can design a table to format your list.

If your lists don't look right, follow these steps.

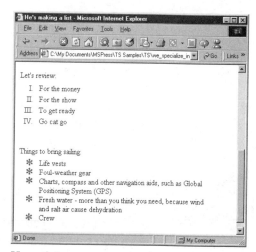

You might want to customize your bulleted and numbered lists with custom bullets, numbers, and spacing.

How to fix it

1. If everything underneath a list is indented, it's because you've omitted the end tag (`</OL>` or `</UL>`) from the list. Add it after the last `<LI>` tag.

2. By default, numbered lists use decimal numbers and bulleted lists use round bullets. If you want to change the bullet style for a `<UL>` tag, set the **type** attribute to **circle** or **square**.

Or, to change the numbering style to roman numerals or letters, set the **type** attribute of the `<OL>` tag to **I**, **i**, **A**, or **a**. The following list uses capital roman numerals:

```
<ol type=I>
  <li>For the money</li>
  <li>For the show</li>
  <li>To get ready</li>
  <li>Go cat go</li>
</ol>
```

> **Tip**
>
> If you use FrontPage, you can set most list options without editing HTML or using style sheets. Click the list you want to change, click Bullets And Numbering on the Format menu, and specify options.

3. If you want to double-space items in the list—for example, if list items are themselves entire paragraphs—end each list item with a line break (**
**) followed by a nonbreaking space ( ):

```
<li>Easy-to-Use  Databases<br> </li>
```

4. For more control over list spacing—to specify custom spacing around and inside your list—you can set CSS margin properties. Unfortunately, because many tags are involved, it might take some experimentation to get all the margins correct. To control spacing around lists, set styles for the **<P>**, **<UL>**, and **<OL>** tags. To control spacing within lists, set styles for the **<LI>** tag. The following **<STYLE>** block adds space between list items but reduces space around lists somewhat: ▶

```
<style>
  p {        margin-top: 6px;
             margin-bottom: 6px; }
  ul,ol {  margin-top: 8px;
             margin-bottom: 18px; }
  li {       margin-top: 0px;
             margin-bottom: 4px; }
  ul ol {  margin-top: 4px;
             margin-bottom: 8px; }
}
</style>
```

The fourth style declaration above sets the margins for an **<OL>** block *within* a **<UL>** block.

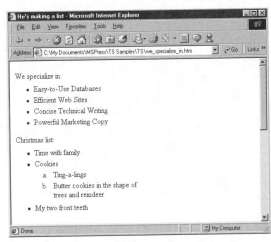

For version 5 and later browsers, you can set margin styles to control list layout precisely.

5. In version 5 and later browsers, you can change the bullet to a picture using the **list-style-image** property:

```
<ul  style="list-style-image:  url(images/
ast.gif);">
```

When you create an image to serve as a bullet, be sure to leave a bit of space around it to help with list spacing.

6. If you want to create a custom list that includes images and works in any browser, use a table. Place images in the cells in the left column, and text in the right column. Use the **cellpadding** attribute to adjust the spacing between list items:

```
<table border=0 cellpadding=5 cellspacing=0>
  <tr>
    <td valign="baseline">
       <img src="images/ast.gif" border=0 width=14 height=15></td>
    <td valign="top">Life vests</td>
  </tr>
```

> **Note**
>
> Netscape 4 doesn't deal with margin styles very well. In lists in particular, you might see problems after setting styles, such as items that don't line up with their bullet or number. If you want to support viewers who use Netscape 4, you might want to use default list spacing rather than setting margin styles.

HTML tag summary

This appendix summarizes the most important HTML tags and attributes, and provides examples where helpful. Tags are organized by function.

In the interest of making this reference concise and easy to use, I've included only those tags and attributes you are likely to need on a regular basis. For a complete list of tags, attributes, and possible values, see the HTML specification at *www.w3.org/tr/html4* or the HTML reference for the two major browsers at *msdn.microsoft.com/workshop/author* and *developer.netscape.com/docs/manuals/htmlguid*.

Basic HTML page structure

An HTML page is a text file with the following basic structure:

```
<!DOCTYPE HTML PUBLIC "-//W3C//DTD HTML 4.0 Frameset//EN">
<html>
  <head>
    <title>Page Title</title>
  </head>
  <body>
    <!--Insert page content here-->
  </body>
</html>
```

The first line is optional, but tells strict HTML validation programs (such as the service at *www.w3.org*) which version of the HTML rules you intend to follow in the code for your page.

Structure and page header tags

<HTML>...</HTML>

Enclose your entire HTML page in this block.

\<HEAD>...\</HEAD>

Enclose the \<TITLE> tag and other general page information tags (such as \<META> and \<STYLE>) in this block.

\<BODY>...\</BODY>

Enclose page content in this block, following the \<HEAD> section. Use attributes to control the appearance of your whole page, including text and background colors.

Sample	Result
`<body bgcolor="#cccc99" text="#003300">`	Sets page background and text colors.
`<body link="#993300" alink="#cc6600" vlink="#993333">`	Sets normal, active, and visited hyperlink colors.
`<body background="images/bkgd.gif">`	Sets a background image.
`<body leftmargin=0 topmargin=0 marginwidth=0 marginheight=0>`	Page appears at top left corner of browser window. (Use all four attributes to support both Internet Explorer and Netscape.)

\<TITLE>...\</TITLE>

Provides the title of your page, which appears in the title bar of the browser.

\<META>

Sets page information variables. When you set the **http-equiv** attribute, your web server sends the variable to the browser (as an HTTP header) before sending your page.

Sample	Result
`<meta http-equiv="Content-Type" content="text/html; charset=windows-1252">`	Browsers with other language settings will display special characters properly.
`<meta http-equiv="Refresh" content="7">`	Browser refreshes page every 7 seconds.
`<meta http-equiv="Refresh" content="7; URL=http://microsoft.com">`	Browser redirects viewer to *microsoft.com* after 7 seconds.
`<meta name="keywords" content="soup, nuts, kitchen sinks">`	Keywords for your page are available to search engines that use them.

<BASE>

Sets a "base" web address for hyperlinks (instead of the page location). Or, use on a frames page to specify the target frame for hyperlinks.

Sample	Result
`<base href="http://www.callahansoftware.com/">`	All relative hyperlinks refer to pages on the specified web site, even if the page isn't located there.
`<base target=main>`	All hyperlinks load their pages into a frame called "main."

<LINK>

Links an external style sheet or creates a relationship with another page or file.

Sample	Result
`<link rel="stylesheet" type="text/css" href="styles.css">`	Page uses styles found in external style sheet styles.css.
`<link rel="shortcut icon" href="favicon.ico">`	Internet Explorer uses the specified icon file for its Favorites menu icon.

<STYLE>...</STYLE>

Provides cascading style sheet (CSS) style rules for the page. For a summary of CSS rules you can create, see Appendix B on page 347.

<SCRIPT>...</SCRIPT> and <NOSCRIPT>...</NOSCRIPT>

Provides script code, such as JavaScript, for your page. Optionally, use a <NOSCRIPT> block to provide alternate HTML for browsers that don't understand scripts.

Sample	Result

``<script language="JavaScript">
  <!--
    if (document.styleSheets)
      window.location='new.htm';
  //-->
</script>```
	This script redirects viewers using Internet Explorer 4 or later or Netscape 6 or later to a page called new.htm; comment indicators cause script to be ignored by older browsers.

<!-- comment -->

Allows you to enter notes in your HTML that don't appear on your page in a browser.

Headings, paragraphs, and line breaks

<P>...</P>

Creates paragraphs with space before and after. The end tag is optional, but recommended (and required if you use style sheets).

Sample	Result
`<p align=center>This is a paragraph.</p>`	Text is centered and has a blank line above and below.
`<p style="margin-top:6;margin-bottom:6">` `  This P is tight with the neighbors.</p>`	Text has 6 pixels between it and other paragraphs.

<H1>...</H1> through <H6>...</H6>

Displays bold heading text. Level-1 headings are large, while level-6 headings are smaller than ordinary text. Headings are left-aligned by default; to center, set the **align** attribute to **center**.

<DIV>...</DIV> and <SPAN>...</SPAN>

Indicates a block of text to which you want to apply a style. Set the style for the block of text using the **style**, **class**, or **id** attributes. Browsers display a line break before and after a <DIV> tag, while a <SPAN> tag can be used on part of a paragraph without breaking a line.

Sample	Result

`<div align=center>`
`  Middle of the road.`
`</div>`
	Section is centered, with a line break before and after.

`<div style=`
`  "position:absolute; top:80; left:80">`
`  Unbearable lightness of being.`
`</div>`
	Section floats on top of other elements on the page, its top left corner exactly 80 pixels from the top and left sides of the browser window.

`This predicament is utterly <span` `  class="crazy"> mad</span>.`	The word "mad" takes on style characteristics defined for the *crazy* class in a style sheet.

\

Breaks to the next line.

Sample	Result
`<br clear=all>`	Browser breaks to a new line, skipping below any objects it happens to be wrapping around.

\<NOBR>...\</NOBR>

Prevents the browser from breaking to a new line. If the contents don't fit on the line, viewers must scroll to the right; if the contents don't fit in a cell, the column expands.

Text formatting

\<FONT>...\</FONT>

Sets the typeface and font size for a block of text. Size is a number from 1 to 7, where 3 is usually the default font size. For more precise font settings, use styles instead of **\<FONT>**.

Sample	Result

`<font size=4 face=`
`"'Courier New', courier,monospace">`
`My old friend the typewriter. </font>`
	Displays text in Courier New (or another listed font if it isn't available), with text size larger than usual.

\<B>...\</B> or \<STRONG>...\</STRONG>

Formats enclosed text in **bold** type.

\<I>...\</I> or \<EM>...\</EM>

Formats enclosed text in *italic* type.

\<U>...\</U>

Underlines enclosed text.

<PRE>...</PRE>

Formats text in monospace (typewriter) font, and displays the text exactly as it appears in HTML (with the same spacing and line breaks).

Sample	Result

```<pre>```
 ```   AGE```
 ```   OF```
 ```   AQUARIUS </pre>```
	```AGE```
	 ``` OF```
	 ``` AQUARIUS```

<UL>...</UL>, <LI>...</LI>

Displays a bulleted list. Lists are indented and have space above and below.

Sample	Result

```<p>I hope we have heard the last of:</p>```
 ```<ul type=square>```
 ``` <li>Conformity</li>```
 ``` <li>Consistency</li>```
 ```</ul>```
	I hope we have heard the last of:
	
	 ▪ Conformity
	 ▪ Consistency

<OL>...</OL>, <LI>...</LI>

Displays a numbered list. Lists are indented and have space above and below.

Sample	Result

```<ol start=4>```
 ``` <li>Cuatro</li>```
 ``` <li>Cinco</li>```
 ``` <li>Seis</li>```
 ```</ol>```
	4. Cuatro
	 5. Cinco
	 6. Seis

Hyperlinks

<A>...</A>

Provides a hyperlink to another page or file. Use the **name** attribute to mark a position on the page to which other links can jump.

Sample	Result
`<a href="matt.htm">Matthew's Page</a>`	Displays an underlined hyperlink (Matthew's Page) to a page called matt.htm in the same folder.
`<a name="news">News about Fiona</a>`	Defines an *anchor* within a page to which other hyperlinks can jump.
`<a href="#news">Read the News</a>`	Display a hyperlink to an anchor.

`<a href="baby.htm" onmouseover=`
`  "window.status='Babies!';return true">`
`  <img src="baby.jpg" width=40`
`    height=30></a>`
	Displays the image baby.jpg as a hyperlink to the page baby.htm; when viewers move the mouse over the link, the status bar displays a message.

<MAP>...</MAP> and <AREA>

Creates an image map with separate hyperlink areas. Use an image map program to help define the link coordinates. As an alternative to this method, most web designers "slice" large images into pieces, assemble the pieces using a table, and then assign a link to each piece.

Sample	Result

`<map name=clickbot>`
`  <area shape=rect coords="26,40,86,177"`
`    href="http://www.microsoft.com">`
`  <area shape=circle coords="67,207,21"`
`    href="http://www.chillbot.com">`
`</map>`
`<img usemap=#clickbot src="robot.gif"`
`  width=200 height=300 border=0>`
	Displays the image robot.gif with two invisible "hotspots" that viewers can click.

Images and objects

<IMG>

Displays a GIF, JPEG, or PNG image.

Sample	Result
`<img src="green.jpg" width=100 height=50 align=right vspace=8 hspace=8>`	Positions the image green.jpg at the right margin so text wraps around on its left. The image appears at least 8 pixels from surrounding text or objects.
`<img src="welcome.gif" width=80 height=30 alt="Welcome to Lewes, DE">`	Displays the image welcome.gif, and provides alternate text for browsers that don't display images.

<HR>

Displays a horizontal rule across the page.

<BGSOUND>

In Internet Explorer, plays a background sound. Use the **src** attribute to specify an audio file, such as a WAVE (.wav) or MIDI (.mid) file.

<EMBED>

Embeds a browser plug-in object to play media or display information. Specify a file to play or an object to display using the **src** attribute, and use attributes to provide parameters to the plug-in.

Sample	Result
`<embed src="Groove.wav" hidden=true autostart=true volume=50 loop=true>`	Plays a WAVE file automatically when the page opens.
`<embed width=280 height=200 src="chomsky.mov" autoplay=true controller=false type="video/quicktime" pluginspage= "http://www.apple.com/quicktime/">`	Displays the QuickTime plug-in and plays the specified movie (.mov) file.

<OBJECT>...</OBJECT>, <PARAM>

In Internet Explorer for Windows, embeds an ActiveX control to play media or display information. Use the <PARAM> tag to provide parameters to the object.

Sample	Result

<pre><object id="real" classid=
  "clsid:CFCDAA03-8BE4-11cf-B84B-0020AFBBCCFA"
    width=300 height=100>
  <param name="src" value="Ocean.ram">
  <param name="hidden" value="false">
  <param name="autostart" value="false">
</object></pre>
	Displays the RealAudio ActiveX control, loading the specified audio (.ram) file so it is ready to play.

<APPLET>...</APPLET>, <PARAM>

Embeds a Java applet. Use the <PARAM> tag to provide parameters to the applet.

Sample	Result

<pre><applet code="chat.class"
  width=495 height=83>
  <param name="server" value="ares">
  <param name="user" value="evan">
  <param name="picture" value="evan.jpg">
</applet></pre>
	Displays an applet whose code is contained in the file chat.class, sending three parameters to the applet.

Tables and frames

<TABLE>...</TABLE>, <TR>...</TR>, <TD>...</TD>, <TH>...</TH>, and <CAPTION>

Creates a table with one or more rows (<TR> blocks) and cells (<TD> blocks). You can optionally add headings (<TH> blocks) to columns, or provide a table caption.

Sample	Result

<pre><code><table border=3 cellpadding=5>
  <caption>The Happy Life</caption>
  <tr>
    <th>Desire</th> <th>Satisfaction</th>
  </tr>
  <tr>
    <td>Greed</td> <td>Generosity</td>
  </tr>
</table></code></pre>
	Data table with a caption, a header row, and one data row.

<pre><code><table cellpadding=0 cellspacing=0
    border=0 width=620>
  <tr>
    <td width=220>
      Narrow left column
    </td>
    <td width=400>
      Wide right column
    </td>
  </tr>
</table></code></pre>
	Two-column page layout table with no space or border between cells.

<FRAMESET>...</FRAMESET>, <FRAME>, and <NOFRAMES>...</NOFRAMES>

Creates a frames page. Use a <NOFRAMES> block to provide alternate HTML for a viewer whose browser doesn't support frames.

Sample	Result

<pre><code><frameset cols="120,*" frameborder=0
    framespacing=0 frameborder=no border=0>
  <frame src="navbar.htm">
  <frame src="main.htm">
</frameset></code></pre>
	Frames page with no borders. The left frame is 120 pixels wide and the right frame occupies the remaining space.

<IFRAME>...</IFRAME>

Displays an inline frame—an area within a page that displays another page.

Forms

<FORM>...</FORM>

Creates a form for viewers to enter information. Use the **action** attribute to specify the page or program to which the form submits information. Use other form tags (such as <INPUT> and <TEXTAREA>) inside a <FORM> block.

Sample	Result

`<form action="search.asp" method="POST">`
`  Search:`
`  <input name=query type=text size=10>`
`  <input type=submit value="Go">`
`</form>`
	Small search form. When a viewer clicks the Go button, the form sends the text value to the Active Server Page search.asp for processing.

<INPUT> and <BUTTON>...</BUTTON>

Depending on the value of the **type** attribute, the <INPUT> tag displays a text box, check box, or radio button for viewer input—or a button or image that submits or resets the form. With a <BUTTON> block, your button can contain any HTML content.

Sample	Result
`ID: <input type=text name=uid size=8> ` `Password:` `  <input type=password name=pwd size=8>`	Two text boxes for viewer input. The first shows text type inside, the second conceals it.
`<input type=checkbox name=xcheez` `  value="please" checked> Extra Cheese`	Check box that is selected by default. If a viewer submits this form, the **xcheez** parameter is set to **please**.

`<input type=radio name=browser`
`  value="ie" checked> MSIE`
`<input type=radio name=browser`
`  value="ns"> Netscape`
	Two radio buttons. If a viewer submits this form, the **browser** parameter is set to either **ie** or **ns.**

`<input type=image src="gobtn.gif"` `  height=16 width=16>`	Image gobtn.gif provides the submit button for the form.

\<TEXTAREA>...\</TEXTAREA>

Displays a multi-line text box for viewer input.

Sample	Result
`<textarea name=story rows=6 cols=20>` `</textarea>`	Text area 20 characters wide and 6 lines high.

\<SELECT>...\</SELECT> and \<OPTION>

Displays a drop-down list for viewer input.

Sample	Result
`Who's on first? ` `<select name=answer>` `  <option selected>What?` `  <option>I dunno` `</select>`	Drop-down list with the first value selected.

CSS property summary

Beginning with the introduction of cascading style sheets (CSS) in Internet Explorer 3 and Netscape 4, web standards started a strategic shift. Rather than using HTML to describe both the information to be presented *and* its appearance, CSS separates the two. You describe the content and structure of your page in HTML, while the instructions for displaying the page go into a style sheet.

The great benefit of styles is that, if you want to make a change to the way an element of your document looks—such as the color of a heading or the spacing around images—you don't have to sift through every line of your HTML to make updates. You just change the style in one place, and every page that uses the style sheet falls into line.

Many web designers have been reluctant to use CSS because not all browsers support it. (See "Browser support for CSS" on page 302.) But now that most popular browsers support at least the core CSS specification, it makes sense to start taking advantage of it. Whether or not you abandon HTML formatting in your pages, you'll enjoy much greater control over formatting and layout by setting the style properties described here.

Note
This list covers the most useful CSS concepts and rules to get you started with styles. For a more complete CSS reference, see *msdn.microsoft.com/workshop/ author/css/reference/ attributes.asp*. For the official CSS specification and many other resources, visit *www.w3.org/Style/CSS*.

Style sheet basics

Style rule format

Style rules specify a *selector*—such as an HTML tag name or a custom class name—followed by one or more CSS property settings in brackets, separated by semicolons.

Sample	Result
`body { background-color: darkblue; }`	Page background is dark blue

Cascading and inheritance

Styles are called *cascading* because many of them apply not only to the element for which you set them, but also to sub-elements. For example, when you set a font style for a table, the cells and paragraphs within the table inherit the style as well—you don't have to set the style for each item. (However, you can always override the table style by using different style rules for items inside the table.)

Sample	Result
`table { font-size: smaller; }`	Font is smaller throughout table

Other style characteristics, such as margins and backgrounds, are not inherited.

Sample	Result

`table {`
`    margin: 8px;`
`}`
	Tables have an extra 8 pixels around the edge, but items inside tables don't have the extra margin

Setting multiple styles

To set a style for more than one selector, separate with commas.

Sample	Result
`h1,h2,h3,h4,h5,h6 { color: white; }`	Text color is white for all headings

Setting styles in context

You can set styles that apply only when they are in certain context—a style for one element inside another.

Sample	Result
`table a { color: maroon; }`	Hyperlinks in tables use maroon text

Specifying units of length

There are several units of length for specifying CSS property values; the most important are **px** (pixels), **pt** (points), **in** (inches), **mm** (millimeters), **em** (the width of a capital "M" in the current font), and **ex** (the height of a small "x" in the current font).

Sample	Result
`body, td { font-size: 16px; }`	Font size for ordinary text is exactly 16 pixels high
`body { margin: .5in; }`	Page has a half-inch margin

`h1, h2, h3 {`
`  border: 1mm solid gray;`
`  padding: .5em; }`
	Headings have a 1-millimeter gray border, and the distance between text and border in cells is relative to font size

Where to set styles

External style sheet

You can set style rules for your pages in an external style sheet (.css) file, which you share between pages. Link a style sheet file from your HTML by placing the **<LINK>** tag in the **<HEAD>** section.

Sample	Result
`<link rel=stylesheet` `  href="stylesht.css" type="text/css">`	Style rules contained in file stylesht.css apply to this page

Style sheet within file

You can set style rules for a single page by using a **<STYLE>** section in the page's HTML file.

Sample	Result

`<style>`
`  <!--`
`  body { background-color: gray; }`
`  -->`
`</style>`
	Sets style rules for this page

Apply style to a single HTML tag

To set the style of one HTML tag, set CSS properties using the **style** attribute.

Sample	Result
`<table style=` `"background-color:blue; color:white;">`	Text is white on blue background in this table only

Create custom style class or ID

You can create custom classes in your style sheet and then apply them in your pages. For example, you might create a class called *quote* for quotations that you want indented a certain amount. Precede classes with a period and IDs with a number sign.

Sample	Result

`.quote {`
`  margin-left: 20px;`
`  margin-right: 20px; }`
	Creates style class called *quote* for use with **class** attribute in HTML

`#bigred {`
`  text-transform: uppercase;`
`  color: red; }`
	Creates style ID called *bigred* for use with **id** attribute in HTML

Apply custom class or ID to tag

To apply a style class to a tag, use the **class** attribute; for an ID, use the **id** attribute.

Sample	Result
`<p class=quote>I hate quotations;` `  tell me what you know.</p>`	Applies style class *quote* to paragraph (and elements inside it)
`<h1 id=bigred>Warning</h1>`	Applies style ID *bigred* to heading

Color and background

Color numbers

Specify colors as you would in HTML, using RGB numbers such as **#000000** (black), **#ffffff** (white), and **#006600** (dark green).

Sample	Result
`h1, h2 { color: #006600; }`	Heading levels 1 and 2 are both dark green

Color names

If you don't like color numbers, select from over 100 enticing color names, such as **darksalmon**, **seagreen**, and **papayawhip**. However, version 4 and earlier browsers only recognize a small subset of color names. (For a complete list of color names, see *msdn.microsoft.com/workshop/author/dhtml/ reference/colors/colors.asp*.)

Sample	Result
`h1, h2 { color: darkgreen; }`	Heading levels 1 and 2 are both dark green

color

Specifies the foreground color for text and other elements.

Sample	Result
`body, p, td { color: #000066; }`	All text in page is dark blue

background-color

Specifies the page background color for any element.

Sample	Result

`table {`
`    color: white;`
`    background-color: maroon; }`
	Tables display white text on maroon background

background-image

Specifies a background image file for the page or other block element (such as a table or cell). Use the format **url(*imagefile*)** to specify a web address or file name.

Sample	Result

`body {`
`    background-image: url(estar.jpg);`
`}`
	File estar.jpg (in same folder as page) appears in the background

`table { background-image:` `url(http://chillbot.com/bot.gif); }`	File bot.gif (on another web server) appears as table background

background-repeat

Determines whether the background image *tiles* (repeats) if it is too small to fit the space. Set to **repeat, repeat-x, repeat-y,** or **no-repeat.**

background-attachment

Determines whether the background image scrolls with the page or is fixed, like a watermark. Set to **scroll** or **fixed.**

background-position

Determines the position of a background image relative to top and left edges of window or other element border. Specify **left**, **center**, or **right**, and then **top**, **middle**, or **bottom**.

Sample	Result
| ```
table {
    background-image: url(war.gif);
    background-repeat: no-repeat;
    background-position: center top; }
``` | Table displays background image, centered and at the top of the table |

background

Sets previous five properties all at once. (Specify values in the order listed above, omitting those you don't want to set.)

Sample	Result
| ```
body {
    background: silver url(war.gif)
        no-repeat fixed center top; }
``` | Page background is silver gray, with image centered at top as a watermark |

Fonts and text

font-style

Set to **italic**, **oblique** (slanted), or **normal**.

font-weight

Set to **bold**, **bolder**, **lighter**, or **normal**.

font-size

Set to **xx-small**, **x-small**, **small**, **medium**, **large**, **x-large**, **xx-large**; **larger** or **smaller**; an exact height in pixels or points; or a percentage of the inherited font size.

Sample	Result
| ```
body, td { font-size: 14pt; }
h1 { font-size: x-large; color:blue; }
h2 { font-size: x-large; }
h3 { font-size: large; }
.footer { font-size: 13px; }
``` | Font size for ordinary text is 14 points, heading fonts are slightly different than usual, and the font size in *footer*-class elements is exactly 13 pixels high |
```

line-height

Sets the height allowed for each line of text. Set to an exact height or a percentage of the default line height.

Sample	Result
`.compact { line-height: 95% }`	Text lines in *compact*-class elements are closer together than usual

font-family

Sets the typeface. To support systems with different fonts, be sure to specify several alternatives (including **serif**, **sans-serif**, and **monospace**, for which most systems provide a font).

Sample	Result
`body, td { font-family: Verdana, Arial, Helvetica, sans-serif; }`	Page uses Verdana font if available; otherwise, uses Arial or Helvetica or the default sans-serif font
`.typewriter { font-family: "Courier New", Courier, monospace; }`	Text in *typewriter*-class elements use Courier New font if available; otherwise, they use Courier or the default monospace font

font

Sets previous five properties all at once (in the order listed above). If you set line height, it should follow font size, separated by a slash (/).

Sample	Result
`body, td { font: 12pt/14pt "Times New Roman", Times, serif; }`	Page uses Times New Roman or other serif font at 12-point size with 14-point line height
`h1 { font: italic bold 18pt Arial sans-serif; }`	H1-level headings use 18-pt bold italic Arial font or the default sans-serif font

text-decoration

Set to **underline**, **overline**, **line-through**, or **none**.

letter-spacing

Allows you to expand or contract space between letters. Set to a positive or negative length, or a percentage of the default spacing.

text-align

Set to **center, justify, right,** or **left**. Use for images, tables, and other objects as well as text.

vertical-align

Set to **baseline, sub, super, top, middle, bottom, text-top, text-bottom,** or **auto**. Use for images, tables, and other objects as well as text.

text-indent

Indents the first line of each paragraph by the length you specify.

text-transform

Specifies capitalization. Set to **capitalize, lowercase, uppercase,** or **none**.

:first-letter and :first-line pseudo-element selectors

Use pseudo-element selectors to provide special formatting for the first letter of an element or the entire first line.

Sample	Result

`p:first-letter { float:left;`
`    font-size:32pt; line-height:28pt;`
`    padding-right:5px; }`
	Create a drop cap (a large capital letter with text wrapping around it) at beginning of each paragraph

`.fancy:first-line {`
`    font-size: larger;`
`    letter-spacing: 1pt; }`
	First line of each paragraph or heading designated as class *fancy* has larger, spread-out type

Hyperlinks

Setting hyperlink styles

To control the display of hyperlinks on your page, set properties for the <A> tag, such as **color, font-weight,** and **text-decoration**.

Sample	Result
`a { color: #993300; font-weight: bold;` `    text-decoration: none; }`	Hyperlinks are not underlined and appear in bold, maroon type

a:link, a:visited, a:active and a:hover pseudo-element selectors

Using hyperlink pseudo-element selectors, you can set properties for different hyperlink states. Set properties for **a:hover** to create a rollover effect when viewers move the mouse over your links.

Sample	Result

`a:link { color: darkslateblue; }`
`a:visited { color: steelblue; }`
`a:active { color: hotpink; }`
`a:hover { color: tomato; }`
	Hyperlinks appear in different colors when they are clicked or followed, or when viewers hover over them with the mouse

Margins, padding, and borders

According to the CSS *box model*, every block-element—tables, cells, paragraphs, and images, for example—has margins, padding, and borders that you can control. Margin behavior doesn't work right in all browsers; in Netscape 4, it's best not to use margin properties at all.

Margin behavior

Margins are the space around the outside of an object. They are transparent, so they appear in the color of the background behind the object. For most objects, margins are zero by default; however, text elements such as paragraphs and headings have default top and bottom margins.

Adjacent margins

When elements with margins follow one another vertically, the space between them is not the sum of their top and bottom margins; it collapses into the larger of the two margins. With side-by-side items, however, margins add up to create more space. You can specify negative margin values; when you do, they subtract space from the margin that would otherwise occur.

Element width | Border

Every block element, such as a paragraph, table, cell, or image, has a series of boxes around it: padding, border, and margin.

Margin | Padding

margin-top, margin-right, margin-bottom, margin-left, and margin

Sets the distance between an object (or its border, if any) and adjacent objects or the edge of the window or cell. Use **margin** to set all four margins at once.

Sample	Result
`body { margin:0; }`	Page appears against top and left edges of browser window

`.quote {`
`  margin-left: .25in;`
`  margin-right: .25in; }`
	Paragraphs of class *quote* are indented one-quarter inch on either side

`h1, h2, h3 { margin-bottom: 6px; }`
`p {`
`  margin-top: 6px;`
`  margin-bottom: 6px; }`
`ul, ol {`
`  margin-top: 8px;`
`  margin-bottom: 18px; }`
`li {`
`  margin-top: 0px;`
`  margin-bottom: 4px; }`
	Page is more evenly spaced: headings and paragraphs are closer together and list items have a bit of space between them

`img { float:right; margin-left: 10px; }`	Images are right-aligned; text wraps around them on the left, but is separated from them by at least 10 pixels

padding

Sets the distance between a paragraph or other element and its border.

border-width

Set to **thin**, **medium**, **thick**, or an exact width. (Setting this property won't provide a border unless you set **border-style** as well.)

border-style

Displays a border around any block-level element, such as a paragraph, image, or table. Set to **solid**, **double**, **ridge**, **groove**, **dashed**, **dotted**, **outset**, **inset**, or **none**.

border-color

Determines border color.

border

Sets previous three properties all at once.

Sample	Result
`.bigframe { border: 4mm ridge gold; }`	Elements of class *bigframe* have a wide, raised gold border
`h1 { border:2px solid; padding:4px; }`	Each heading has a box around it
`table { border:2 solid gray; }` `td, th { border:1 dashed gray; }`	Displays subtle borders around table and cell boundaries; useful for testing tables

Lists

list-style-type

For bullets, set to **square**, **circle**, or **disc**. For numbers, set to **decimal**, **lower-roman**, **upper-roman**, **lower-alpha**, or **upper-alpha**. For neither bullet nor number, set to **none**.

list-style-image

Provides an image in place of a bullet.

Sample	Result
`ul { list-style-image:` `        url(images/bullet.gif); }`	Bulleted lists use an image called bullet.gif in lieu of a bullet

list-style-position

Set to **outside** (the default) for a hanging indent, or **inside** if you want lines after the bullet to flow to the left margin.

Size and position

float

Determines alignment and whether text or other elements are allowed to wrap around an object (like the **align** attribute of the <IMG> tag, but not just for images). Set to **left** or **right** to align the object with the left or right margin and allow text to wrap, or set to **none** (the default) to prevent wrapping.

Sample	Result
`img { float:left; margin-right:10px; }`	Text wraps around all images, with at least a 10-pixel margin on the right side of each
`<div style="float:right; width:120;">` `<img src="mel.jpg" width=120` `height=200> ` `Caption under the picture</div>`	Both image and caption appear against right margin, while other page content wraps around on the left

clear

If a paragraph or object would otherwise wrap around existing elements, set the **clear** property to cause it to start with the next open left or right margin (below other elements). Set to **left**, **right**, **both**, or **none**.

width and height

Sets the dimensions of an object, such as an image or paragraph. Paragraphs always use the specified **width** setting. With **height**, however, when the box is smaller than the paragraph, the text stretches beyond the specified height (unless you set the **overflow** property).

overflow, overflow-x, and overflow-y

Determines whether a paragraph of a specified size is allowed to expand in height to fit the text, and whether scroll bars are displayed to view the overflow. The default setting is **visible**, which allows paragraphs to expand beyond their specified height.

Set to **hidden** to chop off extra text, set to **auto** to display a scroll bar at right as necessary, or set to **scroll** to always display two scroll bars. Use the **overflow-x** and **overflow-y** properties to provide different settings for horizontal and vertical overflow and scrolling.

Sample	Result

`.boxnote { width:160px; height:100px;`
  `overflow:auto; float:right;`
  `border:2px solid navy; padding:4px;`
`}`
	Paragraphs of class *boxnote* are contained in a fixed-size box against the right margin; if the note has more text than will fit, a vertical scrollbar appears in the box

`#mustfit { width:100px; height:12px;` `overflow:hidden; }`	Element with ID *mustfit* will be exactly 100 by 12 pixels; text is cut off if it doesn't fit

position, top, and left

The **position** property causes an element, such as an image or a <DIV> block, to move from the place it would ordinarily fall on the page. Set **position** to **absolute** to position the element a specific distance (in pixels) from the top and left edges of the page, closing up the space it would otherwise have occupied. Set **position** to **relative** to adjust the position of the object, leaving open the space it would otherwise occupy.

Settings for the **top** and **left** properties can be positive (to move down and right) or negative (to move up and left).

Absolute positioning is usually in reference to the top left corner of the page, but you can also set position in relation to another block element. For example, if you set **position** to **relative** for a <DIV> block, absolute positions inside that block refer to its top left corner.

Absolute positioning is most useful in DHTML programming, where you define objects on your page, and then control their position, content, and visibility using JavaScript.

Sample	Result
```<div style= "position:absolute; top:0; left:200"> <img src=spaceship.gif></div>```	The left edge of the image is exactly 200 pixels from the left edge of the window, and the image touches the top margin
```The word <span style= "position:relative; top:-8;">higher </span> is higher than the others```	The word ^{higher} is higher than the others

z-index

Determines which positioned elements overlap others when positioning causes objects to overlap. A larger **z-index** value brings an element "forward" in 3-D space, while a smaller value sends it back behind other elements. A negative value moves elements behind nonpositioned elements on the page.

Sample	Result
```<div style= "position:absolute; top:200; left:200; z-index:2"> <img src="front.gif"></div><div style= "position:absolute; top:250; left:250; z-index:1"> <img src="back.gif"></div>```	Image front.gif partially overlaps back.gif
```<div style= "position:absolute; top:250; left:250; z-index:-1"> <img src="chau.gif"></div>```	Image appears behind content on the page, exactly 250 pixels from the top and left edges of the page

display

Set to **none** to cause an element to disappear from the page, closing up the space it would otherwise occupy. Set to **block** to display the element as a block (the default) or **inline** to display as part of the current line (similar to a <SPAN> tag).

visibility

Set to **hidden** to cause an element to disappear from the page but continue taking up space as if it were there. Set to **visible** (the default) to show the item.

Web authoring resources

As you might have guessed, the best source of information on web page design is the web itself. This appendix lists web sites that I've found useful in my own writing and work. You can find many more web sites on your own by typing any web design topic—from *GIF images* to *audio plug-ins* to *DHTML programming*—into your favorite search page. But beware: time can get away from you, and surfing the web won't get your web pages any closer to being finished.

Web sites and addresses change all the time. If a page I've listed no longer exists, try searching for the company or web site title.

Of special interest

Company or web site	Web address	Notes
Callahan Software Solutions	*www.callahansoftware.com*	Real friendly folks; familiar images and code from this book
Microsoft Office Update	*officeupdate.microsoft.com*	Updates and information for Office and FrontPage
Microsoft Product Support	*support.microsoft.com*	FAQs and searchable knowledge base
Troubleshooting Book Companion Site	*mspress.microsoft.com/troubleshooting*	Updates and information about this book

General information

Company or web site	Web address	Notes
Browser News	www.upsdell.com/BrowserNews	Browser usage statistics
CNET	www.cnet.com	Web developer portal site; try the Web Building area
The Copyright Site	www.benedict.com	Information about copyright law and the web
Digital Web Magazine	www.digital-web.com	Slick magazine
FrontPage World	www.frontpageworld.com	FrontPage resources
HTML Writers Guild	www.hwg.org	Excellent web authoring resources
Internet.com	www.internet.com	Web developer portal site
Internet Corporation for Assigned Network Names	www.icann.org	The domain name officials
lynda.com	www.lynda.com	Lynda Weinmann's books and design tips
Microsoft Press	mspress.microsoft.com	Other web page books
MSDN Web Workshop	msdn.microsoft.com/workshop	Articles and reference material; focus on Internet Explorer solutions
Netscape DevEdge Online	developer.netscape.com	Documentation and Netscape development resources
O'Reilly Web and Internet Resources	web.oreilly.com	Books, news, and resources
Project Cool	www.projectcool.com	Web authoring tips
W3C Design Issues pages	www.w3.org/DesignIssues	Interesting articles
W3C URL specification	www.w3.org/Addressing/URL	All about web addresses
Webmonkey	webmonkey.lycos.com	Excellent reference and tutorials
WebReview.com	www.webreview.com	Web developer portal site; huge archive of articles, so be sure to search for your topic
Yahoo GeoCities	geocities.yahoo.com	Free web hosting
ZD Net Developer Pages	www.zdnet.com/developer	Web developer portal site

Web browsers

Company or web site	Web address	Notes
Extremely Lynx	www.trill-home.com/lynx.html	Lynx is a text-mode web browser, still popular
Microsoft Internet Explorer	www.microsoft.com/windows/ie	The most widely used web browser
Netscape	home.netscape.com/browsers	Netscape runs on a number of operating systems and is the choice of many people
Opera Software	www.opera.com	Opera is a leader in adhering to HTML and CSS standards, and is a favorite of developers
WebTV	developer.webtv.net	WebTV viewer lets you see what your pages look like on TV

Products and tools

Company or web site	Web address	Notes
Adobe	www.adobe.com	Home of Photoshop, ImageReady, and GoLive
AI Internet Solutions	www.htmlvalidator.com	CSE HTML Validator
Allaire	www.allaire.com	Home of HomeSite and ColdFusion
Apache Project	www.apache.org	Apache web server
Bradbury Software / TopStyle	www.bradsoft.com	TopStyle style sheet editor
Chami.com / HTML-Kit	www.chami.com	HTML-Kit editor and other tools
HTML Tidy	www.w3.org/People/Raggett/tidy	Free tool that cleans up your HTML and reports errors
ImagiWare / Doctor HTML	www.imagiware.com/index_tools.html	Doctor HTML and other tools

(continued)

Products and tools *continued*

Company or web site	Web address	Notes
Ipswitch / WS_FTP	www.wsftp.com	WS_FTP file transfer software
Macromedia	www.macromedia.com	Home of Fireworks, Dreamweaver, and Flash
Microsoft FrontPage	officeupdate.microsoft.com/welcome/frontpage.asp	Updates, add-ons, FAQs, and other resources
Microsoft FrontPage Server Extensions Resource Kit	officeupdate.microsoft.com/frontpage/wpp/serk	Server Extensions information and downloads
Microsoft Windows	www.microsoft.com/windows	Information on Microsoft web server software
W3C CSS Validation Service	jigsaw.w3.org/css-validator	Free tool that reports CSS errors; from the official source
W3C HTML Validation Service	validator.w3.org	Free tool that reports HTML errors; from the official source
W3C Tools pages	www.w3.org/Tools	Links to much more software

HTML and CSS

Company or web site	Web address	Notes
Bare Bones Guide to HTML	www.werbach.com/barebones	HTML reference
Chami.com HTML tips	www.chami.com/tips/html	HTML tips
The HTML Reference Library	www.htmlib.com	HTML reference tool
Network Communication Design	www.ncdesign.org	Excellent HTML and CSS guides
RichInStyle	www.richinstyle.com	Extensive CSS information
W3C HTML pages	www.w3.org/MarkUp	The first and last word on HTML

(continued)

HTML and CSS *continued*

Company or web site	Web address	Notes
W3C Style Sheet pages	www.w3.org/Style/CSS	The first and last word on CSS
WebCom	www.webcom.com/html	HTML reference and resource links
Web Design Group	www.htmlhelp.com	Excellent HTML reference

Multimedia and images

Company or web site	Web address	Notes
Apple QuickTime	www.apple.com/quicktime	Great movie player
Corbis	www.corbis.com	Stock photography
Microsoft Developer Network Multimedia	msdn.microsoft.com/downloads	Look in the graphics and multimedia section for many free sounds and images
Microsoft Office Clip Gallery	www.microsoft.com/clipgallerylive	Free images and sounds
PhotoDisc	www.photodisc.com	Stock photography
Real Networks	www.realnetworks.com www.realnetworks.com/devzone	RealServer, RealProducer and other media tools and information
RealPlayer	www.real.com	Popular media player
Sonic Foundry	www.sonicfoundry.com	Audio and video editing and encoding software
Syntrillium	www.syntrillium.com/cooledit	CoolEdit audio software
Terran	www.mediacleaner.com	MediaCleaner video production and encoding software
Windows Media	www.microsoft.com/windows/windowsmedia	Windows Media Player, tools and information
Xing Technologies	www.xingtech.com	AudioCatalyst MP3 encoder

Scripting and Java

Company or web site	Web address	Notes
Chami.com	www.chami.com/tips/javascript	Javascript tips
CodeBrain.com	www.codebrain.com	Java, Perl, and JavaScript resources and scripts
Comprehensive Perl Archive Network (CPAN)	www.cpan.org	Perl treasure chest
Earthweb JavaScripts page	javascripts.earthweb.com	Scripts and tips
HTML Guru	www.htmlguru.com	Dynamic HTML tutorial
Java Boutique	javaboutique.internet.com	Free Java applets
Javascript.com	www.javascript.com	Scripts and tips
JavaScript Gate	www.javascriptgate.com	Scripts and tips
The JavaScript Source	www.javascriptsource.com	Scripts and tips
Matt's script archive	www.worldwidemart.com/scripts	CGI and Perl resources and free scripts
Microsoft Developer Network Web Workshop	msdn.microsoft.com/workshop	Development resources for Internet Explorer
Netscape JavaScript Documentation	developer.netscape.com/ docs/manuals/javascript.html	Official JavaScript manuals
Sun Microsystems Java Technology Pages	java.sun.com	Java development resources
WebCoder.com	www.webcoder.com	Tutorials and tips
Webdeveloper.com	www.webdeveloper.com	Articles and tips
Web Developer's Journal	webdevelopersjournal.com	Articles and resources

Index

network places, 247
<NOBR> tag, 321, 325, 339
<NOEMBED> tag, 290
<NOFRAMES> tag, 143, 344
noresize attribute, 147
<NOSCRIPT> tag, 289–90, 337
numbered lists, 332–33, 340, 357

"Object doesn't support this property or method" error, 284
"Object expected" error, 284, 289
<OBJECT> tag, 30, 228, 238, 343
ODBC. *See* Open Database Connectivity (ODBC)
Office. *See* Microsoft Office
Office Server Extensions, 267
offline vs. online, 44
<OL> tag, 332–33, 340
onion skinning, 8
onload attribute, 288
onmouseout attribute, 185
onmouseover attribute, 185
Open Database Connectivity (ODBC), 95–96, 98, 102–5
Opera, 54, 363
optimizing
   animations, 5
   images, 194–95
<OPTION> tag, 134–35, 137, 346
Oracle DBMS, 99
ordered lists, 332–33, 340, 357
overflow property, 358
overflow-x property, 358
overflow-y property, 358

padding, 355–56
padding property, 356
page
   banners, 36, 38
   breaks, 213
   headers, 91, 335–37
   layout strategies, 212
   margins, 58
   templates, 78, 88–89
   transitions, 10, 56
page-break-before property, 213
page-break-inside property, 213

paragraphs
   boxes, 325, 358
   formatting first letter or line, 354
   HTML tags, 338–39
   indenting text, 323, 354
   space between, 327
<PARAM> tag, 228, 238, 343
password protection, 275
Perl, 99, 295
permissions. *See* security
Personal Web Server (PWS), 98–99, 269, 274
PhotoDraw. *See* Microsoft PhotoDraw
photographic images, 19–20, 63, 71, 197
Photoshop. *See* Adobe Photoshop
PHP scripting, 98–99, 269, 295
pictures. *See* images
ping command, 46
plug-ins, 54, 227, 236–39, 342
PNG images, 16, 25, 195, 197, 342
positioning elements, 357–59
position property, 219, 358–59
PostgreSQL, 99
POST method, 138
PowerPoint. *See* Microsoft PowerPoint
preformatted text, 124–25, 340
<PRE> tag, 125, 340
previewing in different browsers, 52, 58
printing
   from browsers, 213
   from FrontPage, 165
   reports, 172
_private folder, 132
progressive JPEG images, 196
projects, sharing files, 85, 88–90
proxy servers, 45
<P> tag, 327, 338
publishing webs, 263–68
PWS. *See* Personal Web Server (PWS)

QuickTime. *See* Apple QuickTime
QuickTime Player, 225, 230, 236
quotation marks ("), 328

radio buttons, 131, 134–35, 345
RealAudio files, 229

About the author

Evan Callahan owns Callahan Software Solutions, a consulting firm specializing in Microsoft Access databases and custom web design. Evan worked for Microsoft Corporation from 1989 to 1995, where he created documentation and sample applications for Microsoft Access and Visual Basic. He received a B.A. in philosophy and comparative literature from the University of Washington.

Evan was born and raised in Seattle, Washington, where he today lives with his wife, Margaret, and daughters, Fiona and Grace. In his spare time, he enjoys hiking, sailing, making music, and being close to family and friends.

Evan's other books published by Microsoft Press include *Microsoft Access 2000 Visual Basic Fundamentals* and *The Power of Intranets*.

The manuscript for this book was prepared and galleyed using Microsoft Word 2000. Pages were composed using Adobe PageMaker 6.52 for Windows, with text in ACaslon Regular and display type in Gill Sans. Composed pages were delivered to the printer as electronic prepress files.

Cover designer

Landor Associates

Interior graphic designer

James D. Kramer

Principal compositors

Paula Berg
Jean Trenary

Manuscript editor

Jeff Wagner

Technical editor

Robert Tennant

Indexer

Carl Siechert

Proof of Purchase

0-7356-1164-5

Do not send this card with your registration.
Use this card as proof of purchase if participating in a promotion or
rebate offer on *Troubleshooting Your Web Page*. Card must be used in conjunction with
other proof(s) of payment such as your dated sales receipt—see offer details.

Troubleshooting Your Web Page

WHERE DID YOU PURCHASE THIS PRODUCT?

CUSTOMER NAME

mspress.microsoft.com

Microsoft Press, PO Box 97017, Redmond, WA 98073-9830

OWNER REGISTRATION CARD

Register Today!

0-7356-1164-5

Return the bottom portion of this card to register today.

Troubleshooting Your Web Page

FIRST NAME   MIDDLE INITIAL   LAST NAME

INSTITUTION OR COMPANY NAME

ADDRESS

CITY   STATE   ZIP

(   )

E-MAIL ADDRESS   PHONE NUMBER

U.S. and Canada addresses only. Fill in information above and mail postage-free.
Please mail only the bottom half of this page.

start faster **go farther**

DATE DUE

For infor
proa
mspr

Mic

Printed
in USA

HIGHSMITH #45230